Mystical \

The Life and Works of Mabel Collins

'I'm not really bad, I'm just drawn that way.'[1]

'I grumble at them, I drive them away, I shut myself off from all these mystical vampires, who suck all the moral strength out of me-no! all the same they rush to me like flies to honey.'[2]

MYSTICAL VAMPIRE

The Life and Works of Mabel Collins

By

Kim Farnell

Mandrake

Copyright © 2005 Mandrake & Kim Farnell

First paperback edition 2005

All rights reserved. No part of this work may be reproduced or utilized in any form by any means electronic or mechanical, including *xerography, photocopying, microfilm*, and *recording*, or by any information storage system without permission in writing from the publishers.

Published by
Mandrake of Oxford
PO Box 250
OXFORD
OX1 1AP (UK)

A CIP catalogue record for this book is available from the British Library and the US Library of Congress.
1869928857

Contents

	Picture credits	6
	Acknowledgements	8
1	Minna mine with the brown, brown eyes ...	9
2	Marrying the man from the Post Office	27
3	Walking with Egyptians	37
4	It was a dark and stormy night	49
5	Herrings in a barrel	63
6	Penitent squirrels	79
7	Watch the birdie	91
8	Love and the Ripper	101
9	Ink stains lingering	119
10	A brilliant tangerine	127
11	Rose scented vows	139
12	One Life, One Law	151
	Endpiece-a personal note	163
	The Works of Mabel Collins	165
	Sources and references	171
	Notes	189
	Index	231

Pictures

Studio portrait of Mabel taken in 1911.   7

Saint Peter's Church, Knowl Hill, where Mabel married.   26

Lord Vancourt's Daughter. Cover of an American pirated version of Mabel's book first published in 1885. Hence the spelling error on the cover, the English version reads "Vanecourt."   36

View of Crown Hill in early 1890s.   62

View of Crown Hill early 20th century.   118

Mabel as a young woman, from a pastel portrait by Louise Jopling drawn 1891 and exhibited at The Grosvenor Gallery 1892.   126

The Priory, Woodchester. Catherine Metcalfe's family home.   154

Cintra Lawns, now the Brent House Hotel. Catherine Metcalfe's town house in Gloucester Road, Cheltenham where Mabel died.   154

Mabel's grave. Cheltenham Cemetery and Crematorium, Bouncers Lane, Cheltenham.   159

Acknowledgements

Many people helped me in the writing of this book. I would like to thank Alan Bain; the Theosophical Library of Pasadena especially Jim Belderis; Joyce Cummings; Kim Morgan; Ivor Edwards; Caroline Gerard; Robert Gilbert; Michael Gomes; James Gregory; Eileen Gunn of the Royal Literary Fund; the late Melvin Harris; Katinka Hesselink; Aisling Lockhart of the Manuscripts Department, Trinity College Dublin; Mogg Morgan; Ernest E. Pelletier of Edmonton Theosophical Society, Canada; Jean Povey of Cheltenham Cemeteries and Crematorium; Juan Revilla; James Santucci; the Theosophical Society in London particularly Karin Vintney; the British Library and staff; the British Newspaper Library and staff; Kent State University, Ohio; Penn State Harrisburg Library, USA and above all, Leslie Price, who talked me into turning a tentative enquiry into a book, Russ Chandler for his help in editing the text and Garry Phillipson for his proofreading.

On a personal note, a thanks to my children, Adelais and Rory for allowing Mabel to take me away from them so often and for such a length of time.

And this is for Geo, just because.

And my thanks to everyone who has offered their views, ideas, thoughts and help and my apologies if I have inadvertently missed you out of the list above!

Studio portrait of Mabel taken in 1911.

CHAPTER ONE

Minna mine with the brown, brown eyes[3] ...

"Summer is sweet", wrote Mortimer Collins in 1875. And one of the sweetest summers he saw was the one when his daughter was born one late morning in 1851.[4]

That daughter was to become known to the world as Mabel Collins. Depending whom you spoke to, she was a novelist, fashion icon, theosophist, anti-vivisectionist, the lover of Jack the Ripper...the list goes on. One thing Mabel wasn't was boring. Theosophists remember her for having the audacity to attempt to sue Helena Blavatsky for libel and for being ejected unceremoniously from the Theosophical Society for "flirtation". Ripperologists know of her as the lover of Robert D'Onston Stephenson, a candidate for having been Jack the Ripper. Those interested in reading spiritually enlightening literature will have heard of her as the author of *Light on the Path*. Students of nineteenth century literature know her as a popular romantic novelist.

Mabel continues to be a footnote in numerous fields of study having all digits planted firmly in numerous pies. Yet next to nothing has been written about her life. In fact, when I began to ask questions about who Mabel was, I was told that her life was undocumented, there was nothing known about her and she would forever remain a mystery, destined to permanent footnote status. She deserves better than that.

Mabel was not actually born as a Mabel. Although that name now has connotations of elderly aunts with scented handkerchiefs, in the mid to late Victorian era it was highly fashionable.

She was, in fact, born Minna Mabel Collins on 9th September 1851 at St Peters Port, Guernsey. Her father was Edward James Mortimer Collins, known as Mortimer Collins, a popular poet and journalist at that time. Her mother was born as Susanna Hubbard, the daughter of a Russian Merchant and banker. Any attempt to understand Mabel and her life must begin with the story of her father. The family Mabel was born into throws most of our preconceptions of Victorian life out of the window. The Collins were in no way typical Victorians as we tend to view them, prudish, strait laced and constrained. Even today, a century and a half later, Mortimer would be seen as a maverick.

The changes that were to occur in the nineteenth century had barely begun when Mortimer was born on the 29th June 1827. He was an only child, the son of Francis Collings, a Plymouth solicitor. The family wasn't particularly wealthy and lived in Kingscombe, a small port at the head of the estuary of Salcombe, near Plymouth on the southwest coast of England. Salcombe was a small waterfront town whose main industries were shipbuilding and sailing. A typical seafaring town, it comprised mainly seamen's and fishermen's cottages, with a few houses belonging to sea captains and rich landowners. There were a few food shops, workshops and houses of craftsmen who catered for local needs. Salcombe's isolated location meant both people and goods arrived and departed from Salcombe via its one major route - the sea. The town was rapidly expanding when Mortimer was born.

Mortimer's grandfather, (also called Francis Collings - as was his great grandfather), worked as a customs officer.[5] Francis was known for his great swimming ability. The family delighted in telling the story of how he had saved a life owing to his prowess in the water. A rise in customs duties in the 1780s had made smuggling increasingly worthwhile, and a fall in the numbers of customs officers made smugglers bold. They became more than ever determined to resist attempts to limit their activities. Revenue officers waiting in ambush to disturb a smuggling run faced ever greater risks. Working as a customs officer during this period was an adventure in itself.

The writing bug hit the Collins family with Mortimer's father, Francis. In 1826 he published a volume of hymns entitled *Spiritual Poems*.[6] A collection of melancholy, evangelical verses, they could hardly be more different to the writings later to be produced by Mortimer and his daughter.

Mortimer's mother was born Elizabeth Branscombe, of a local Plymouth family. Her mother was named Elizabeth Mortimer and it was for his maternal grandmother that Mortimer was named. Elizabeth was apparently high-spirited when younger but it was said of her that an illness treated by bloodletting with leeches did her an injury from which she took a long time to recover. Throughout Mortimer's youth, he would know his mother as "delicate".

However delicate Elizabeth really was, she outlived her husband. Francis died of consumption, when Mortimer was only twelve years old. The bereft Elizabeth sought solace in the welcome of the Plymouth Brethren and was to remain a member until her death in 1872. The Reverend Dr Robert Hawker,[7] a vicar in Charles, Plymouth and a friend of the Collings family, was instrumental in her decision. He had written a book entitled *The Poor Man's Commentary on the Bible*[8] in 1822 and although he remained a member of the Church of England, Elizabeth and others believed that he was instrumental in the establishment of the Plymouth Brethren.

In the early years of the nineteenth century some Christians had begun to feel uncomfortable with the clerical hierarchy and wished to simply read their Bibles and gather in a simple manner, as they saw Christians did in the New Testament. Numerous Christian sects were established in this period, the Plymouth Brethren being only one. As they were based locally, they were a natural choice for someone who demanded a greater simplicity from their Christian practices, as did Elizabeth.

The sect was started in the 1820s by four men, John Darby,[9] Edward Cronin,[10] John Bellett[11] and Francis Hutchinson[12] who held their first meeting at Hutchinson's house at Dublin, Ireland. Their continuing meetings attracted attention and other gatherings sprung up. Among them one at Plymouth became the most well known and people in the district began to call them "brethren from Plymouth". This resulted in the designation "Plymouth Brethren".

There was no paid ministry although a talent for preaching was recognised. Women of the Brethren keep silence and don't worship audibly. Communion and baptism were practiced but their meetings were, and are, highly unstructured and evangelical in nature. The words of the Bible are taken literally by Brethren, although nowadays there are arguments about what exactly the literal value of those words is. The rules of the Brethren are extremely strict. The man of the family rules the home and women must be submissive. Contact with non Brethren members is discouraged and the group practiced exclusion, cutting off those who refused to adhere to their rules. Calling each other sister and brother, the Brethren were constantly alert to the Second Coming. So much so that it was forbidden to make any long-term plans, such as signing a lease in case that be viewed as a lack of confidence in Christ's imminent arrival.

A number of Christians, particularly in Devonshire, joined the Plymouth Brethren in the first half of the nineteenth century, although the movement never to grew to a large size. The occultist Aleister Crowley[13]'s family were Brethren as was that of the astrologer Alan Leo[14] and Sir Robert Anderson[15] the Scotland Yard detective, known for his involvement in the Jack the Ripper case some years later.

Mabel came to know her grandmother well in later years and described her in her semi autobiographical novels *Our Bohemia* and *In the Flower of Her Youth*[16]."…black dress…white hair smoothed away under a large white cap…belonged to the Plymouth Brethren. Their gloomy creed, which assigns half creation to eternal flames…Like all bigots Gran was incapable of argument."[17]

Mortimer's world was suddenly defined by a set of rules over which there was no question. School was his potential escape. Like that of many of his peers, Mortimer's educational background was never so grand as he tried to make it sound. In the end he was largely self educated. Although he was sent to private schools, including Totteridge Park School in Hertfordshire, on the Middlesex border, Mortimer detested school life and twice ran away to stay at his grandmother's home.

Elizabeth and her brothers were worried that Mortimer was occupying himself with unsuitable reading matter, and made several attempts to wrestle it from him. So far as Elizabeth was concerned, they had a Bible, what more could any decent being need? Their attitude only fired Mortimer's enthusiasm further. He managed to teach himself Greek and Latin and to study poetry. His holidays, such as they were, were often spent with members of his mother's family. The time he spent with his mother was occupied by her dragging him to Brethren services to lay him back on the path of salvation and away from the path of wickedness that his classical studies directed him towards. As soon as Mortimer was able to do so he dissociated himself completely from the Brethren.

The Collins family were in dire financial straits. When Mortimer's father fell ill they had no income and had to rely on relatives in Chatham and London to house and support them. There was no choice but for Mortimer to enter the world of employment just before his eleventh birthday. On 5th May 1838 he became a reading boy at the printing house of Gilbert and Rivington, where he was responsible for reading manuscripts aloud to the reader who corrected the proofs. He worked there for eight weeks until his mother decided that he should leave. It seems a strange choice of employment in any event considering that his mother objected to his reading anything other than the Bible. Perhaps it took her a little time to realise exactly what his work entailed.

Mortimer and Elizabeth moved to Holborn, London and she set him to work in a shop. He eventually put his foot down – shop work was beneath him. After some argument he agreed to take the position of monitor in a private school. The school was kept by the Reverend Richard Harris[18] in Westbury, Wiltshire. Mortimer remained there for two years from 1843 to 1845.

Monitors were used in schools because there weren't enough teachers to cope with the rising numbers of pupils. This system was greatly economical, as it enabled the teacher to be responsible for large numbers of pupils. Along with a few other, brighter, students, Mortimer was taught a particular task and activity. It was then his responsibility to teach a group of children. The teacher taught another group of monitors and when Mortimer had finished his task, one of those would begin to teach and he would learn the next activity. Most of the work was based around learning the three R's – reading, writing and 'rithmetic. Monitors earned a small salary as well as receiving an education. For many, this work was the first step towards becoming a teacher. Not only was Mortimer continuing his education – he also managed to earn a living.

It was at this point in his life that Mortimer saw his first published work. A translation from Ovid appeared in the *Bath and Cheltenham Gazette* on 10th April 1844. Now he had started to write nothing would stop him. As well as poems, Mortimer submitted a regular series of essays to the *Gazette*, under the name of "Bystander". His work was soon published in

Fraser's Magazine and *Punch*. In leaner times he continued to teach at the school to increase his income.

By 1847 Mortimer was thinking of marriage. After all he'd be of age the following year and could see no reason to delay. Turning twenty one meant that he was leaving the era of childhood and becoming a man. He would have all his legal rights. Although since 1823 girls had been able to marry from the age of twelve and boys from fourteen, the memory of twenty one being the age for marriage before that date stuck fast. And most people married around that age in the mid nineteenth century. Mortimer wouldn't have to seek Elizabeth's consent for any prospective wife once he gained his majority.

Not that he had anyone in particular in mind at this point. However, his travel writings – descriptions of places he had never, nor would ever visit – inspired him enough to make him visit Paris shortly before his twenty first birthday. The occasion clearly needed marking in some way. Strangely, he is reticent about this occasion. Perhaps reality lacked the glamour of his fantasy visits.

It was about time that Mortimer fell in love. He wanted to marry and what was marriage without love? All he needed to do was find a suitable candidate for his affections. He was writing more and more prolifically, but his main income was still derived from teaching, moving from post to post. A good connection led to his being offered a job in Lechdale.[19] He arrived at the appointed time for a meeting with the headmaster. Unfortunately, the headmaster had been taken ill and sent his wife down to meet Mortimer. The moment he saw the headmaster's wife Mortimer fell in love and vowed that this would be the woman he would marry. He must have thought the fates were really smiling down on him when the headmaster died from his illness three weeks later.

Susanna Crump, née Hubbard, known as Minna, was the daughter of William Hubbard, a Russian merchant and banker. As a young girl her beauty led to several offers of marriage – to the extent that one suitor threatened to shoot himself if she wouldn't run away with him. She didn't and he didn't. Susanna's father decided that she was so much trouble he needed to get her married off as soon as possible. A visiting minister, the Reverend J H Crump, fell in love with her while preaching and proposed to her as soon as his sermon was over. Susanna's father was far more impressed with this proposal than she was and although Susanna objected her father finally wore her down. A week after her marriage Susanna threw her ring at her new husband and swore never to wear it again. Eventually the couple made their peace and settled into a placid marriage. Susanna's time was largely spent in helping her husband to keep school, enjoying time spent with the boys there. When she met Mortimer Susanna was forty, nineteen years older than him. She was the mother of six children, the oldest of whom was little younger than Mortimer himself. After her husband's death she would sit with the young tutor reading poetry in the evenings.

With the headmaster's death the school had to be sold and Susanna took a picturesque cottage at Knowl Hill,[20] between Maidenhead and Reading. Mortimer was out of work again and after searching for a while found a new post and began work in Northamptonshire. In the autumn of 1849 he wrote to Susanna proposing marriage – she refused immediately. When their families found out they were horrified at the idea of this mismatched couple. If they married Mortimer would be taking on a ready made family and a wife much older than himself when he had problems earning enough money for his own survival.

Elizabeth couldn't resist interfering. She wrote to Susanna and one of her brothers travelled to Susanna's house to dissuade her from marrying. Unfortunately, they succeeded in having precisely the opposite effect. It had been a long time since Mortimer had taken much notice of his mother's wishes. And all this fuss persuaded the contrary Susanna that marriage to Mortimer did, after all, hold some attraction. She decided to accept his proposal and spent the ensuing weeks calming irate relatives. Susanna's family were no more impressed than Mortimer's – she would be marrying beneath her station.

On more than one occasion the romance almost ended. In Spring 1850 Mortimer found lodgings close to Susanna's home. He walked the nine miles there each morning to meet her for breakfast and walked nine miles back at night. Finally, on 9th May 1850 the couple were married at Wargrave Church, two miles from Knowl Hill, with Susanna's daughter as bridesmaid. Although Susanna knew her new husband was much younger than herself it wasn't until he signed the marriage register that she realised just how young he really was. Somehow Mortimer had managed to avoid mentioning his age.

On the day of the wedding the new family left Knowl Hill. Susanna had a small income and Mortimer found work on the *Lancaster Gazette*.[21] The couple spent a brief honeymoon in Morecambe,[22] taking a house

15

there. A few weeks after their marriage three of Susanna's children came to join them. Two others followed for six weeks of holiday and the sixth finally turned up having been ill. Although money was short, entertainment was cheap. The family spent many happy hours together on the beach.

It was hard to manage such a large family on Mortimer's low income. Susanna managed to raise some money and the couple decided to buy a school in Launceston.[23] Although they had never seen the school, they spent a small fortune that they could ill afford in transporting the old fashioned furniture Susanna had inherited from her father, only to arrive to find the school comprised two pupils. It was a complete disaster. After three months they realised they had to give up.

They heard of another school for sale in Guernsey, in the Channel Islands. Mortimer went to visit it, and was so impressed that he decided to buy a partnership and wrote for his wife to join him. She packed the silver, which was all she could afford to transport, and began to follow with her two youngest children. Bad weather meant that the steamer from Plymouth was delayed and Susanna and her children had to take lodgings while they waited to cross. Unfortunately, that left her waiting when someone the family owed money to finally managed to catch up with her. He'd already seized the furniture but still wanted more towards the money he was owed. Susanna had to hand over her silver and arrived in Guernsey penniless.

Guernsey is one of a group of islands off the coast of Normandy. The Channel Islands are formed of two bailiwicks – the first being Jersey and the second the group of islands comprising Guernsey, Alderney, Sark, Herm and Jethor, along with other small islands, some still uninhabited today. While part of Great Britain, the Islands are not part of the United Kingdom and remain self-governing. Although English was spoken on Guernsey the official, and most commonly spoken language was French. It would not be until 1921 that English became the legal language of the Islands. The form of French spoken – Guernsiais – was a dialect similar to that spoken by the Normans in the 11th and 12th centuries in England.

When the Collins moved there, Guernsey was as much a foreign country as France. The population was increasing rapidly as it had become a popular holiday resort for the English in the 1830s and 40s. A regular steamer service had begun in the 1820s and interest in Guernsey was heightened by the first Royal visit there in 1846. And the lack of income tax until 1922 attracted many to move to the Islands.

MYSTICAL VAMPIRE

Guernsey is the hottest spot in the British Isles during the summer. Its wild sweeps of sandy bays were as much an attraction to Susanna's children as they are to children today. Numerous rock pools allowed them to while away hours fishing for small fish and baby crabs and to discover starfish and shrimps. Only forty square kilometres big, Guernsey was to struggle to maintain its steadily increasing population. In decades to come, locals would leave the island in droves to settle on the mainland. At this time, however, mainlanders were settling in Guernsey and changing its face forever.

Although Susanna and Mortimer persisted with the school in Guernsey, its bad reputation meant that this too turned out to be a disappointment. After a year, the principal of Queen Elizabeth College in St Peters Port, Dr Bromby,[24] offered Mortimer the position of headmaster of the lower school, responsible for its younger pupils.

The college was founded in 1563, with a grant from Elizabeth I, who gave the school her name. The school had its ups and downs and nearly went out of business a number of times, but was rechartered in 1824 when the new building was constructed. The architect was John Wilson, who was also responsible for St James' Church across the road. Run by the Church of England, this prestigious boy's college, offered an English type education to wealthy Guernsey parents. The school still exists today. Mortimer's new position was highly successful. As well as teaching at the school he took private pupils and taught his stepdaughter and stepson.

Susanna fell pregnant in early 1851. Life was treating the family well when Minna Mabel Collins was born. Mortimer worshipped her from the first. Calling her Mabel, or May he wrote endless poems and sonnets for her.

Well do I love September: best for this –
   A daughters kiss
First knew I in that pleasant time:
First saw beneath September skies
   My Mabel's eyes,
Fall often sung in careless rhyme[25]

Mortimer's obsession with writing, coupled with his complete lack of business sense, meant that Susanna realised that she had to take responsibility for the running of the household and all practical matters. Mortimer was a large and powerfully built man. Six foot tall in his socks, he lived with his head permanently in the clouds. He spent several hours each day writing, several walking when he had the opportunity, and needed little sleep.

Minna's early childhood was spent in a country which, although British on the surface, was as different to England as any other continental country. There was no close family nearby and the Collins spoke a different language to many of those around them.

Mortimer was filled with boundless energy. With his school teaching, private tuition, chess playing and endless writing it was amazing he still found time to spend with his family. His devotion to his daughter was unquestionable.

> Oh God! Who lovest everything!
>   Be good to little May;
> Sweet slumber to mine eyelids bring
>   When daylight flies away.
>
> O make me happy, give to me
>   A tender heart and true,
> And let me love to learn from Thee
>   The things I ought to do
>
> And wake me when the pleasant light
>   Awakes the birds and bees,
> And carrollings of pure delight
>   Are heard among the trees.[26]

After two years Dr Bromby decided to move to Melbourne, Australia. As soon as he left his deputy took the post of headmaster and gave Mortimer his notice. Mortimer established a new school and took some of his former pupils with him. Without sufficient capital the project was doomed to failure and it slowly became clear that this might be the time for the family to leave.

In early 1856 Mortimer decided to devote himself totally to his writing and the family returned to England. On leaving Guernsey he left his stepdaughter behind at school where she languished unattended for several months. She finally returned to England to be met by her step father.

Life in England began with Mortimer trying to buy a newspaper in Shrewsbury. When the deal fell through Mortimer travelled to Leamington to establish a periodical of his own. He continued to write poetry and to lecture.

While working in Leamington Mortimer found his social life taking wing. He had become highly fashionable and frequently held court at a local watering place. With his admirers he frequented a number of coffee rooms in local hotels and was au fait with all the gossip. Drink became a larger part of Mortimer's life and he lived far beyond his meagre means.

This enchanted life couldn't continue, and one day Mortimer walked out into the countryside and disappeared. It was getting harder and harder for him to cope. Susanna had developed a hip complaint and she was obliged to withdraw further and further from the world. Until now she had acted as Mortimer's business manager as well as constant companion. With the onset of Susanna's condition Mortimer was again alone. Managing his finances had never been Mortimer's strong point and without Susanna's guidance, he soon fell into problems. In the spring of 1857 Mortimer had no choice but to leave his friends and enemies from Leamington behind.

The Collins went to live at a relative's house near the Thames, by now completely penniless. Mortimer had been expecting to find work in London but on arrival he found that the man who had offered him the job had died. Moving from lodging to lodging Mortimer desperately continued to try and make a living from his writing. The family took a large unfurnished house in Barnes. Their state was such that they sat on boxes and used skewers for forks. Susanna managed to obtain a little money but their financial problems continued.

Things became desperate. Mortimer accepted a private tutorship in Carlisle. He continued to write verse for London papers but even with the little money Susanna had access to, and Mortimer's tutoring fees, the family couldn't afford to live. Susanna's banker cousin paid for them to travel back to Plymouth and Mortimer took a job as editor of the *Plymouth Mail*.

Mortimer entered into Plymouth life with a vengeance. But bad luck was following him around. An Exeter paper that was in competition with the *Plymouth Mail* happened to be owned by the brother of a newspaper proprietor in Leamington. While in Leamington Mortimer had gleefully attacked this proprietor in print. A solicitor had been sent to track Mortimer down but lost the trail in Carlisle. Mortimer was tracked to Plymouth and thrown into prison. Susanna's cousin again came to the rescue and paid several hundred pounds to secure Mortimer's release.

And just as it seemed things couldn't get any worse – they did. The family's few possessions were still in storage in London – when Mortimer sent for them he found that the person responsible for their safekeeping had decamped with them to America.

But even now Mortimer refused to change his ways. Money flowed through his hands like water. He was reduced to borrowing from the sheriff's officer at a rate of sixty per cent interest. And once he realised that he wouldn't be able to repay that debt the family had to decamp again.

Next came a job in Nottingham. Mortimer's stepdaughter was by now old enough to work for him. It was not such a great change, as he had always liked to work with his family in the room. Although Susanna read everything he wrote she was gradually coming to have less and less interest in his work. By now Mortimer had begun to lie to Susanna. He denied his foolish spending and instead claimed he was not being properly paid. Mortimer continued to take out loans using Susanna's small income as security.

Mortimer was relying more and more on drink and often claimed that the slippery streets made it hard for him to go to and fro his office. Mabel and her half sister spent many hours escorting him and holding him upright. Much of his free time by now was spent in London. The next few years were riddled with visits by bailiffs and attempts to keep one step ahead of his debtors.

In 1861 the family moved to Wandsworth in London. Money soon ran out and the cottage at Knowl Hill, where Susanna had lived in the early days of their romance, was taken again. Mortimer was followed to the cottage and again thrown into prison for debt. The pattern of his life was now set – stay and work in one place for a while, overspend, run into problems with debts, spend time in prison, run away and then finally move to a new town where the whole process could begin again.

By 1866 Mortimer obtained a job as joint editor of the *Globe* and began living the life of a bachelor in London while the rest of his family remained at Knowl Hill. Although he would visit at weekends, with Susanna's health failing further he was spending more and more time alone. It was in his room at Knowl Hill that he continued to write his poetry and Mabel later recalled falling asleep to the sound of her father's pen scratching the paper. She knew better than to interrupt him while he was writing. By the time she was twelve years old Mabel had begun writing romances and verse. She had never attended school – what education she had was from her father, poetry and philosophy formed the main content of her lessons.

Mortimer soon became familiar in the London haunts of journalism. Many of his hours were spent in taverns meeting with other writers and journalists. Mortimer's way of dealing with a now unhappy marriage was to simply deny its existence. As far as his contemporaries were concerned he was a bachelor. Of course, this also meant him not acknowledging his daughter. He had said that he himself should be responsible for educating Mabel as he didn't agree with the system of education on offer. But this also made it easier for him to keep his family life a secret. As he had to spend *some* time with his family, there were those who believed Mortimer to have a skeleton securely locked in a cupboard. But very few were to discover what that skeleton actually was. The "King of Bohemia"[27] would have suffered severe damage to his reputation of a lively man about town if it were generally known that he had a wife and child along with a large collection of stepchildren.

Playing the role of the King involved late nights setting the world to rights in a number of taverns around London. And in that process Mortimer would imbibe a large amount of alcohol. One night in particular he managed to cause a fracas at the Alhambra Theatre. While out with Bertrand Payne[28] he got into an argument and the attendants at the theatre had the problem of trying to remove him. Fortunately, as Payne was more sober than Mortimer, it didn't develop into the major fight it may otherwise have done. But the police were called, and the two men were taken to Vine Street police station and charged with being drunk and disorderly. Tey were bailed out and had to appear before a magistrate the following morning at Bow Street. In the end the charges were dismissed. But all of London soon heard of the event and although in some circles the episode simply added to Mortimer's reputation, in others it led to his being despised. Dante Gabriel Rossetti[29] referred to him as "a creature...a dead dog..."

Susanna and Mabel took no part in this side of Mortimer's life. Apart from taking responsibility for Mabel's education, Mortimer appears to have had little to do with his daughter. It is difficult to work out when he did take the time to teach Mabel. He would spend several hours each day in writing, many evenings in the company of his friends. And if at home he would begin writing again at 10 pm, usually continuing until 2 am.

His life with his family at this time warrants no mention in Mortimer's prolific writings – apart from a fictionalised account of his teaching of Mabel in the novel *Frances*.[30] "…her father delighted to teach her at home. So she knows a lot of things other girls don't know, and is ignorant of an infinite number of things…She knows her Shakespeare; she can read Chaucer; she can enjoy the Odyssey and the odes of Horace…She can play neither croquet nor the guitar." A lover of the classics, a staunch Tory and conventionally religious, Mortimer ensured that Mabel's education would stand her in good stead if she were to mix with poets but be of little help in the real world.

But it is also clear that Mortimer had a great affection for his daughter - "Girls should tell their fathers all their troubles."[31] – shown by a letter he wrote to her for her fifteenth birthday:-

> MY DARLING MAB, The eternal want of pence
> That vexes poets like a pestilence –
> Me at this moment cruelly condemns
> To offer you no gift of gold or gems
> So if with carelessness your young eye looks
> Upon a couple of two well-known books
> Why I'll forgive you. One is Horace, done
> Into good English verse by Conington –
> Horace who by a half prophetic ken,
> Wrote verse that suits our country gentlemen;
> Him in the Latin never will you read –
> Try him in English, and the next indeed
> Tho' in his brain is gone Horation stuff,
> For a Horace has not quite backbone enough:
> My dear friend Locker. Poet true is he.[32]

In 1867 Susanna died. A year later Mortimer married Frances Cotton and his life changed irrevocably. This was "a marriage of completion – the true union of soul with soul."[33] The couple spent barely a minute apart and Frances devoted the rest of her life to working as Mortimer's secretary and co-writing his novels. Mortimer was head over heels in love. He wrote endless love poems dedicated to Frances. The cottage at Knowl Hill had been bought in 1862 and Mortimer took his new wife there to begin their married life.

It was a picturesque dwelling. Two stories high in an acre of land, it was surrounded by trees and a large garden. A long low room on the ground floor formed the focus of the house. Mortimer and Frances had a desk in each of the bay windows. A long dining room nearby saw numerous dinner parties and the first floor held a number of small bedrooms usually filled with visitors.

Mortimer spent hour upon hour writing. He didn't encourage his guests to sleep much, although conversation would go on until the early hours he would be up by 8 am, clamouring for attention. Wearing his black velvet coat, white waistcoat, an open shirt, light brown trousers and his straw hat, Mortimer spent hours indulging himself in his other interest, walking. The family didn't fit easily into village life as Mortimer was an enigma to the locals. He had no visible means of income and yet seemed constantly to be receiving vast numbers of books. An argument with the local vicar did nothing to endear him to those around him.

One of his closest friends at this time was Edmund Yates,[34] who he had known since 1860. He wrote for many of Yates' publications. Another friend was the novelist R D Blackmore,[35] author of *Lorna Doone*. Writing occasionally for the *Dublin University Magazine* led to its then editor, John Francis Waller,[36] forming a close friendship with Mortimer and frequently staying at his house.

Mortimer split his time between writing, walking and caring for his three dogs while simultaneously entertaining his many and frequents guests. Frances' devotion to him, and their active social life, left Mabel barely acknowledged.

But Mabel worshipped her father regardless. He called her his "baby" and starved of company of her own age Mabel thought of him as her best, if not only, friend. The King of Bohemia had his princess and Mabel revelled in playing this role to their many visitors. Occasionally, Mortimer's mother would call and stay for a visit now that he had a stable address, and cast a gloomier atmosphere over the house.

Although Mortimer has been credited with having spiritualist beliefs it is clear from his writings that the contrary is the case. "Spiritualists…present us with an imbecile creature who has gone backward instead of forward…they cannot believe in the soul – unless souls will come back and lift dining tables and play accordions in the dark…It appears to me that spiritualists ought to form…Royal Hysterical Society…"[37]

However, although Mortimer's views about spiritualism are damning, he wasn't as conventional in his beliefs as it may at first seem. His writings demonstrate knowledge of astrology beyond that of a mere dabbler.

> *Raphael*: I am adventurous who would fain be indolent.
> *Astrologos*: Venus and Mars conjunct at your nativity
> Gave love of luxury, with power of princeliness;
> With you my lord 'tis always fight or festival.[38]

Life was treating Mortimer and Frances well. They spent many happy years together, in which Mabel appears to have been almost incidental. Mortimer's life revolved around his writing life and the many people he met on his long and frequent walks. Frances recalled a happy summer in 1870 when the family, along with a Dr Steele and the dogs were left stranded - after taking a boat across the river they were unable to find anyone to ferry them home again. Mortimer found a boatman to row them back and insisted that he joined them for dinner that evening – to the consternation of his mother who was staying at Knowl Hill.

This idyllic life, to which Mabel clung was shortly to end. Mabel had no idea how to be a lady. She was better trained to write verse and read books while walking. Although she could translate from classical Greek she had no knowledge of how to darn her stockings or cook a meal. Her grandmother occasionally made attempts to turn her towards more ladylike activities, but Mabel took little persuasion from Mortimer to spend time on the river or edit his latest writing. It was clear that Mortimer had done too good a job on his daughter for her grandmother to bring her back into the fold but as a growing young woman Mabel was starting to show some interest in her looks and femininity. "I don't think you've the making of a Plymouth sister in you baby…If Gran can't convert you to her religion it seems she can to feminine follies."[39] Gran was despairing of Mabel however – "Oh, that I could bring her to the Lord! Oh, that I could convince her of her state of sin and show her the awful doom of eternal flame which lies before her. "[40]

Mortimer was a great fan of falling in love and marrying early. And encouraging Mabel to do just that would take her off his hands and let him enjoy the lifestyle he craved. A growing daughter could only serve to remind him of how quickly the years were passing.

And at this point Mabel met Kenningale Robert Cook, the son of Robert Keningale Cook, the Church of England Canon of anchester. He was six years older than her and instantly smitten. A good looking young man, although not from a wealthy background, he affected the airs of a gentleman. He seemed to be well enough educated for Mortimer's tastes, and it was Mortimer's judgment Mabel was trusting to when she chose Robert. She had to trust someone's judgment; her knowledge of the ways of the world was minimal.

By February of 1871, Robert had proposed and the couple became engaged. Mabel spent time at the Canon's home in Smallbridge where her father sent her a Valentine's Day greeting.

"I mean to send a Valentine,
E'en tho' it seem ridiculous
Unto a little maid of mine
Who's staying at Ponticulus.

Tho' flatterers sometimes say to me
Of verse I've the complete art,
I guess that she would rather see
Some verses from her sweetheart…

…"Good morrow to my Valentine,"
In polyglot fasiculus:-
A hope that little maid of mine
Won't tire them at Ponticulus"[41]

The marriage took place on 3rd August 1871 at St Peters Church[42] in Knowl Hill. "My annotations on things in general, will, I fear, be brief today; and for this reason…that a little girl of my acquaintance will be passed onto a gentleman and poet, 'with the authors compliments'. How is a man to interest himself in trivial matters under such circumstances?"[43] The wedding was a small affair. The family walked to the local church and there were few guests.

Five years later Mortimer's happy life with Frances was also to come to an end. After a bout of rheumatic fever he decided to visit Mabel and her husband in Richmond. Even while so ill he didn't want to stop writing. Finally, his heart gave up the battle and on 28th July 1876 Mortimer died and was buried the following Tuesday in Petersham churchyard.

Frances lived until 1886 and spent much of her time compiling her husband's work and letters. Her cousin, F Percy Cotton, edited Mortimer's poems for publication and spent much of his time setting the poems to music. Today Mortimer's work is almost forgotten.

Mabel had begun a new life. Away from her family as a new bride, the world was to open its doors to her.

Saint Peter's Church, Knowl Hill, where Mabel married.

CHAPTER TWO

Marrying the man from the Post Office

Considering the chaotic state of Mabel's early life, she may have considered the prospect of marriage to someone so seemingly respectable as Keningale Robert Cook, the chance of a lifetime. He had a degree in law, and so the chance of a good professional career, wrote poetry and, best of all, had Mortimer's approval. He was also an ardent spiritualist and so was to leave a lasting effect on Mabel's life.

But was she so sure about this marriage? In her book *In the Flower of her Youth*,[44] which is semi autobiographical, the character representing Mabel, Lil Warrington, says "Doesn't it seem rather rash to take a vow at seventeen which one has to keep all ones life?" Mabel's alter ego, Lil, pops up in a number of different novels. And it's Lil who offers us another reason why Mabel chose to marry at this time, "It is a difficult thing for a woman who loves her father, as did Lil, to accept a stepmother with a good grace at all."[45]

Keningale Robert Cook was the son of a clergyman, the Canon Robert Keningale Cook, Vicar of Smallbridge and the Dean of Rochdale. At this time Rochdale was a small town, and Wardle, where the Cooks were based, was an isolated hamlet on the edge of the moors, with only a glorified cart track leading to the Halifax Road. Smallbridge itself had a reputation for being one of the rowdiest areas in Rochdale. It had a huge number of ale houses, which may be relevant.

Canon Cook was no small town, retiring priest. He was responsible in 1858 for the erection of the church of St James the Apostle in Wardle. This was the culmination of a campaign beginning in 1842, when the Wardle National School was erected. In June 1843, Canon Cook wrote to the Bishop of Manchester explaining his desire to build a church in Wardle.

Owing to Cook's efforts, endowments were secured, and by July 1855 plans for a church had been accepted. The foundation stone was laid on 16th May 1856 at a service conducted by Dr Molesworth,[46] Vicar of Rochdale. The donor of the site, James Whittaker, was ill and so the stone laying ceremony was performed by Canon Cook.

Coins were placed into the cavity and a plate bearing the inscription, "This chief corner stone of a new church, to be built to the glory of God, and dedicated to St. James the Apostle, was placed here by James Whitaker Esq. of Wardle; and the first Masonic Cube by Brother Albert Hudson Royds,[47] Esq. P.M CELRRIII, P.G.J.M. East Lancashire and D.P.G.C. Lancashire, on the sixteenth day of May, being Friday in Whitsun - Week, in the year of our Lord Christ MDCCCLVI: And in the nineteenth year of the reign of Her Majesty Queen Victoria".

When the stone had been laid, AH Royds, and several Freemasons, laid the first cube stone. The proceeds of a collection taken among the Masons were to be used for the completion of the spire. The silver trowel used to lay the first stone was intended as a present to Mr Whittaker and inscribed, "Presented to James Whitaker Esq. in commemoration of laying the foundation stone of St. James' Church, Wardle, Friday, 16th May, 1856. R.K.Cook, M.A. Incumbent Treasurer".

The consecration of the church in 1858 was a lively affair, after the consecration service itself about two hundred people indulged in a warm meal followed by toasts and speeches led by Robert Healey of Hurstead.

Canon Cook found time during his campaigns to father a son. Robert was born in Lancashire in 1845 and educated at Rugby school. One of the leading private schools in England, established in 1567, Rugby had become much larger and gained in popularity in the nineteenth century. Robert attended Trinity College in Dublin[48] from January 1863 when seventeen, as a pensioner – that is he paid a fixed fee for his education there. He obtained his bachelor's degree in the winter of 1866 and would gain his Masters and Bachelor in Laws as well as his Doctorate in Laws in 1875.

His family's lack of ready money meant that Robert had been unable to attend Oxford University, as he would have liked. Instead he joined many other financially challenged students in enrolling at Trinity. He was obliged to pay eight visits to Dublin and sit eight termly exams to gain an ordinary degree. Degrees with honours were only available to full time students. Robert didn't have to attend lectures under this arrangement, but simply pay a total fee of £84. Although that sounds low, it is equivalent to about £5,400 in today's terms. A student pursuing a law degree at Trinity in 2004 would pay fees of £3,805 a year.

The University of London offered the same arrangement but required eleven visits rather than eight and charged substantially higher fees. Robert was by no means alone in gaining his qualifications in this way.

Although Robert was continuing with his studies he needed to make a living. From 1869 he had been employed by the Post Office dealing with money orders. He was to hold this job until at least 1873. By the mid nineteenth century, the General Post Office was big business. As well as the obvious tasks related to delivering mail, the chief district offices of the Post Office transacted business relating to money orders and savings banks. The Post Office was a huge employer. The main office at St Martin's le Grand in East London had a Secretary's Office; Medical Department; Solicitors', Surveyors', Telegraph, and Engineering Departments; Receiver and Accountant General's Office; Money Order Office; Savings Bank Department; Circulation Department and Returned Letter Office. By 1858 3,200 officials were employed in London alone.[49] Part of the Civil Service, the Post Office required candidates to be examined by the Civil Service Commission. Overtime was payable for extra hours and after twenty or twenty five years, workers could retire with a pension. Working for the Post Office was eminently respectable and completely safe. Robert could be guaranteed years of employment — though perhaps not so much excitement as he may have wished.

By 1875 Robert managed to obtain a post as a stockbroker in the City of London. Although he didn't stay with his first firm and moved on in 1882, he continued in this line of work. His literary aspirations didn't wane, and in 1878 he applied for the post of Librarian to the Society of

Writers in Edinburgh. Unfortunately, his lack of success left him obliged to carry on working within the field of finance.

By the time of his marriage Robert had already completed and published a book of verse, *Purpose and Passion*.[50] This was a collection of poems dated from 1869 onwards. To say that this didn't meet with great acclaim is rather understating its reception. A review of the book in the *Athaeneum* in April 1870 ran: "Mr Cook, in his preface, hangs out so big a bush we wish he had given us better wine and less bush. His poems are deficient in two essential particulars; they lack beauty and clearness. And this is the result, not of designed obscurity, but of inability in the author to express himself adequately. None of the poems are complete in themselves and the completed parts want finish. The aim and purpose is uncertain. The form too in which Mr Cook casts his thoughts or half thoughts, is unmusical…(His) present performance gives evidence that we may expect more perfect work from him hereafter."

Robert appears to have been undaunted by this scathing review – although it would be some time before he had any poetry published again. Now a published writer he continued to sell his work wherever he could. Within weeks of marrying Mabel he had an article published in *Fraser's Magazine*.[51]

Throughout 1871 and 1872 he wrote innumerable pieces for Amelia Lewis' magazine *Woman*. Mabel had written since she was very young, and this magazine saw her first published writings. Contributing to *Woman* seems to have been something of a family affair, Robert's sister Louisa also wrote occasionally for the magazine, and Mortimer contributed to the first issue with subsequent issues carrying advertisements for his books.

Almost every issue contained Mabel's or Robert's writing. Their articles covered a range of subjects but were primarily concerned with education, the role of women and the arts. Although Robert may have considered this to be the beginning of a literary career for him, it was Mabel who was to eventually become the writer of the household.

Although still called Minna, or Minnie, at home, gradually she was to become known as Mabel. When Mortimer died a gap appeared in the world of romantic fiction that his daughter was more than able and willing to fill. Over the next decades Mabel's novels were to appear with unremitting regularity. Like her father she drew heavily on her own experiences for her novels and created alter egos, like the aforementioned Lil Warrington, to act as her voice.

1877 was a milestone year in many ways for the Cooks. Robert bought the *Dublin University Magazine,* Mabel had her first novel, *An Innocent Sinner,*[52] meet with great success, and Frances would publish her biography of Mortimer.[53]

Mabel was totally unimpressed with Frances' biography of her father. She took advantage of the *Dublin University Magazine* to air her disquiet. "A widow, however well disposed, is not the best estimator of her husband."[54] She was mainly annoyed with Frances' presumption in publishing verses written for Mabel by her father without permission. Although the article is unsigned, it is clear from its content that it is Mabel's work. She was further angered by the impression given that Mortimer wrote "wedding verse on satin" – so far as Mabel was concerned, this was demeaning her father's memory. A series of articles were to follow in the *DUM* about the life of Mortimer, which itemised more or less his every move since birth, and were interspersed with selections of his verse. These were signed by "K.M.C.", which suggests a collaborative effort on Mabel and Robert's parts. The collaboration does seem a little unbalanced though, considering how like the rest of Mabel's writings these articles appear.

In early 1877 Robert had bought the *Dublin University Magazine* from James Waller, a long time friend of Mortimer's. The magazine had gone through a number of editors and owners in its lifetime. Launched in January 1833, it had struggled for a number of years. Robert's efforts to restore it to former glories were in vain, and after struggling through 1877, by the following year it was effectively no more and closed in June 1878. Its end was hastened by Robert's translation of "Aenon"[55] causing the University to issue a formal disclaimer of involvement with the magazine. His translations of Sappho's works did nothing to increase his popularity.

In its early days The *DUM* had a strong reputation in literary circles: it was the first to publish the writings of Oscar Wilde and Robert wrote to Wilde in 1877, "I hope in 12 months time the *DUM* may be restored to its true position again and will be able to pay its contributors…"[56] Robert's time as editor had got off to an optimistic start. He persuaded Christina Rossetti to write in his first issue and produce writing on demand. Alarmed at the developing anti-Christian tone of the magazine, she wrote to Robert six months later asking that their "quasi agreement" be cancelled.

Although Robert's literary efforts appear to have been tinged with an air of disaster, Mabel was launching on a roller coaster of success. *An Innocent Sinner* attracted enthusiastic reviews, which the publisher ensured were prominently placed on the dust jacket. "Miss Collins who writes with correctness and vigour, has chosen in 'An Innocent Sinner' to rely for interest on an entirely new combination of circumstances."[57]; "The book is one that ought to be both read and studied."[58]; "…decidedly remarkable and well worth reading…"[59], "…there are both prettiness and ingenuity in the novel which Miss Mabel Collins, the clever daughter of a gifted father has written."[60]

Written shortly after Mortimer's death, *Sinner* contained a number of references to his work. Quotations from Mortimer's writings were used throughout the text as headings for various chapters. Also Mabel's faith in Robert had not yet diminished. Quotations from *Purpose and Passion* as well as extracts from his translation of Sappho's work were scattered throughout the book. The only other writer to be quoted was Bulwer-Lytton.[61]

Although Robert persisted in his literary efforts, his work was being eclipsed by his wife's. In 1879 Mabel had two more books published, *In This World*[62] and *Our Bohemia*.[63] Many of Mabel's books were two or three volumes in length, and once she had begun to produce her novels there was nothing to hold her back. Many were first seen in serialised form in magazines such as *Short Cuts* and *Temple Bar*. Novel after novel appeared in quick succession: *Too Red A Dawn* in 1881,[64] *Cobwebs* in 1882,[65] *In The Flower of Her Youth*[66] and *The Story of Helena Modjeska*[67] written jointly with John Lillie in 1883; *Viola Fanshawe*[68] and *Idyll of the White Lotus* in 1884,[69] *Lord Vanecourt's Daughter*[70] and *The Prettiest Woman in Warsaw*[71] in 1885.

Ever emulating her father, Mabel regarded fountain pens as too new fangled and preferred to write with an old fashioned pen, dipping it in ink at regular intervals. Her books were published in the US as well as in Britain and widely reviewed. She was seen as Mortimer's natural successor.

Much of Mabel's work was autobiographical. *Cobwebs* is set in Campden Hill,[72] where the Cooks lived in 1881 and features a character who decides to go on the stage because of financial problems. Much of the book is about the problems caused by a man allowing his wife to work.

It was rumoured that Mabel herself tried acting for a short time in the 1870s.

Mabel's novels are best classed as Victorian sensation fiction. Popular from about 1860 onwards, this genre of fiction relocated the Gothic novel to modern, middle class England. Typically it featured cliff-hanging conclusions to chapters with plots involving guilty family secrets, bigamy, insanity and murder. Energetic heroines and hypersensitive heroes are also typical. The term is a pejorative one although highly descriptive. Because Mabel's writing was often featured in serial form before appearing as a book, each chapter ended with the required cliffhanger to encourage the reader to buy the next issue of the magazine. Writing was a highly popular pastime amongst educated Victorian women and came much easier to Mabel than most, following as she did in her father's footsteps.

> "At no age, so far as we are aware, has there yet existed anything resembling the extraordinary flood of novels which is now pouring over this land - certainly with fertilising results, so far as the manufacture itself is concerned. There were days, halcyon days - as one still may ascertain from the gossip of the seniors of society - when an author was a natural curiosity, recognized and stared at as became the rarity of the phenomenon. No such thing is possible nowadays, when most people have been in print one way or other - when stains of ink linger on the prettiest of fingers, and to write novels is the normal condition of a large section of society."[73]

Often it appears that Mabel is describing the sort of woman she aspired to be – rather than necessarily the one that she was – but the line is a fine one. "The heroine of this class of novel is charming because she is undisciplined, and the victim of impulse; because she has never known restraint or has cast it aside, because in all these respects she is below the thoroughly trained and tried woman."[74]

Undisciplined Mabel was clearly frustrated in her marriage. In *Illusions,* published in 1905, she vents some of her feelings about Robert. "His sneers were very powerful and I had never been able to bear them…A woman is never a man's friend…(he has) an overwhelming longing for physical life and physical exercise and physical power and supremacy…"[75] Their marriage was failing. It was never clear exactly why the couple separated. In *In the Flower of Her Youth,* Mabel depicted the character representing Robert falling in love with another and she, to free him from his bonds while avoiding the scandal of divorce, fakes her own death.

The couple separated finally in 1880. Mabel clearly hadn't faked her own death so what really happened? She is extremely discreet about the realities of their separation in her writings. But one source baldly states that they separated in 1880 when Robert went mad.[76] Mabel's' writings were no longer simply an occasional diversion – the money she made from them provided an income which was never quite enough for her to live off. It is unknown whether Robert attempted to support his wife financially after they separated, but in that era it would have been unlikely for him to do otherwise. However, money had never flowed freely for him, and if Mabel was to maintain a decent lifestyle, she needed to at the last subsidise her income.

Mad or not, Robert hadn't given up his attempts at writing. In 1881 another collection of his verse, *The Guitar Player,*[77] was published and met with a lukewarm reception. He also wrote two romantic plays *The King of Kent*[78] and *Love in a Mist.*[79] There is no record of either of these ever being performed. He corresponded with a number of authors. Walt Whitman,[80] for example, sent him copies of his poems at Robert's request.[81]

Robert's final work, *The Fathers of Jesus*[82] took him more than ten years to complete and was published shortly after his death. This rather strange occult work contained chapters on the Book of Thoth, Aryan Ancestors, Buddhism, Essenes, and ones with tempting headings such as *A Ray from the Sphere of Plato* and *The School of Pythagoras.* This set of essays on ancient religious and philosophical systems and their bearing on Christianity was his life's work.

By the time of Robert's death in 1886 the Cooks' marriage had failed and the couple were living separate lives. Robert died on 24th June 1886 "at his little property, Arnewood Rise, on the borders of the New Forest".[83] His father was with him when he died from an internal abscess after a long and painful illness. A rather strange obituary appears in *Light*[84] in July 1886 where it states that his wife "Miss Mabel Collins, besides one or two clever novels wrote some very original short stories wherein Spiritualism, or some facts based on it, were prominent motives *(sic)*" and, "All that he wrote was written like a scholar, and a man of thought, whose literary aims were high. Had he made letters his profession, he would certainly have taken higher rank as a writer than he did; on thither *(sic)* hand it is far from improbable that certain of his poems and the best of his prose writings will be preserved in the criticism of an age more liberal in thought, and more courageous in speculation, than the present."

As Mabel was working on her fourteenth book at this time she would no doubt have questioned being attributed with "one or two clever novels". She was a highly popular writer by this time, both in Britain and the US. Today Robert's only claim to posterity is his editorship of the *Dublin University Magazine,* which he succeeded in hastening towards its end. Apart from Mabel's spiritual works, which shall be addressed later, her writing has also not stood the test of time. But making "letters his profession" was never an option for Robert. And despite the adulation of spiritualist magazines such as *Light* he was a man who once worked for the Post Office, married to a famous novelist. Doubtless not the epitaph he would have desired.

Lord Vancourt's Daughter. Cover of an American pirated version of Mabel's book first published in 1885. Hence the spelling error on the cover, the English version reads "Vanecourt."

CHAPTER THREE

Walking with Egyptians

Life and the Universe show Spontaneity;
Down with ridiculous notions of Deity!
Churches and creeds are all lost in the mists;
Truth must be sought with the Positivists.

Wise are their teachers beyond all comparison,
Comte, Huxley, Tyndall, Mill, Morley, and Harrison;
Who will adventure to enter the lists,
With such a squadron of Positivists?

Social arrangements are awful miscarriages;
Cause of all crime is our system of marriages;
Poets with sonnets, and lovers with trysts,
Kindle the ire of the Positivists.

Husbands and wives should be all one community,
Exquisite freedom with absolute unity;
Wedding rings worse are then manacled wrists,
Then he was a MAN - and a Positivist.

If you are pious, (mild form of insanity,)
Bow down and worship the mass of humanity,
Other religions are buried in mists;
We're our own gods, say the Positivists.
Mortimer Collins

But let us step back a few years and take a look at what married life meant to Mabel. She had settled into a marriage offering unremitting boredom. Each morning, Robert would leave for work while she tried to fill the hours until his return. In the early days Mabel didn't spend so much of her time writing. The daytime hours hung heavily on her. "It is a commonly accepted fact that a young married lady, whose husband is tolerably 'well off', cannot possibly have anything to do."[85]

Destined to be childless, she did not even have the distraction of children to care for. Mabel described the life of a middle class housewife in *Woman* 23rd March 1872 –"She breakfasts with her husband in the morning, sees him off about nine or ten o'clock. Then she gives orders to her servants and looks after her house for an hour or two. We will not enter into the question whether her servants manage *her* or not. After these duties are performed; what more? A walk or drive; a little practising; but how universal is it that married ladies do not attempt to keep up their music - a book for an hour or so perhaps – crochet or tatting! By-and-bye comes dinner; and her husband again, tired with the day, dull-brained with the smoky city atmosphere. She, after the inanities of *her* day, has no intellectual stimulus to give him. The pair talk a little perhaps, but of what? For he cannot tell her of what he has done; the mysterious ways in which he makes his money are far beyond her, he thinks; and she has absolutely done nothing. So after dinner, he reads his *Times,* or goes to sleep, or perchance, asks her to sing one of the old songs she used to sing. She may sing it, or she may say she doesn't practice, and has lost her voice; so he goes back to the politics and city news, which are beyond her, and the libel cases &c., which are not fit for her."[86]

The few activities on offer to women of her ilk held little attraction for Mabel - comprising occasional shopping, visiting and perhaps the odd evening at the theatre. This was the most exciting schedule on offer. A year into her marriage Mabel was making the case for married women to have their own career, stating her belief that it would actually promote intimacy between couples rather than estrange them.

In *In the Flower of Her Youth,* Mabel describes Robert as a quiet young man who liked to spend his time writing verses. Each day he would go to his office like a machine, each evening come home and complain about it. Although he enjoyed spending his time writing Robert was no saleable author. His monotonous life was punctuated by long evenings of study.

Mabel was popular in her circle, a tall, graceful woman with auburn hair and a delicate colouring. She looked younger than her age throughout her life. And on embarking into married life she felt her brain was atrophying.

There was nothing unusual about Mabel's predicament. The role generally imposed on middle class women was that of the angel of the hearth, an entity whose role as wife and mother was pre-eminent and inevitable. She was there to tend to her husband's needs when he returned home from work and protect her children. Robert had few needs that could be met by Mabel and no children were to appear. Victorian houses were zones of privacy and segregation. The world at large was kept at bay by thick curtains, inner lace curtains; held off by overstuffed furniture and mocked by wax fruit and candles. It was easy to feel suffocated. Working women often sought solace in drink – an option not easily open to a woman of Mabel's class. Women only worked when it was impossible for the family to survive otherwise. It would not be until the First World War that it would be acceptable for a woman like Mabel to seek employment and by then she would be too old. Granted, Mabel had her writing, which must have alleviated some of her frustrations. But there was certainly room for more in her life.

In these circumstances it was not at all difficult for Robert to persuade Mabel to attend séances. Soon after they married he took Mabel to events where "…Such strange and often terrible happenings occurred, that she gave it up once and for all."[87] But she was not to give it up immediately. In fact, Mabel soon became a renowned medium herself. She attended spiritualist gatherings and soon gained the admiration of those around her. Robert had been interested in spiritualism for some time and spent many hours in studying it. But it was Mabel who was to develop the abilities he jealously desired.

At this distance it may appear strange for Mabel to enter such a world. Her father had written against spiritualism, and owing to his early years amongst the Plymouth Brethren, had a horror of involvement with strange sects. However, it is worth bearing in mind that the role spiritualism played in Victorian England was vastly different to that of today.

The nineteenth century was a time of great spiritual turmoil in England. Despite the image of Victorian Britain being a God fearing society, only a small percentage of the population were practising Christians. With the doubts about Christian doctrine and the advancement of natural science, many religious revivals were characterised by a tendency to identify true spirituality with mysticism or occultism. The spiritual was moving away from religious institutions. Although the established churches were in decline, interest in religion itself had never been stronger. Another obsession of the period was the search for a single key that would solve the mysteries of the universe. And, ironically enough, the desire to find unity in diversity caused numerous movements to spring up.

Spiritualism itself had begun in 1848 when two daughters of the Fox family of New York began receiving what they claimed were spirit messages in the form of rapping and knocking sounds. Kate and Margaret Fox interpreted these messages and replied to them by means of a simple code. They soon had a large and enchanted audience. The fashion for séances had begun. In later years the Fox sisters were to admit that they had produced the sounds themselves. But by then it didn't matter. Spiritualism had grown way out of their control.

In a short space of time spiritualism had arrived in Europe. It rapidly became part of an alternative lifestyle including vegetarianism, feminism, dress reform, homeopathy…Daniel Dunglas Home's[88] visits to Europe in 1855 sealed the movement in that area of the world.

It went further than supplying a religious outlet for spiritually frustrated spinsters however. There was a quest to prove the validity of spiritualism scientifically. A number of organisations, including the London Dialectical Society[89] and the National Secular Society,[90] along with the Society for Psychical Research,[91] supported by the psychologist William James[92] in the USA, took a close and sympathetic interest in the progress of spiritualism.

There were a whole variety of people under the banner of mediums: some took money for their services while commonly, financial recompense was refused. Mediums could relay the words of the departed through the laborious process of alphabet rappings, or the more common and effective trance utterance. As a medium's reputation spread they could acquire a circle of devoted sitters, who would seek out their powers as much as several times a week. Hundreds of private mediums discovered their powers in their own drawing rooms. And it was almost as if mediumship was catching – as soon as one person in a household demonstrated their abilities, everyone else living there would soon follow suit. The doubtful legality of mediums' activities, coupled with the very real problem of being accused of insanity, led to many mediums being extremely private about their activities. The threat to their social position – and in some cases, their jobs – was an added attractant towards secrecy for certain mediums.

Mediumship was primarily a feminine activity. Housebound and frustrated women, barred from gainful and stimulating employment by social conventions, and living within the limited horizons allowed by their domestic responsibilities, leaped on the escapism offered by involvement in the spiritualist movement. No single creed existed for spiritualists, and so it was easy to ally your own personal beliefs with mediumship.

Victorian England was in a state of crisis as far as religion went. Christianity was being buffeted from all sides with doubts raised by recent scientific discoveries. The inherent divinity of humanity was under question. The move towards materialism was seen by many as making a mockery of morality and accepted social sanctions. In the earlier part of the century a fascination with apocalyptic prophecies and signs had led to the formation of such groups as the Plymouth Brethren. By the later half of the century, with Christianity under threat, spiritualism was to take a similar role in the lives of many. Perhaps Mabel had not moved so far away from her family's background as it first appears.

And although often only passing comment is made in histories of spiritualism, it is worth bearing in mind that the spiritualist movement coincided with the birth of the women's rights movement. The two were intertwined. In the north of England, spiritualism was very much a political movement, having as it did, a strong affinity with the works of Robert Owen.[93] Although not all feminists claimed to be spiritualists, all spiritualists advocated women's rights to a greater or lesser extent – within spiritualist practice women and men were equal. Finally, death was a women's issue, centring as it did around the home.

Mabel was described as a medium by many, implying that she was able to open the lines of communication with the dead whilst in a trance state. As in later years she was violently opposed to spiritualism, little documentation remains about this part of her life. AP Sinnett says that "she was amongst those gifted with the faculties that put consciousness into relation with other realms of nature besides those cognised by the physical senses..."[94]

From 1872 to 1876, Florence Marryat,[95] or Mrs Ross-Church, was the editor of *London Society*, a writer like Mabel, and a staunch believer in spiritualism. In December 1860 she had given birth to a daughter who survived for only ten days. The child was born with a cleft palate, and Florence was told that her recent troubles and stresses had been the cause of the deformity.

Florence first made contact with her daughter again at a séance with Mrs Holmes in 1871. A young girl "much muffled up about the mouth and chin appeared, and intimated that she came for me, although I could not recognize her. I was so ignorant of the life beyond the grave at that period, that it never struck me that the baby who had left me at ten days old had been growing since our separation, until she had reached the age of ten years."[96]

Two days later the same spirit face appeared at another of Mrs Holmes' séances. Florence still denied the child was anything to do with her. A few weeks later Florence attended a private séance given by the medium Florence Cook. Again, the child appeared and Florence Cook said that she had some sort of deformity about the mouth. After Florence returned home, she wrote to Miss Cook and received in response a letter that told her the girl was closely connected to her.

Florence remained unconvinced. She tried to make contact herself but failed. She had been told by her close friend John Powles that it was indeed her child, and that her daughter was not yet in heaven. Florence could not understand why an infant should not go directly to heaven, but was later to come to the view that her daughter had training to undergo before she could do so. Mabel was to convince Florence that she had made contact with her daughter in 1873.

Robert knew Florence through writing for *London Society*. The Cooks then had a cottage in Redhill, Surrey and Robert brought an invitation to Florence to spend the weekend with them. So far as Florence was aware, the Cooks knew nothing of her past and dead daughter as she chose not to talk about it. Florence went down to Redhill, and after dinner the three of them sat and chatted about spiritualism and she was told that Mabel was a powerful trance medium.

MYSTICAL VAMPIRE

Florence was immediately interested and Mabel entered a trance with Robert taking shorthand notes. She listened while old friends of the family spoke through Mabel, until Mabel suddenly grabbed her attention by leaving her seat and falling to her knees while kissing Florence's hands and face and sobbing violently.

Florence had no idea what was happening. Mabel returned to her seat and one of her guides speaking through her said that the spirit was unable to speak because of its emotional state, but would try again later. Mabel continued and suddenly, in the midst of other communications, Florence heard her sigh, "Mother!"

Florence began to get excited. She started to respond but Mabel raised her hand to silence her and began to speak. Florence had a conversation with her dead daughter through Mabel. Her daughter said that she was lonely and missed her and looked forward to the two of them going to heaven together and picking blue flowers. She said she had tried to speak before but failed, she could now because Mabel was different to the other mediums.

Mabel got a little cross with the child and scolded her for making things out to be worse than they were. The child said that Florence should not be sad as she would have had more sorrow if her daughter had lived and that it was better that she died. She said goodbye and Florence asked Mabel to describe her appearance. "Her face is downcast. We have tried to cheer her, but she is very sad. It is the state in which she was born. Every physical deformity is the mark of a condition. A weak body is not necessarily the mark of a weak spirit, but the prison of it, because the spirit might be too passionate otherwise. You cannot judge in what way the mind is deformed because the body is deformed. It does not follow that a canker in the body is a canker in the mind. But the mind may be too exuberant - may need a canker to restrain it."

Florence remained convinced that neither Mabel nor Robert knew that she had lost a child or knew any of her friends who could have told her the story. Of course, as Florence had clearly been attending numerous séances to try and contact her daughter, the Cooks could easily have found out the story.

But the episode was not yet over. A short time later Florence was at her solicitor's, seeking his advice. The following morning she was astonished by Mabel running into her room announcing that she had received a message from her daughter that she had been begged to deliver without delay. The message was that her daughter had been with her at the solicitors and that Florence should not take the advice offered. Mabel said that she had no idea what the message was about but thought it best to deliver it at once, especially as she was coming into town anyway. Florence was convinced. She saw no way that anyone could have known of what had transpired between herself and her solicitor.

Florence was now convinced that her own sorrows and stresses had caused the death of her daughter. She believed that she was able to lift her child from her state of depression and so spent as much time as she could trying to communicate with her. Throughout the following years she attended numerous séances and made some sort of contact with her each time. Florence was convinced that she was regularly in contact with her daughter.

Mabel's experiences while working as a medium and in attending the séances of others led her to believe that the practice was highly dangerous.

> "Spiritualists are people who call spirits from the vasty (*sic*) deep…I have gathered together episodes from real life, which reveal some of the dangers that lie in the path of those who practice what is called spiritualism…I have expressed my conviction that the practice is dangerous…if disembodied spirits of men or women were all that visited the séance room, the seekers for communication with them might only incur the danger of being selfish…any form of selfishness is the first step in black magic…elemental beings…they are non human…spirits arising from the forces which surround men, from earth, air, fire, water…some of the elemental beings are friendly to man and protect him…others are definitely his enemies."[97]

But this was to come later. In the early days Mabel was a seeker of truth. She wrote in 1906 "It is many years ago (perhaps a quarter of a century) that I first accomplished the feat of getting out of my body and realising myself apart from it…I had given hours of concentration, during many months, to one definite aim, that of acquiring knowledge. I did not at all imagine that I had to go out of my body in order to obtain the kind of knowledge I wanted – truth"[98] She describes being led by the hand in her astral body to a hall of learning where she saw jewels and writing. The writing that she returned to note down was eventually to form the text of *Light on the Path*.

It was in 1878 that Mabel was to have the experience that she documented and that was to lead to the writing of *Idyll of the White Lotus*. She described how a procession of priests appeared as her inspiration and that she wrote the first seven chapters of *Idyll* automatically. In the preface to *Light on the Path* she also states "Once as I sat alone writing, a mysterious Visitor entered my study unannounced and stood beside me…He spoke from knowledge, and from the fire of his speech I caught faith. I have written down his words; but alas, I cannot hope that the fire shall burn as brightly in my writing as in his speech." *Light on the Path* and *Idyll* are regarded as classics of theosophical writing and their role within theosophical history is discussed below. At this stage Mabel had no thoughts of theosophy and was concerned with seeking truth through spiritualist practice.

Mabel's experience is best told by herself:- "I was living in a house in the Adelphi that looked upon the river when Cleopatra's Needle[99] was brought into London by that ancient highway and set up on the Embankment. It was placed just beneath my windows. In the first moment I saw it I became aware of a face in it, which I soon discovered was not visible to anyone else. It was an Egyptian face, full of power and will, and intensely alive. The effect was very strange, because it was just the same width as the Needle, and it gave an idea to me of an imprisoned being, too large for the space in which it was confined. I cannot attempt to offer any explanation of this, I can only state that I have never seen the Needle without seeing the face, and that I have seen it sometimes with the eyes closed and the expression of deep Egyptian calm upon it, but more often with the eyes open, looking hither and thither with an inscrutable glance."

> "Immediately after the arrival of the Needle I became aware of long processions of white-robed priests who came in at the door of the house and up the stairs and into the room in which I was, and stood around me. This happened constantly, and I grew accustomed to the gleam of the white draperies amid the gloom which generally hangs over that part of London."

"I was at work upon a novel at the time, writing incessantly. My sister-in-law was staying with me, and she was busy upon some drawing, which kept her equally occupied. We generally worked at the same table, she with her drawing board on one side of it, and I at the other, writing, as has been my habit, very rapidly, and throwing the pages aside without taking the time to dry the ink upon them. One day we were at work in this manner when I saw the procession of priests come in at the door of the room. I looked up at them for a moment and saw that they were ranging themselves all around as usual. Then I returned to my writing, for I was working against time, and did not want to spare even a few moments to look at this wonderful array of Egyptian priests, with their composed, purposeful faces, in their most beautiful robes of glistening white. I had often described them to my sister-in-law, so I did not stay even to tell her of their presence, but went on busily writing. She looked up at me and noticed a change in my appearance; I had become rigid, or like one turned to stone as she expressed it; my eyes were fast closed, but I wrote on and on, as quickly as ever; and she watched me cast page after page aside, the ink all wet."

"This continued for some considerable time, and then at last I opened my eyes and dropped the pen. I was very tired, but I was absolutely unaware of the fact that I had been unconscious – or, out of the body – or whatever one may choose to call it. She said nothing, but watched me still, and saw me take up a page of my manuscript to look at and discover to my unutterable amazement that it was not, as I believed, a page of the novel I was writing, but something entirely and absolutely unknown to me. Page after page I picked up and regarded with the same amazement. I found that I held in my hand, complete, the prologue and the first chapter of the *Idyll of the White Lotus*. My sister-in-law is no longer in this world to tell this tale herself, but it is well known in her family, for she often talked of it. To me it was a very wonderful experience, as I had never until then known what it was to be absolutely taken from my body in order that my hand and pen might be used by another intelligence without my being – if I may so express it – even present."[100]

One cannot help but wonder at Mabel's easy acceptance of a procession of Egyptian priests strolling through her house at regular intervals. And the point has been oft made that this account did not appear until after the death of her sister-in-law, making it impossible to seek confirmation of the experience.

The experiences continued until Mabel had seven chapters completed. The writing was originally published as part of *Cobwebs* in 1882. Because of Mabel's annotation "The papyrus unfortunately ends here", the myth sprang up that the manuscript was found by her written on a papyrus – as if her experiences were not strange enough! It was during 1884-5, when Mabel was ill and there was "much trouble" in her life that the work was finally finished.

The text of *Light on the Path* was acquired in a similar manner, and again Mabel's sister-in-law was present. "…I was one day taken away from my body, taken out of the place I was in, to another and very different place, where I found myself moving about in another and very different body, and using its senses with a similar difficulty to that experienced by a child in using it newly acquired senses. I was led by the hand like a child, by a powerful being who showed me what to look at and stood in front of one of the walls. I looked at it with great delight, for it was incomparably beautiful. It blazed with jewels; from the floor to the dim distant roof, every inch of this glorious wall is crusted thickly with them, and the sparkle and flash is bewilderingly beautiful. I was told to look with care and then I saw that the jewels were arranged in patterns and designs. It needed more than my own attention, it needed actual help from my guide, to enable me to see that these patterns and designs were letters formed into words and sentences. But I was enabled to see this, and told to remember very carefully as much as I could read, and to write it down the moment I returned to my body."[101]

The two experiences differed in that the second time Mabel was actively attempting to attain a different condition of consciousness. She continued for many years to repeat these experiences, particularly in 1893, when she states she was almost constantly out of her body – this led to *The Story of the Year*.[102] Another book *The Scroll of the Disembodied Man*[103] was written by Mabel undergoing the experience jointly with Dr Helen Bouchier in 1902.

In later years, the method by which Mabel obtained the text of *Light on the Path* was to cause a major argument within the Theosophical Society. And the fact that she suffered at least one nervous breakdown over the next few years, one that she herself wrote about in 1889, has led to questions about Mabel's state of mind. At this distance in time there is no way that we can ascertain the truth of the matter and whether or not her claimed abilities were genuine. What is certain is that many around Mabel fully believed that they were.

But incredible though these stories are, Mabel was for much of her time a married woman who wrote novels. Her psychic experiences did not form anywhere near such a large part of her life as did her writing. Robert would still come home from his office at night and Mabel would still have to lead the life of a Victorian middle class housewife.

By 1881 the Cooks were living opposite the artist and writer, Isabelle de Steiger, "Mrs Cook was a charming creature, and they lived in a little old-fashioned Victorian villa, standing in a large square garden, full of apple and pear trees, roses and canary creepers. It was smothered in greenery, shading the rustic verandah with which all homes then were furnished."[104]

Keeping two servants allowed Mabel to divide her time between her psychic and literary efforts. By this stage she was developing a life of her own away from Robert's supervision. When Robert died Mabel was left to live the life of a respectable widow.

In his will Robert left Mabel a little over £2,651. When the will was re-sworn two years later the sum rose to a little over £3279. With the income Mabel earned from her books, although not a rich woman, she would be able to live comfortably for a few years.

CHAPTER FOUR

It was a dark and stormy night[105]

A month before Mabel was born, in 1851, a young Russian woman spent her twentieth birthday on the beach in Ramsgate.[106] She had made her escape from the hard work demanded by her employer to whom she acted as companion, and armed with her sketchbook and pencils had fled to the new resort that was rapidly becoming popular with Londoners.

In warm weather the beach at Ramsgate was so crowded that it was difficult to pick a path through the throng. Women lay on their backs at the water's edge and let the waves fling their bathing dresses over their heads. Young gentlemen employed opera glasses to enjoy the view and the staid British press delighted in the apparent lack of decency shown by their behaviour.

Our young woman spent a day and a night there, drawing scenes of the water and sailboats. She also noted in her sketch book, "Nuit memorable! Certaine nuit, par au clair – de lune qui se couchait a Ramsgate 12 Aout 1851 lorsque je recontrais M le Maitre – de mes rêves!!" *(Memorable night! On a certain night by the light of the moon that was setting at Ramsgate on August 12 1851, when I met M the Master of my dreams!!)*[107]

It isn't totally clear who the man of her dreams actually was. Years later Helena Petrovna Blavatsky[108] would claim that it was the first fleshly manifestation of Mahatma Morya. He was Blavatsky's childhood protector, and she saw him as her personal Master.[109] The story is confused by her own differing version of the story where she first came across Morya in London. It's been suggested that the man she saw at Ramsgate was the novelist Edward Bulwer-Lytton, who was to have a heavy influence on her work. Or perhaps it was a romantic encounter. After all, on the second page of her sketchbook she wrote of a man and woman, out doors on a beautiful summer night with the man saying, "I love you – words formed of a divine perfume of the soul." And she added that he would later have regretted having uttered these words. But, "Love is a vile dream, a nightmare," she added on the next page. Happiness lay in the acquisition of supernatural powers.

In some ways it isn't important precisely who the encounter was with. After all, Helena was to rewrite her own history on numerous occasions in future years. It's almost impossible at this juncture to judge how much of what she said is true. But there was an encounter that she claimed to be with a Master. And it would be through the Masters that she would later have a connection with Mabel.

Over the next few years Helena Blavatsky would lead a well travelled and exciting life. Even the most sceptical of accounts made it clear that she was destined to become renowned for SOMETHING. Her life story has been written on many occasions, so here we gloss over the years she spent back in Russia, her travels through India and Egypt, the likelihood or not of her visit to Tibet. According to her own accounts there were few parts of the world she did not grace with her presence at some point over the next few years. Along the way she picked up a variety of skills, becoming renowned as a spiritualist and medium for one.

By 1875 she had ended up in America, where, along with Henry Steel Olcott[110] and William Quan Judge[111] amongst others, she founded the Theosophical Society. Societies with spiritualist and occult agendas were sprouting up at an alarming rate during this time. There was no reason to suppose then, that this particular one would be more influential than any other.

The word "theosophy" comes from the term "theosophia" and means "knowledge of the divine". The objectives of the Theosophical Society are: "to form a nucleus of the universal brotherhood of humanity, without distinction of race, creed, sex, caste, or colour; to encourage the study of comparative religion, philosophy, and science; to investigate the unexplained laws of nature and the powers latent in man." At the time of the formation of the Theosophical Society, Blavatsky was living in New York. On 7th September 1875, George Felt, an engineer and architect, gave a lecture in Blavatsky's rooms. During the discussion which followed, Olcott expressed his opinion that it would be a good idea to form a society that pursued and promoted occult research. Everyone attending was happy with this idea and Judge proposed that Olcott be the Chairman while Olcott in return proposed Judge as Secretary. The next day this was formally agreed and sixteen people gave their names as being willing to form and belong to such a society. A constitution and bye laws were drawn up and presented to a meeting on 12th September. It was decided to name the new organisation The Theosophical Society. The first meeting under this name was held on the 16th October, in the drawing rooms of Emma Hardinge Britten, a well known spiritualist.

The Theosophical Society reached England in 1878. Its early meetings were held at the Great Russell Street home of the British National Association of Spiritualists, from which many of its early members were claimed. It's likely that it was through this connection that Mabel first came into contact with theosophy. Numerous writers contributed eagerly to spiritual and psychic research during this period. Charles Carlton Massey,[112] impressed with what he had seen of theosophy in the US, opened the first European branch of the Theosophical Society in London. He resigned from the society in 1884, after finding that his discovery of what he thought to be a precipitated letter had been staged. The second president, George Wyld, also abandoned theosophy in its early years. It may never have taken off in England if it weren't for the enthusiasm of Alfred Sinnett.[113]

Sinnett met Blavatsky in 1879 while in India as the editor of an Anglo-Indian daily paper, *The Pioneer*. He was already a spiritualist and not long after meeting her was receiving precipitated letters from the Masters with almost monotonous regularity. These letters became the basis of his books *The Occult World* and *Esoteric Buddhism* published in 1880 and 1883. His enthusiastic campaigning for theosophy lost him his job in India and he returned to England in April 1883 where he quickly made himself and his home a centre of theosophical activity in London. Only a year later he manoeuvred Dr Anna Kingsford[114] out of office as president of the Theosophical Society, and to most intents and purposes was theosophy in England.

On his arrival in England Sinnett had become intimate friends with the Arundales in Notting Hill. Francesca Arundale[115] was a former spiritualist and friend of Charles Massey. She lived with her mother Mary and six year old nephew, George. Drifting through Allan Kardec's[116] reincarnationist groups, into Anna Kingsford's coterie and finally finding herself deeply immersed in theosophy, Francesca made her work for the Society a full time occupation. Her home in London was soon a gathering place for theosophists. Sinnett decided not to return to India after spending the summer in Europe and finally settled in London in October of 1883, happy to use his home from January 1884 as a theosophical base.

During February of 1884 the Theosophical Society was under attack at their headquarters in Adyar, Madras when Blavatsky was charged with forgery in producing letters from her teachers as well as trickery in the production of phenomena. Worldwide publicity put the Society under extreme pressure and the Society for Psychical Research sent to India a young man named Richard Hodgson[117] to investigate and report on the situation. But in London theosophy was as strong as ever. It would not be until the following year that the reports that would shake the Theosophical Society would be published.

Mabel's marriage was failing and she had separated from Robert four years earlier. She was now in her late thirties, tall and slim with flowing auburn hair and a beautiful oval face. And she was an interesting character in her own right. By now a renowned novelist and respected medium, her psychic abilities and standing in society opened many doors for her. By February 1885 she had moved out of the marital home and was living in Clarendon Road. Spiritualism no longer appealed to Mabel. Her experiences had left her worried about what precisely she was dealing with when she was involved in séances. In later years she was to be vehemently opposed to any mediumistic practices, describing spiritualism as,

> "...one of the greatest menaces to true religion in the present day and that it is the most subtle of the devil's efforts of the century."[118]

She believed that elemental beings would come into séances and pretend to be the spirits of the dead. These elementals were not human, but spirits that arose from the elements.

"They delight in getting possession of a human body, evicting its rightful tenant. Mad houses contain many of them; a family is made utterly wretched when one gets possession…They are without human feelings or human sympathies and entirely disregard human laws."[119]

Considering that Robert was said to have gone mad after his experiences in spiritualism, one cannot help but wonder whether Mabel is describing episodes in her marriage.

Mabel had been first introduced to theosophy in 1881, when Robert was lent a copy of Blavatsky's *Isis Unveiled* by Isabelle de Steiger,[120] who at that time lived opposite the couple.

On Tuesday afternoons the Sinnetts were "at home" to visitors. The hours were crowded with friends wanting to talk about theosophy. Mabel was one of many. "On the 31st January 1884, we moved into our new house, 7 Ladbroke Gardens – 'Mabel Collins' was one of us and very helpful at that time in our studies as she was extremely sensitive and under the direct influence of the master Hilarion."[121]

It was a strange and varied group that filled the Sinnetts' rooms: "I remember very well the strange crew that filled Sinnett's drawing room at the gatherings, the astrologers, the mesmerists, the readers of hands and a few, very few only, of the motley spiritualist groups."[122] Although there were numerous people passing through the doors, there were only a small number of regular visitors, Mabel amongst them.

Theosophy was becoming highly fashionable. Members would gather to study the works of Blavatsky and other theosophical authors, and discuss their meaning. Much of this writing was obscure and difficult to understand. It was probably more frustrating to Mabel than most, considering that she had no problem in writing spiritual works in an accessible fashion. Mabel satirises one such meeting in *The Mahatma*.

"She was asked by the old lady to read Mr Waters writing aloud…she did so, in a high-pitched, monotonous voice, and with elaborate emphasis:

"*In the beginning of all things, there was nothing.*
There was less than nothing, for there was no mind to realise the nothingness.
In the beginning, there was not chaos, for there was no conscious-

ness with which to know there was chaos.
In the beginning there was neither light nor dark nor cold nor shape nor form.
Nor yet was there any knowledge that these things were not.
In the beginning there was not the spirit of the world, which has created and built it up.
Nor was there any fire, nor anything of which chaos could be made.
In the beginning there was neither movement nor stillness.
Nor was there anything which could move or be silent."[23]
Quite.

Mabel described to Sinnett her experiences of the Egyptian priests who crossed her room while she was working on *The Idyll of the White Lotus*. Once the seventh chapter was completed the priests had stopped visiting. Although she was anxious to complete the work it was seven years before she was able to do so. In 1884-85, amid many problems and illnesses, "the work was taken up again by a mysterious power outside myself for whom I was a chosen instrument, and it was finished in the same manner that the first seven chapters were written, without my being aware of a single word."[124]

Mabel sent her work to *Banner of Light*,[125] a New York spiritualist magazine, which published it. The original was written in Greek characters. Isabelle de Steiger assumed that Mabel must have been writing English in Greek characters, as modern spiritualism didn't tend to throw around classical language tuition. Though it may not have been something she regularly put to good use, Mabel had, of course, been taught Greek by her father years earlier. She showed the manuscript to a Mr Ewen, and Gerard Finch,[126] then President of the Theosophical Society in England arranged for it to be published as a book. Mabel said that the work had been "inspired" by "some one" whose appearance she described. Mr. Ewen showed the manuscript to Colonel Olcott, with whom Mabel Collins talked and told him the story of how it came about. She told Colonel Olcott that the work had been written by her either in trance or under dictation, and described to him the appearance of the inspirer. Finch arranged for *Idyll* to be published in booklet form and distributed it amongst theosophists.

Blavatsky would be eager to claim the intervention of the Master Hilarion[127] in Mabel's work. "...when I met her she had just completed *The

Idyll of the White Lotus, which as she stated to Colonel Olcott, had been dictated to her by some "mysterious person". Guided by her description, we both recognised an old friend of ours a Greek, and no Mahatma, though an Adept; further developments proving we were right..." [128]

The Masters, or Mahatmas, are integral to the theosophical belief system. Blavatsky claimed that she had been instructed by them to form a society for the purpose of making known to the world certain teachings. She said that they were men possessed of the highest wisdom, who had a knowledge of the laws of life and death and of the phenomena of nature, and who were able to control the forces of nature and produce phenomena according to natural law as they desired. They were located in Tibet, but existed in all parts of the world. They were amongst the few who had reached sainthood and become members of the hierarchy responsible for governing the world. As teachers they supervised apprentices who had devoted themselves to humanity. The Masters often communicated their wishes by precipitated letters, mail that would drop from an astral post box.

The Master Hilarion is responsible in particular for science. Another Master translated the aphorisms in *Light on the Path* from Sanskrit into Greek and Hilarion then obligingly translated them for Mabel. Hilarion is an ancient Greek although he often stays in Egypt. It was Hilarion who was given credit for Mabel's work.

In later years Mabel was to satirise theosophists and their dealings with the Masters in *The Mahatma: A Tale of Modern Theosophy*.[129]

A facsimile of a page of the original writing was published by Sinnett to show how unlike Mabel's normal handwriting this manuscript was. When Mabel described how this manuscript had been produced, she said that she had been absolutely taken from her body in order that her hand and pen might be used by another intelligence.

In April of 1884 year Blavatsky came to London just before a meeting to replace Anna Kingsford as president with Finch at Sinnett's behest was to take place. In the middle of this acrimonious meeting Blavatsky arrived and caused the whole meeting to become filled with excitement. She went home with the Sinnetts and floods of eager visitors followed her to their door.

Bertram Keightley[130] was present at this meeting and later described what happened. "The first time I ever saw Mme. Blavatsky was in 1884, shortly after I had joined the Theosophical Society. A meeting had been called and was being held in the chambers of a member in Lincoln's Inn. The reason for the meeting lay in differences of opinion between Mr. Sinnett on the one hand and Mrs. Kingsford and Mr. Maitland on the other. Colonel Olcott was in the chair and endeavoured to adjust the differences of opinion, but without success. By him were seated the contending parties, Mohini M. Chatterji [131] and one or two others, facing a long narrow room which was nearly filled with members of the Society. The dispute proceeded, waxing warm, and the room steadily filled, the seat next to me being occupied by a stout lady who had just arrived, very much out of breath. At the moment someone at the head of the room alluded to some action of Mme. Blavatsky's, to which the stout lady gave confirmation in the words "That's so". At this point the meeting broke up in confusion, everybody ran anyhow to the stout lady, while Mohini arrived at her feet on his knees. Finally she was taken up to the end of the room where the "high gods" had been enthroned, exclaiming and protesting in several tongues in the same sentence and the meeting tried to continue. However, it had to adjourn itself and so far as I know, it never reassembled. Next day I was presented to Mme. Blavatsky, who was my stout neighbour of the meeting. Her arrival was totally unexpected and her departure from Paris was, she told me long afterwards, only arranged "under orders" half an hour before she left. She arrived at Charing Cross without knowing the place of meeting, only knowing she had to attend it. "I followed my occult nose," she told me, and by this means got from the station to Lincoln's Inn and found her way to the rooms on foot. Her arrival was singularly opportune, for it broke up a meeting, which declined to be peaceful, in spite of all the oil, which Colonel Olcott was pouring on its troubled waters." [132]

The likelihood of Blavatsky walking anywhere at this point in her life was low owing to her ill health. Invitations had been pouring in to visit London for some time. Francesca Arundale, Isabelle de Steiger, the Sinnetts, as well as numerous people she hadn't met, had recently written to invite her. She'd refused these as well as a formal invitation to attend the meeting. But if anything Bert had underplayed the excitement. "The members wildly delighted and yet half-awed at the same time, clustered around our great Founder, some kissing her hand, several kneeling before her, and two or three weeping hysterically." [133]

Things were not running smoothly with the Theosophical Society. Sinnett himself had numerous rows with Blavatsky but was to later claim he couldn't remember what they were about, "Rows were so frequent that a much better memory than mine might be pardoned for not keeping count of them all." [134]

But Blavatsky had arrived, the light was turned away from other theosophists and yet in the midst of all this excitement, Mabel was to produce what was to be generally accepted as the most classic of all theosophical works.

Mabel was in every way a foil for Madame. Every bit a lady, she looked much younger than her thirty-five years. During the summer of 1884 Archibald and Bertram Keightley, who were to become instrumental in the Theosophical Society, met Blavatsky. They both became very close to Mabel. Exactly how close that was is open to conjecture. However, the relationship between Mabel and both Arch and Bert was described as intimate – certainly from Bert's point of view as he pointed out later, "I have known Mabel Collins intimately from the date of the publication of *Light on the Path*."[135] Rumours were later to fly around that Mabel had become engaged to Bert – or perhaps that was simply a polite way of describing the black magic sex rituals the two were supposedly involved in? But Mabel's sexuality was not under question at this point.

Mabel's best known spiritual work *Light on the Path* was written in 1884. She said that this book was the result of her hard work trying to gain some knowledge. When outside her body, she felt like a child beginning to discover her recently acquired senses. She was led by the hand by a powerful being that showed what she should look at and how to understand what it was. She saw that the walls of a huge room, which she called the "Hall of Learning", were covered by precious stones and, with the help of her guide, she realised that they formed phrases. They told her to try to remember carefully these phrases and to write them down as soon as she returned to her physical body.

On 8th November 1884, Mabel met Blavatsky shortly before she returned to India. Blavatsky herself was later to say that they met on two or three occasions during the autumn of 1884, always in the presence of others. It doesn't appear that any great friendship was struck at this time. Theosophists were thick on the ground in London during that autumn, and great numbers of them enthusiastically met Blavatsky. It would have been strange if Mabel hadn't been amongst those. Almost a thousand people had attended the reception Sinnett held for Blavatsky at Prince's

Hall, Piccadilly on 21st July. Small wonder too, that Blavatsky couldn't remember having met Mabel until November.

The two women must have made a strange contrast. Mabel could not have been more different to Blavatsky. "Except for being immensely obese, in consequence of her gross habits, she was not a particularly ill-favoured old witch when I met her in 1884. Remarkably small, pretty hands and feet for such a curiosity, though with long, dirty nails; suspicion of pug in the saucy nose; pale, restless eyes; flossy yellow hair, tending to kink; Tartar face with high cheekbones, fat chops, and a dewlap, the latter always hid by hand or fan in her photographs; stature medium; weight perhaps 250 pounds; harsh, strident voice; conversation profane and witty; temper abominable; odour of tobacco abiding; dress a sort of a compromise between the robes of a Norma and a *robe de nuit* — such is the general impression she made upon me in 1884, when she was about 53."[136]

As far as Blavatsky was concerned the Master Hilarion had again appeared to Mabel Collins in 1884 and had dictated to her the conclusion of *The Idyll of the White Lotus* and the whole of *Light on the Path*. Mabel said that *Light on the Path* had been written under "Sri Hilarion" beginning in October 1884 and that the small essay on Karma, published as an appendix, had been written on 27th December 1884. It was later claimed that *Light* wasn't begun until November of 1884, three days before Blavatsky was to depart for India. Whatever the specific date, Mabel called on Blavatsky at this time and showed her a couple of pages of the working manuscript of *Light*. Sinnett by now was totally convinced that Mabel was under the influence of the Master Hilarion.

Until this time Blavatsky hadn't taken Mabel any more seriously than any of the other theosophists hanging onto her skirts. But the work Mabel was producing was gaining a lot of attention. Blavatsky was quick to ensure that credit was given to the Masters before Mabel could attribute it elsewhere. "...she saw before her, time after time, the astral figure of a dark man (a Greek who belongs to the Brotherhood of our Masters), who urged her to write under his diction. It was Hilarion, whom Olcott knows well. The results were *Light on the Path* and others."[137] Attributing *Light* to Hilarion neatly solved the problem of Blavatsky's opposition to spiritualism and Mabel's insistence that she had acted as a medium for the true writer. There was no conflict if the messages came directly from one of the

Masters. Mabel was later to believe that she had been manipulated by Blavatsky and described her actions in her later fiction.

> "The Countess had seen a great opportunity in his development as a visionary and fanatic, and had determined to utilise it to the very utmost, and to be held back by no scruple. She saw that she could accomplish all she desired if people were as credulous as she thought them."[138]

Mabel happily accepted Blavatsky's version of events at this time. In February of 1885 she was calling on friends in Cambridge and paid a visit to Mrs. C. A. Passingham, the president of the Cambridge Theosophical Society. She spent the afternoon and part of the evening at her house. "She expressed a wish to leave early, as she had an 'appointment' with 'Hilarion'..." Apparently Hilarion was to dictate the next part of *Light* at 8 pm that evening. Mabel also told Mrs Passingham that *Light* was written under the influence of, 'a person whom she had long known, but had only lately identified as being that of an 'adept.'

Light on the Path, published in April 1885 was headed "a Treatise written for the personal use of those who are ignorant of the Eastern Wisdom, and who desire to enter within its influence. Written down by M.C., Fellow of the Theosophical Society." As it was the first, and at that time only, apparently simple and direct statement of the rules of practical occultism, and as it was plainly hinted that the book was inspired, it attracted immediate attention. It was to immediately become a theosophical classic. Before being published however, *Light* was read in draft form to Sinnett's group. So although Blavatsky's claims that she did not see *Light* until some time after it was published bear a ring of truth, the material contained within *Light* was available and talked about some months before its publication.

Untangling the story of how *Light* was written is rather like trying to knit with spaghetti. In time to come the Theosophical Society was to be immersed in a major argument about whether or not the Masters were involved, whether Mabel had been honest, and whether Blavatsky had put pressure on her to say that her work was inspired by the Masters. As soon as one thread in the tale is grasped, it slips from hold and three more threads appear to confuse. For the rest of her life Mabel was to carry *Light* around with her. And it was to have effects on her life she could not possibly have foreseen.

But writing inspirational texts couldn't possibly take up all of Mabel's time. She was one of the signatories to a letter from the London Lodge requesting that an inner group be set up for esoteric studies. Interestingly, the letter is also signed by Robert's sister, Louisa Cook. So Mabel may have been a little more respectable than it at first appears. Louisa was clearly accompanying her to theosophical meetings and is likely to have been the person who was with Mabel when she had the visions that lead to the writing of *Idyll*. It was early August of 1884 when theosophists petitioned the Masters, expressing their "implicit confidence in the Masters and their teachings and unswerving obedience to their wishes in all matters concerned with spiritual progress." An inner group was established but wasn't very successful. The Esoteric Section of the Theosophical Society wasn't to be born until autumn 1888.

Two of the signatories to the letter, Isabelle de Steiger and Ralph Palmer Thomas were to meet their esoteric needs through joining the Golden Dawn. Louisa also kept herself busy – she was working on her book *Geometrical Psychology or the Science of Representation: An Abstract of the Theories of Diagrams of B.W. Betts,* which was to be published in 1887.

Though theosophy and theosophical socialising took up much of Mabel's time, she continued to write her novels. The semi-autobiographical *In the Flower of Her Youth* had been published in 1883, along with *The Story of Helena Modjeska. Viola Fanshawe* appeared in 1884, and 1885 saw the publication of *The Prettiest Woman in Warsaw* and *Lord Vanecourt's Daughter.* This was to be Mabel's last novel for five years. Although she continued to write, her outpourings were directed towards theosophical outlets.

However well known she was to become on the theosophical scene, to most of the world Mabel was a romantic novelist. Her books were published in the USA as well as Britain and she was gaining a reputation of her own, rather than having to try and hold onto her dead father's coattails.

The Story of Helena Modjeska, is a little different from her usual work in that it is a biography. Helena Modjeska, Madame Chiapowska (1840-1909), was a popular Polish actress and the founder, (in 1876), of a short-lived art commune in Orange County, California. Modjeska had gone to California in 1876 with her husband, Charles Bozenta Chiapowski. Their Polish agricultural colony in Anaheim was a financial failure in the drought and depression of 1877. Modjeska learned some of her former roles in English and made a sensational stage debut in San Francisco in August of that year. For nine months of the year she travelled throughout America, and although she never lost her Polish accent, became America's most distinguished Shakespearean actress of the 1880s and 1890s. She appeared on the London stage for the first time in May 1880. Although the book was to appear with Mabel's name on the cover, it was originally written in collaboration with John Lillie and serialised in *Temple Bar* magazine in 1882. When the book appeared Modjeska was at the height of her fame and sales were guaranteed. And sales of *The Prettiest Woman in Warsaw* were no doubt not too badly hindered by the statement in the American press that this also was about Modjeska, especially with the denial printed on the British edition. So perhaps Mabel was moving into new literary fields, taking on a biography? It appears not – in a brief attempt at acting Mabel had taken the role of Helena Modjeska. Her fiction remained solidly based on her own experiences and personal knowledge.

1884 was a year of unrest. While Blavatsky was meeting dignitaries at her reception in July, five thousand people gathered in Hyde Park to protest against the closure of sugar refineries, a protest to continue until early 1886. Counter demonstrations led to riots and shops being looted in February of 1886. The uprisings were to continue into 1887. Trafalgar Square was filled with sleeping homeless and protestors at regular intervals. By the 13th November feelings were running so strong that two deaths and a hundred injuries resulted in the riots on that "Bloody Sunday". Feelings were high against the government and the Queen.

Against this volatile atmosphere, society lady Mabel was a highly successful novelist, part of the inner circle of theosophists, ever rising. This was a different world where hours could be spent analysing the finer points of the Master's desires while people were dying on the streets, fighting for their rights. She seemed destined to take an integral role in the Theosophical Society, perhaps even to become one of its leaders. Her confidence in the theosophical role she had adopted led her to invite Helena Blavatsky to stay at her home in early 1887 when she returned to England. Mabel was to remain a while in the cosy world of theosophy. But no one could have predicted what was to come next.

View of Crown Hill in early 1890s.

CHAPTER FIVE

Herrings in a barrel

The Victorian period saw the real birth of the middle class as a force in politics and social structure. For the first time the middle class was not merely large, but a vast majority, sweeping every structure away in its path. On the surface it was morally and religiously conservative. In modern, popular perception Victorians spent their time covering table legs to avoid offence, travel was difficult and communications were nowhere near as easy as they are today. The telephone and email has made it possible to contact people in moments and travel is relatively simple now. Those poor Victorians.

But this was an era when an office worker could post his wife a letter mid morning to tell her he would be home late for dinner. Where passports weren't required for foreign travel, when thousands amused themselves by conducting long and frequent correspondence with almost strangers. And when it wasn't at all unusual to drop by a slight acquaintance's home and stay for several weeks.

It's also popularly accepted that the Victorian British adored their queen. The late nineteenth century was actually a period of civil unrest. Several riots and demonstrations took place in and around Trafalgar Square between early 1886 and November 1887. On 8th February 1886, the Fair Trade League held a meeting in Trafalgar Square to demand protective tariffs and public works to cure unemployment. About twenty thousand people, many of them dock and building workers, assembled. When the Social Democratic Federation interrupted the meeting and led part of the crowd in the direction of Hyde Park, another part of the crowd marched west, bent on mischief. In the looting that followed, roughly £50,000 of damage was done – about £35 million in today's terms. Over the next two days, a dense fog covered London, increasing the nervousness of West End shop owners.

In the summer of 1887, a large number of homeless, unemployed vagrants began to camp in Trafalgar Square. The police force was reluctant to remove them at first. The fact that charitable organisations in the West End provided the squatters with donations of free food made the problem worse. On 8th November, after many heated arguments with the Conservative Home Secretary, Henry Matthews, Sir Charles Warren, the head of the Metropolitan Police, took decisive action to disperse what he called the "veriest scum of the population,"[139] he banned all meetings in and processions to Trafalgar Square. On "Bloody Sunday," 13th November 1887, the Metropolitan Federation of Radical Clubs organised a series of marches and demonstrations to protest the government's policy of coercion in Ireland. The police violently dispersed the marchers before they reached Trafalgar Square.

The reaction of the West End to "Bloody Sunday" was, on the whole, positive.

It was against this background that Mabel renewed her acquaintance with Helena Blavatsky. During the period when Blavatsky was out of England, Mabel had continued her theosophical involvement. When it became apparent that someone was needed to host Blavatsky during her next stay in England Mabel was delighted to have the honour of being able to offer her services.

Early in 1887 Blavatsky was alone in Ostend. The Countess Constance Wachtmeister,[140] who had been staying with her, had to return to London on business and was sorely missed. When Blavatsky received a letter from Edward Douglas Fawcett offering help with her work she was more than happy to accept his offer.

Fawcett was shortly joined by the Keightleys. Archibald Keightley was a doctor, and the nephew of lawyer Bertram Keightley, who at 27 was a year younger than him. They came from a wealthy Liverpool family in which the teachings of Emmanuel Swedenborg were greatly admired.

Having studied at Cambridge, the two were attracted by spiritualism and after seeing an advertisement for Sinnett's *Esoteric Buddhism* gained an introduction to its author. They joined the Theosophical Society in 1884, around the same time as Mabel. Bert had spent much of 1884 following Blavatsky around Europe.

Both Arch and Bert had been worried about the sorry state of theosophy in London. There were few active members left, meeting once a week for discussion. As Sinnett was refusing to re-activate the Society they believed that the best answer to their problem was for Blavatsky to come to London and teach them occultism.

> "In the early months of 1887 there were some few members of the TS in London who felt that if theosophy did not receive some vital impulse, the center there would be confined to a few individuals only who were pursuing and would continue to pursue their studies. There were many anxious discussions as to how a vital interest could be awakened in the truths of theosophy, and how attention should be restored to the ethical philosophy. We all felt that we were working in the dark and that we were ignorant of the real basis upon which the philosophy rested."

"Obviously we required a leader who might intelligently direct our efforts. We then determined each separately to write to H. P. Blavatsky, who was then in Ostend, laying before the Founder of the TS and the messenger of the Masters the position as each of us saw it. We asked her to reply in a collective letter giving us advice as to what to do. She replied, however, to each individual, writing letters of eight to twelve pages. The result of this was that we all wrote and asked her to come over and direct our efforts. She had told us that she was writing *The Secret Doctrine* and must finish that before undertaking other work. Nevertheless we wrote to her that there was, we believed, urgent need of her directing presence, and that she could finish *The Secret Doctrine* in London as well as or better than in Ostend."[141]

As Blavatsky didn't sound too convinced in her responses, Bert went to Ostend during late February or early March to try and persuade her. She agreed to come to London at the end of April, providing that a house could be found for her to work in peace. Soon after Bert returned, Arch went over to Ostend and also called on Blavatsky. She invited him to stay and asked him to work on *The Secret Doctrine*. He returned to England with the promise that Blavatsky would leave for England on 1st May.

Money had held Blavatsky back from returning to London, but the Keightleys managed to convince her that was no longer a problem. If she agreed to come a beautiful house, free of charge, would be hers. They would personally transport Blavatsky and her belongings across the Channel.

At the end of March, Blavatsky caught a cold that led to bronchitis and developed into a kidney infection. Ashton Ellis, a member of the London Lodge who was also a doctor, was cabled and hurried to Ostend to treat her. Although his ministrations may well have contributed to Blavatsky's recovery, he lost his job at Westminster Dispensary for leaving without permission.

Packing now commenced for the trip to London. When Bert Keightley arrived in mid April, followed by Arch a few days later, Blavatsky's books and papers still needed to be packed. As the rooms she was staying in were already let, she had no choice but to leave. Packing was a hard job, as no sooner was any book, or part of manuscript packed, than she would demand its return, determined to write until the last moment. But the Keightleys were full of enthusiasm as they told Blavatsky about "Maycot", a little cottage in Norwood owned by Mabel who was honoured to be sharing her home with Blavatsky.

On 1st May Arch and Bert, with Blavatsky's maid Louise, wrestled the boxes and trunks down to the steamer and carried Blavatsky aboard. Blavatsky wrote of her journey to William Judge soon after arriving at Maycot.[142]

"Oh *thy* prophetic Soul!" Didn't know old HPB was for 17 days hovering between life & death; drawn irresistibly by the charm *beyond* the latter & held by her coat-tails by the Countess & some London Lodges? Nice intuitional friend. Anyhow, *saved* once more, & once more stuck into the mud of life right with my classical nose. Two Keightleys & Thornton (a dear, *real* new Theosophist) came to Ostende, packed me up, books, kidneys & gouty legs & carried me across the water partially in steamer, partially in invalid chair & the rest in train to Norwood in one of the cottages of which here I am, living (rather *vegetating*) in it till the Countess returns. ...Very, very seedy & weak; but rather better after the mortal disease which *cleansed* me if it did not carry me off. Love & sincere, as usual, & for ever. Yours in heaven & hell. "O.L." H.P.B."[143] The day after her arrival she was at work on *The Secret Doctrine* at 7 a.m.

Maycot, on Crown Hill in Upper Norwood, was described as small, pretty and charming. Crown Hill no longer exists as a street name, it is now called Crown Dale and lies between Beulah Hill and Knights Hill in Norwood. Norwood was originally part of the Great North Wood – hence its name. The area began to be developed in the early nineteenth century. Between six and seven miles from the City and West End of London, Norwood was too distant in the early years of the nineteenth century for commuting, except for the wealthy. This meant that the area became populated by bankers, solicitors and merchants. Detached villas, such as Maycot, began to appear in the 1820s and 30s. Although most of these have now gone, they were replaced by luxury detached houses in the early twentieth century. The first railways station in the area, The Jolly Sailor, opened in South Norwood in 1839. Once the Crystal Palace was moved to Sydenham in 1854, half a dozen new stations opened. Trains had to be the main mode of transport, as trams could not penetrate into the range of hills. The imminent arrival of the Crystal Palace in 1852 made land shoot up in value, and there was a scramble for new housing. Basic amenities such as water and gas became available as suppliers were persuaded to invest in Norwood. When Mabel was living in the area, it was a middle class suburb. There were a few lower class areas, but they were set aside in specific places. The high point of Norwood as somewhere fashionable to live had already passed and it was beginning to decline as the demand for the huge houses that were its speciality fell away.

Mabel was known to have a taste for the precious. She liked tiny, old fashioned houses, rustic verandas shaded by roses and creepers and elaborate interior decoration. One of her later homes in the West End was described in a newspaper article as, "a perfect cage, delightfully appointed for the little bird it holds."[144] Maycot lay near the glass nave and twin towers of the Crystal Palace. The squares and gardens were scented with grape clusters of lilac, and yellow rain of laburnums under soft green leaves. The eternal smoke pall was thinned to a grey veil shining in the afternoon sun, with the great Westminster Towers and a thousand spires and chimneys piercing through. Every house had its smoke wreath, trailing away to the east. The back of the house looked out onto a small private park, common to the occupants of all the houses surrounding it.

Mabel was waiting and ready to welcome Madame into her home. Glamorous, willowy Mabel, with her flaming hair and ivory complexion. Ultra fashionable Mabel, who could wax lyrical for hours about the correct hat trimming for the season. Accomplished and creative Mabel, by this time the author of nine books, a renowned and respected medium and occasional actress. Mabel was waiting impatiently while her good friends, Arch and Bert, adventured to bring the woman she revered as her spiritual teacher to her home. The moment came, and she opened her door to an obese Russian mystic, who smoked like a chimney, and swore like a trooper. Granted, she could do so in several languages.

Mabel's house was thrown upside down immediately. As walking up and down stairs was so painful for Blavatsky, she was unable to take any of the upstairs rooms. The dining room and a room adjacent were hastily turned over to Blavatsky's use. As soon as she arrived Blavatsky demanded that her writing materials be got ready so she could start work the next morning. Mabel and the Keightleys had to rush around making sure that everything was just so. The next day began with Blavatsky complaining that the books she needed weren't yet unpacked. And so the routine began. Blavatsky would rise before 7 am. She would work until called for her midday meal, which could be asked for any time between twelve and four, a constant annoyance to Mabel's cook. And probably no aid to Mabel's digestion. As Mabel was to describe, "Her taste was for comfort of all kinds, and she cared nothing as to how she obtained it…Her black hair streaked slightly with grey…her eyes…glittered like stars. When she was excited, her shrivelled face and attenuated body appeared to be mere accessories to this peculiar brilliance of expression."[145]

There was no doubt that playing host to Blavatsky wasn't a task to be taken on lightly. Mabel and the Keightleys, who were also now staying at Maycot, were constantly on call to answer her whims. People would call to meet Blavatsky, and she would agree or not to see them depending on her mood at that moment. If the answer was no, it was left to Mabel or one of the Keightleys to break the news. At 6:30 pm each evening, Mabel and the Keightleys, would join Blavatsky for dinner with the day's guests. Once the table was cleared out would come tobacco and everyone would smoke and talk, Blavatsky holding court with tales of her travels and experiences, while laying out cards for her endless games of patience.

At least Mabel had been given an idea of what to expect. Francesca Arundale[146] had written about the frustrations of having Blavatsky as a houseguest in 1884, and as Mabel knew Francesca it seems highly unlikely that Mabel was unaware of the difficulties she may encounter. Not knowing whether there would be twenty people for dinner and having to constantly follow Blavatsky around the house to pick up her lighted matches that she dropped everywhere, before the house caught fire, were just two of the problems described by Francesca. But Francesca was such a starry eyed theosophist by that time that nothing would have put her off. "I never felt afraid of HPB in spite of the very strong language she sometimes used. One always somehow felt it was *surface* strong language."[147]

But Mabel couldn't have predicted just *how* difficult Blavatsky was to be, and it seems unlikely that she made the distinction of *surface* strong language. And lit matches were certainly not *surface*. Blavatsky hated Maycot, and didn't trust Mabel.

> "I am in the enemy's camp, and this says all…This house is a hole where we are like herrings in a barrel - so small, so uncomfortable, and when there are three people in my two rooms we tread uninterruptedly on each others corns. When there are four we sit on each other's heads. Then there is no quiet here, for the slightest noise is heard all over the house."[148]

Matters weren't helped by the fact that visitors overwhelmed the small cottage. Visitors arriving at West Norwood station[149] could hear Blavatsky yelling abuse at Mabel as they walked up the road. Blavatsky had taken a strong dislike to everyone in Mabel's household as she wrote to her sister; "Here I am planted among the fogs of Albion. Literally *planted*, because I did not come here of my own free will. I have been dragged over by my *admirers,* nearly in my bed or in their arms. They make a regular hobby of me. To their mind, they won't be able to find their way to the Kingdom of Heaven without me. They sent a deputation with a petition from seventy-two Theosophists who have firmly made up their minds to deprive poor Ostende of my 'ennobling' presence and 'beneficent magnetic fluid' — *excuse du pen!* I grumble at them, I drive them away, I shut myself off from all these *mystical vampires,* who suck all the moral strength out of me — no! all the same they rush to me, like flies to honey. 'We have become aware,' they say, 'of the spirit of holiness and moral perfection in your *atmosphere*. You alone can enlighten us and give life to the hybernating and inactive London Society.' Well, now they have got what they wanted; I have come and thrown more fuel into the furnace — I hope they won't repent it. I sit at my table and write, whilst they all jump about and dance to my music."[150]

They jumped and they danced. The fact that it was never intended that the visit lasted longer than two or three months appears to have persuaded Mabel to grin and bear things. Other people had hosted Madame; Mabel was made of strong stuff and didn't want to be outdone. And however difficult she was as a houseguest, Blavatsky was still Mabel's spiritual teacher.

For some reason Blavatsky decided that Mabel and her housemates needed something more to do. She set Mabel, the Keightleys and Thomas Harbottle about the task of helping her to finish *The Secret Doctrine*. Arch, Bert and Mabel read every line of Blavatsky's writings, screwed up their courage and told her it was "a confused muddle and jumble".[151] Blavatsky was furious. She asked Mabel if she agreed with the Keightleys. Mabel did. Blavatsky told the whole group to go to hell. Her resentment and bad temper worsened. But they began to organise the material. Some of the three foot high manuscript was set aside to be used elsewhere. The rest was put into a semblance of order. Throughout the summer they worked reading, re reading, copying and editing and sending Bert to check references at the British Museum. It would finally be published on 20th October 1888.

Maycot was overwhelmed with visitors from the start of Blavatsky's visit. Some of them gained private interviews; others joined the company already present when they arrived. The Sinnetts called on the first day and stayed for three hours, calling again later in the month. Hopefully, Mabel hadn't anticipated being able to get on with much work herself, because it became impossible. There simply wasn't any time.

Charles Johnson, the twenty year old son of a Protestant Member of Parliament from Ulster, who had planned to become a missionary until reading Sinnett's *Esoteric Buddhism*, was an early visitor. With William Butler Yeats[152] and Claude Wright he had formed the Dublin Hermetic Society in 1885. He wanted to know whether the Mahatmas really existed.

"HPB was just finishing her day's work, so I passed a half hour upstairs with her volunteer secretary, a disciple who served her with boundless devotion. I had known him two years before. So we talked of old times…So the half hour passed, and I went downstairs to see the Old Lady. She was in her writing room, just rising from her desk, and clad in one of those dark blue dressing gowns she loved. My first impression was of her rippled hair as she turned, then her marvelously potent eyes, as she welcomed me: "My dear fellow! I am so glad to see you! Come in and talk! You are just in time to have some tea!" And a hearty handshake."

"Then a piercing call for "Louise," and her Swiss maid appeared, to receive a voluble torrent of directions in French, and HPB settled herself snugly into an armchair, comfortably near her tobacco box, and began to make me a cigarette. The cuffs of a Jaeger suit showed round her wrists, only setting off the perfect shape and delicacy of her hands, as her deft fingers, deeply stained with nicotine, rolled the white rice paper around Turkish tobacco."[153]

Charley spent several hours in discussion with Blavatsky. After Louise had brought in tea and toast, Bert joined them. Almost immediately Blavatsky turned on him and poured torrents of abuse in his direction telling him he was greedy, idle, untidy, unmethodical, and generally worthless. When he tried to defend himself she flared up and declared that he "was born a flapdoodle, lived a flapdoodle, and would die a flapdoodle."[154] Bert soon bolted from the room.

Despite observing Blavatsky's treatment of Bert, Charley was so inspired that not only did he form the Dublin Lodge of the Theosophical Society, but in time to come he married Blavatsky's niece, Vera Zhelihovsky.

He introduced his friend, William Butler Yeats, to Blavatsky. William's visit involved a great deal of waiting. After being left in an outer room for some time he was finally admitted, only to find that he had to wait until Blavatsky had finished the conversation she was having.

Not all visitors were made welcome. Mabel was sitting one evening with Blavatsky when Isabel Cooper Oakley[155] arrived.

"But this is what happened last night about 6 p.m. As Mrs. Cook was with me, Mrs. Cooper Oakley was announced! As I knew you had refused giving her my address I was disagreeably surprised - but -. Well, she came in smiling - beaming, her very hat raising its blooming arms heavenward in glee and joy. "Take care!" I heard my inner voice say, and I did."[156]

A few months previously Isabel and Mabel had had a huge fight. Isabel's face dropped when she saw Mabel was there, "her face became gloomy as night."[157] An odd reaction in some ways considering she was calling at Mabel's house, and could hardly have been surprised at her presence. But they shook hands before Isabel asked Mabel to leave the room so that she could speak privately with Blavatsky. Isabel insisted that Blavatsky had sent her a vision demanding that she visit. Blavatsky insisted that there was no way she would have done such a thing. In fact, she had taken great care to prevent Isabel from finding out her address, which was no doubt why Isabel insisted she had found Maycot psychically.

For the next half hour Mabel and Bert hid in a room upstairs. Mabel had no desire to speak to Isabel and Bert certainly wasn't going to involve himself in any trouble.

"Well she went on producing psychic *plants* for half an hour — and though upon entering she only shook hands with me, now took me tenderly under the chin and looked lovingly into my eyes. And now I see some new villainy against me at Adyar. Sure to."[158]

As soon as the front door was heard to close, Mabel and Bert came downstairs and started to chat with Blavatsky. Blavatsky asked them to be careful what they said in case Isabel overheard. But as Mabel and Bert had just watched Isabel walk up the street, they carried on chatting. And then a moment later Isabel rapped on the door claiming she had forgotten something. Of course, they were all convinced that Isabel had been listening at the door.

Alice Leighton Cleather[159] asked Bert to arrange her visit. He tried to put her off but she was insistent. Living in Eastbourne, Alice had very little money and had to scrimp and save to be able to afford the rail fare. She managed to borrow a room to stay in for a couple of days, and leaving her husband and children behind made the journey. Meeting the well known novelist Mabel was an added bonus to her trip. Alice was under the misapprehension that Mabel was the niece of the renowned author Wilkie Collins, and so part of a major literary family.

Bert met Alice at the station and as they walked up the road they could hear raised voices "ricocheting" down the road. Mabel and Blavatsky were having a slight difference of opinion. Left standing on the doorstep Alice then heard Bert being torn up for bringing a stranger to call at such a bad time. In vain did he point out that she had made the appointment and that Alice had had a long journey. Alice had to return to Eastbourne with her savings gone.

> "I well remember Mr. Keightley telling me on our way out to Norwood that, in their frequent "arguments," she and HPB could be "heard halfway down the road"—when the windows were open! We walked from Western Norwood station and, sure enough, when we got within about a hundred yards of Maycot, I heard loud and apparently angry voices floating—or rather ricochetting—towards us down the road. I was rather aghast, and Mr. Keightley's murmured remark that he was afraid "the old Lady" was in "one of her tempers" was not reassuring, particularly as he added that she would probably refuse to see me! *She did:* Nothing would induce her to, I could hear her saying so when Mr. Keightley went in (leaving me outside on the doorstep), and rating him soundly for bringing a total stranger to call at such an inopportune moment. In vain he reminded her that she herself had made the appointment, and that I had come up from the country on purpose to keep it. No, she was adamant, also angry (at least I thought so then). So I had to return sadly to London, and thence to Eastbourne, my "savings" gone, and my "high hopes" dashed to the ground. Truly I was greatly upset, as I imagined I must be "unworthy." All the same, I by no means abandoned my determination to see HPB in the end—worthy or unworthy."[160]

Alice wasn't the only one who travelled some distance to meet Blavatsky, although others had a better reception. Walter Old, later to be known as the astrologer Sepharial,[161] turned up at noon one sunny day. He immediately felt at home with her, and Blavatsky asked Walter to call her HPB. They sat together and smoked Blavatsky's cigarettes while she asked him about his studies in theosophy and occultism and told stories about theosophy and the characters involved. Walter thought her to be the most interesting person he had ever met, and a few months later he moved into theosophical headquarters.

Three weeks after Blavatsky's arrival a new theosophical lodge was born. With Sinnett's lodge sleeping, London theosophists wanted to be part of a more active group that could publicise theosophy. The story oft quoted is that seven signatures were needed to establish a new lodge but as Blavatsky said, there were only six of them. It took Mabel to point out that Blavatsky herself could sign the application and be the seventh signatory. However, the minutes of that meeting on 19th May are signed by ten, including Blavatsky. Gerard Finch was elected as president, G Thornton as vice president, Arch as secretary and treasurer with Blavatsky, Thomas Harbottle, Mabel, Bert, W Hamilton, Edouard Coulomb and Mabel's sister in law, Lousia Cook forming the council. Every Thursday evening Mabel, Bert and Arch joined the members flocking into Blavatsky's room and listened as Blavatsky answered the many questions put to her. Some of her answers were later to be published as *Transactions of the Blavatsky Lodge*. It wasn't the easiest of experiences for those who chose to question Blavatsky.

> "The procedure under such circumstances is worth recalling. You would, as I did, present your thesis or remarks. It would be received vehemently, be opposed with a variety of eloquence—an eloquence calculated to upset your balance, and the impression given that you were a most evilly designing person, aiming to upset some of Mme. Blavatsky's most cherished plans of work. But with your sincerity of purpose becoming plain, there would come a change in Mme. Blavatsky. Her manner would change, even the expression of her face. "Sound and fury" evaporated, she became very quiet, and even her face seemed to become larger, more massive and solid. Every point you raised was considered, and into her eyes—those wonderful eyes—came the look we learned to recognize. That look was one to be earned as a reward, for it meant that the heart had been searched and that guile was not found, also that HPB was in charge."[162]

Sinnett was furious at these new developments. He announced that anyone who wished to be part of the new lodge was no longer welcome at his. Half of his membership immediately defected. The relationship between Blavatsky and the Sinnetts had deteriorated in any event, especially when she realised that Patience Sinnett had given Isabel Cooper Oakley the address of Maycot. Not that it would have been particularly difficult for Isabel to find it out anyway. Fourteen theosophists joined the new lodge.

> "The Blavatsky Lodge was originally started as a body of people who were prepared to follow HPB implicitly and a pledge embodying this was drawn up. We all took it and the meetings began. Every Thursday evening they were held in Mme. Blavatsky's room, which was thrown into one with the dining room. Members flocked in, so that the rooms were too small, the interest being in the questions which were propounded for Mme. Blavatsky to answer… The meetings…were out of the ordinary. The discussions were informal and all sat round and asked questions of Mme. Blavatsky. All sorts and conditions of men and women were present, and one part of our delight was for Mme. Blavatsky to reply by the Socratic method—ask another question and seek information on her own account. It was a very effective method and frequently confounded the setter of the conundrum. If it was a genuine search for information which dictated the question, she would spare no pains to give all information in her power. But if the matter was put forward to annoy her or puzzle, the business resulted badly for the questioner. The meetings took up a lot of time, but Mme. Blavatsky enjoyed the contest of wits. All nations would be represented in those rooms on Thursday nights, and one could never tell who would be present. Sometimes there would be unseen visitors, seen by some but not by others of us. Results were curious."[163]

At its second meeting on 25th May the Blavatsky Lodge decided that a new magazine was in order. Blavatsky had set the ground by bemoaning her difficulties in getting her views expressed in *The Theosophist*, under the editorship of Col. Olcott in India. But what was it to be called? Suggestions abounded - *Truth*, *Torch*, *Lightbringer*, to name but a few. After long discussions it was decided to call it *Lucifer*. Some vehemently objected to the name as being diabolical and improper. From then on, its title was guaranteed.

The first issue of *Lucifer* featured a discussion between "a well known novelist" and Blavatsky, received and recorded by "one of the editors" – in other words, Mabel. Everyone involved was perfectly aware of how such a magazine title would be received.

"A Well-known Novelist. Tell me about your new magazine. What class do you propose to appeal to?
Editor. No class in particular: we intend to appeal to the public.
Novelist. I am very glad of that. For once I shall be one of the public, for I don't understand your subject in the least, and I want to. But you must remember that if your public is to understand you, it must necessarily be a very small one. People talk about occultism nowadays as they talk about many other things, without the least idea of what it means. We are so ignorant and—so prejudiced.
Editor. Exactly. That is what calls the new magazine into existence. We propose to educate you, and to tear the mask from every prejudice.
Novelist. That really is good news to me, for I want to be educated. What is your magazine to be called?
Editor. Lucifer.
Novelist. What! Are you going to educate us in vice? We know enough about that. Fallen angels are plentiful. You may find popularity, for soiled doves are in fashion just now, while the white-winged angels are voted a bore, because they are not so amusing. But I doubt your being able to teach us much."[164]

The Blavatsky Lodge also decided to start a publishing house to publish not only the magazine, but also *The Secret Doctrine*. Seven hundred pounds were contributed by members towards starting this project but there was almost as much argument about what to call this venture as there was about the name of the *Lucifer*. Mabel was appointed as co editor of the new magazine and suggested in a fit of pragmatism that rather than *Mystic Publishing Company* or *Octagonal Publishing Company*, the new venture be called *The Theosophical Publishing Company*.

As if Mabel didn't have enough to think about, Arch was then stricken with erysipelas, a skin infection that used to be known as St Anthony's fire, and had to take to his bed. As Blavatsky's doctor called to see her, he popped in to give his judgment on Arch. For once, Blavatsky braved the stairs, walking up to the second floor to offer Arch a glass of water, and persuade him to lie on the couch in her room. While lying there he saw a flash of crimson lightening pass by his head.

Blavatsky was becoming an expensive guest. Although she refused cash when the Keightleys or Mabel offered it, she made no contribution towards her room or board. Arch and Bert paid for a professional typist to work on Blavatsky's manuscript and with Mabel covered all Blavatsky's living expenses. Maycot could no longer bear the number of visitors arriving. And it was too far out of London to be convenient. It was time to think of moving on. Blavatsky had been simply waiting for the Countess to return to her and the Countess would soon be arriving.

The Keightleys located a house in Notting Hill at 17 Lansdowne Road for Blavatsky to move into and become the new centre of theosophy. This was convenient for them as Arch owned a house nearby and Bert lived with his mother in Notting Hill. On the 15th September Constance Wachtmeister arrived with her two Swedish servants. *Lucifer* was to be launched within days. After three days of packing the household was moved to Notting Hill. Apart from Mabel – she was left alone at Maycot. Alone for the first time in over three months.

KIM FARNELL

CHAPTER SIX

Penitent squirrels

With *Lucifer* beginning to take off, much of Mabel's writing was directed towards it. For example, *The Blossom and the Fruit* appeared there in serial form throughout 1887 and 1888. However, Mabel still had to find a way of making a living and however worthy it was, *Lucifer* was not going to help her. Even in 1889 *Lucifer* was struggling financially. "The magazine, Lucifer, I do not think is paying expenses yet. It is a very costly thing to get up, and its circulation has necessarily slow growth."[165]

From July 1887 Mabel was writing for *The World*, a paper owned by Frances Yates, who had been a friend of her father's. *The World* consistently carried glowing reviews of Mabel's books. Her weekly column *Tea Table Talk*, written under the name of *Flower o' the May*, considered clothes, cosmetics, recommended a spa for pet dogs, discussed how often a pair of gloves ought to be worn, (once only according to Mabel), and described the latest fashions at great length. She would recommend sun creams, advise on hemlines and spend many column inches waxing lyrical about hats.

At some points she sounded mildly obsessive about the terminology used by other fashion writers. So far as Mabel was concerned a milliner had a larger remit than hat making and she developed this point at great length. In fact, she was happy to develop any of her points at length. "I had not space to say half of what I wanted to say last week about hats, so

I must return to the subject. I am glad that only one milliner among the leading few in London, so far as I know, has had the temerity to exhibit the dog-bonnet, a monstrosity which has been worn of late in Paris – by some people."[166]

At time it can be a little difficult to join in her enthusiasm about some of the clothes she describes. "A quilted silk bonnet is one of the daintiest and simplest things I have seen this year... The squirrel brown silk is quilted just like the inside of a cloak and there are wide soft silk strings which appear to go right through the bonnet and across the back of it... Two squirrels tails stand up in front, and are not sewn or pinned on, but actually tied into their place by the cream coloured ribbon which makes a small, smart bow just above the hair in front."[167] It was doubtless delightful, as Mabel said. But squirrel tails standing up on the forehead perhaps don't make the same sort of fashion statement today. In pursuit of such news Mabel would dash around London in hansom cabs.

For the next two years Mabel was to remain co-editor of *Lucifer*. And theosophical life continued, albeit on a larger scale, much as it had at *Maycot*. Blavatsky stayed firmly planted at Lansdowne Road, writing throughout the day, much of her outpouring being edited by Mabel for *Lucifer*. As one of her more intimate friends, Mabel would often be there later into the evening, chatting with the theosophists who lived in the household, and occasional visitors such as Sinnett.

Mabel's place had been taken by Constance Wachtmeister who ran the household with frightening efficiency. The Keightleys were equally firmly planted there. Blavatsky had to impose a few of her own rules – one being that the household went to bed at midnight. She was also to recommend celibacy for those who aspired to become one of her chelas.

The Thursday evening meetings increased in popularity. Non members were admitted strictly by invitation – and the cards of entry were in constant demand. Unfortunately Blavatsky's social skills hadn't improved along with the change in location. Bert occasionally rebelled, although he always regretted it later. But he never failed to notice how Arch didn't suffer the sharp end of Blavatsky's tongue in the way that he did. When he asked why she never scolded Arch, Bert was told that it was because he had a blue liver, though she never explained what that meant.

There was no doubt that theosophy was becoming highly fashionable. Scores of people poured into the new headquarters to meet the famous Madame. 'At Homes' were held on Saturdays when there would be a succession of guests, and during the week the dinner table was often set for twenty. *Pall Mall Gazette* editor WT Stead,[168] William Butler Yeats and George W Russell (AE)[169] were amongst the visitors. George RS Mead[170] became a member of the household as Blavatsky's private secretary. The Wilde family drifted in and out of the theosophical world with Oscar Wilde's wife, Constance joining the society.

It wasn't all fun and games however. For much of early 1888 Blavatsky was working on *The Secret Doctrine* with the help of the Keightleys, and the Blavatsky Lodge continued to meet on Thursday evenings. "The meetings of the Blavatsky Lodge were out of the ordinary. The discussions were out of the ordinary…All nations would be represented in those rooms on Thursday nights, and one could never tell who would be present."[171] But not all of the visitors were as solid as others.

> "…I remember that the rooms gradually filled until there was no vacant seat. On the sofa sat a distinguished Hindu, in full panoply of turban and dress. The discussion proceeded and apparently our distinguished guest was much interested, for he seemed to follow intelligently the remarks of each speaker. The President of the Lodge arrived that night very late, and coming in looked around for a seat. He walked up to the sofa and sat down — right in the middle of the distinguished Hindu, who promptly, and with some surprise, fizzled and vanished!"[172]

Mabel was living at Clarendon Road at this time, and her garden backed onto that of Lansdowne Road. So although she was not part of the household she and Blavatsky apparently developed the habit of signalling one another across the gardens when they wanted to talk.

The formation of the Esoteric Section of the Theosophical Society was announced by Olcott in the October and November 1888 issues of *Lucifer*. The Esoteric Section of the Theosophical Society was a group solely under Blavatsky's direction, separate and distinct from the Society proper. Members of the section were not taught practical occultism or how to perform psychic phenomena. But as all its activities were carried out under a strict pledge of secrecy, it is unclear how many were being taught there.

So, when on 15th February 1889, Mabel's name suddenly disappeared from *Lucifer* it was inevitable that everyone would want to know why.

Mabel herself kept quiet about the matter. Nothing appeared in *Lucifer* or other theosophical publications to explain what had happened. Gradually, the scandal began to emerge.

One of the main players in the drama was Vittoria Cremers, an American, the widow of Baron Louis Cremers who was at one time attached to the diplomatic corps at the Russian Embassy in Washington. In 1886 Vittoria had come across a copy of *Light on the Path*, which prompted her to immediately join the Theosophical Society. In 1888 she went to Britain and met Blavatsky. As Vittoria had previously been involved with publishing Blavatsky asked her to take over the business side of *Lucifer* – it would only be a short time before Vittoria achieved her ambition of meeting Mabel.

Vittoria moved into the Theosophical headquarters at Lansdowne Road, and after getting to know the Keightleys was introduced by them to Mabel. According to Vittoria, she became firm friends with Mabel and began to spend time at her home. The only version we have of Vittoria's relationship with Mabel is through her unpublished memoirs. Apart from a mention or two by WB Yeats in his letters, Vittoria has cast no permanent mark on theosophical history.

Stories were going around that the original version of *The Blossom and the Fruit* contained an ending that endorsed black magic. According to Blavatsky, she had to intervene before it was published and rewrite the final chapters. Considering how much of Blavatsky's work was rewritten again and again by the Keightleys and Mabel, amongst others, it's a little difficult to accept this.

Whatever the truth of the matter, Vittoria was called in to see Blavatsky one day. She was told that Mabel was being asked to leave the society because of her conduct with the Keightleys. While Vittoria sat wide eyed Blavatsky related how Mabel had been engaged to Arch and the two had taken part in Tantric worship and black magic. The trouble they got themselves into apparently meant that Blavatsky had to intervene to rescue them.

Vittoria refused to break her friendship with Mabel and had to leave the Society herself. Mabel was understandably furious when she heard what was being said about her. Vittoria made sure that Mabel didn't stay in the dark for long by rushing to see her and giving her a full, and embellished, account.

MYSTICAL VAMPIRE

The accusations of tantrism were particularly stinging. There was a strong association between black magic and tantrism. Tantra is often used as a general term that relates to the traditional practice of sex as a spiritual evolutionary scheme. There are many different accounts as to how this may manifest. In some contexts tantric sex simply refers to fellatio. Since Richard Burton's translation of *The Kama Sutra* was made available in 1883 there had been a rising interest in sex and the spiritual. It's more than likely that Mabel would at least be aware of the ideas being discussed. Whether or not she practised them, or what in fact she was specifically being accused of practising is another matter entirely. Blavatsky began to claim that even *Light on the Path* contained dangerous teachings based on tantrism. No one defined precisely what was meant by tantrism.

At this point it seems that a doctrinal difference had simply gone a little wild, and was more interesting than many in-house theosophical rows. But the stories weren't to stop there.

Mabel had also begun a friendship with Michael Angelo Lane. Lane was a newspaper reporter from St. Louis. A staunch theosophist from 1885 he had come to London after hearing about the Esoteric Section and stayed there several weeks. As a member of the Esoteric Section he went from lodge to lodge revelling in the spread of tales of what was happening in the inner sanctum.

Mabel herself had not initially been allowed to join the Esoteric Section. After pleading with Blavatsky she was allowed to join as a probationer but within four days was dismissed for her "treachery and disloyalty". Part of that treachery was to flirt with Lane. WB Yeats wrote in a letter to John O'Leary in May 1889, "Mme B expelled Mrs Cook (Mabel Collins) a most prominent theosophist writer and daughter of Mortimer Collins, also the president of the lodge for flirtation; and expelled an American lady for gossiping about them. Mme B is in great spirits, she is purring and hiding her claws as though she never clawed anybody. She is always happy when she has found a theosophist out and clawed him."[173] Yeats also wrote to Katherine Tynan telling her that Lane and Mabel had been expelled for flirtation and that Mabel's husband was till alive! He contradicts Vittoria's version of events by saying that she was expelled for gossiping about what was happening.

The situation had actually blown up in March and April of 1889. Vague accusations of tantric activities and flirtation with a fellow theosophist sound fairly harmless though surely?

"When I first began to frequent her house, as I soon did very constantly, I noticed a handsome clever woman of the world there, who seemed certainly very much out of place, penitent though she thought herself. Presently there was much scandal and gossip for the penitent was plainly entangled with two young men who were expected to grow into ascetic sages."[174]

So, according to Yeats, Mabel's relationship with the Keightleys went way beyond a little chummy late night editing. Mabel was, of course, an independent widow at this time. Although she had paid lip service to conventionality there is no reason at all to assume that after the breakdown of her marriage to Robert she took the celibate role that Blavatsky recommended to her acolytes. But did Blavatsky actually expect her to be celibate? It seems not – although one Keightley may have been acceptable, two was excessive.

"The scandal was so great that Madame Blavatsky had to call the penitent before her and to speak after this fashion, "We think that it is necessary to crush the animal nature; you should live in chastity in act and thought. Initiation is granted only to those who are entirely chaste," But after some moments in that vehement style, the penitent standing crushed and shamed before her, she had wound up "I cannot permit you more than one."[175]

Vittoria's claims that she had a more intimate relationship with Mabel than Mabel really ought to have had time to schedule, considering what she was accused of, wasn't likely to help. Although this wasn't to emerge publicly for some time, Aleister Crowley was later to delight in telling this part of the tale.

"One of the closest followers of H. P. B., and in the sphere of literature unquestionably the most distinguished, with the possible exception of J. W. Brodie-Innes, was a woman named Mabel Collins. Her novel, *The Blossom and the Fruit*, is probably the best existing account of the theosophic theories presented in dramatic form. One of the great virtues acclaimed and defended by this lady was that of chastity. She did not go quite as far as the girl made famous by Mr Harry Price upon the Brocken a few years ago, whose terror of losing the jewel of her maidenhood was such that she thought it unsafe to go to bed without the protection of a man; but Mabel Collins had considerable experience of this form of chastity a deux; at the same time, reflecting that one of the points of H.P.B.'s mission was to proclaim the Age of the Woman, she occasionally chose a female for her bed-fellow."[176]

Vittoria certainly played a part in bringing the scandal to everyone's attention. Crowley reported that she boasted of worming her way into Blavatsky's confidence with Mabel to betray her at her first opportunity. However, Vittoria's importance in the affair was never so great as she claimed, though her part in it was to remain for posterity in a fictionalised form "Didn't I down ole Blavatzky? Sure I did. An ain't this like eatin' pie after that?"[177]

It is all too easy to judge Mabel according to present day views of Victorian sexuality. We often have in mind a prudish society where women's sexuality was, at the best, an aberration. But it was also one where the free love movement went hand in hand with spiritualism, one where Blavatsky could speak of tantric sex and know that the term with its implications of group sex, sodomy and bestiality would be understood. Mabel was never the most conventional of women, and a number of her friends in later life were happy in lesbian relationships including Frances Power Cobbe, who lived with sculptor Mary Lloyd for thirty six years.

Whatever the facts of Mabel's entanglements, it appears clear that Blavatsky had seized an opportunity to be rid of her. Why? Blavatsky must have known about any goings on between Mabel and the Keightleys since they all stayed together at *Maycot*. Vittoria's stirring could easily have meant that it was impossible to ignore what was going on any longer, but one event that occurred at this time seems to have passed most commentators by. In late March Blavatsky met Annie Besant for the first time.

Annie was friendly with WT Stead and through him was asked to review the *Secret Doctrine* for the *Pall Mall Gazette*. Annie never did anything by halves and asked Stead for a letter of introduction to Blavatsky which she forwarded with a note asking for permission to call. On 15th March 1889 Blavatsky wrote back enthusiastically asking Annie to call at practically any time she wished – and to bring anyone she wanted with her.

Annie was already known over half the world as one of the most remarkable women of her day. She was an agitator in radical political circles, a champion of science, an atheist, feminist, social and educational reformer, author and the first prominent woman to wage war on behalf of birth control. She was acclaimed as the greatest woman speaker of the nineteenth century. Becoming disillusioned with life Annie had recently begun to take an interest in psychology, hypnotism and spiritualism. She was poised for change when offered the *Secret Doctrine* to read.

In late March Annie called on Blavatsky for the first time. At the final moment of her visit, as Annie and her friend Herbert Burrows turned to leave, Blavatsky cried "Oh, my dear Mrs Besant, if only you would come among us!" Although Annie was transfixed she didn't call again until the end of April. On the 10th May 1888 Annie visited the office of the Theosophical Publishing House, asked Constance Wachtmeister for an application form, filled it in and hurried straight to Lansdowne Road. She knelt at Blavatsky's knee saying, "…will you accept me as your pupil, and give me the honour of proclaiming you my teacher in the face of the world?"[178]

The rest, as they say, is history. Although the news of Annie's conversion did not break until June, there was no doubt from the onset that she would play an integral role in the Society. In years to come she would be elected as president and lead theosophy into the twentieth century. She would become more renowned than Blavatsky herself and was to be seen as one of the most important women in the twentieth century. But that is Annie's story – Mabel simply could not compete with the potential Annie offered to theosophy in the first moments of her meeting Blavatsky. Mabel's downfall coincided precisely with the first appearance of Annie. And to play completely safe Blavatsky sent Bert over to America, where he remained until late 1890. She was a little coy about precisely why she had got rid of Mabel. "As regards Miss Collins, I also state that this lady received in London during March and April, a serious official rebuke for grave cause, in the Theosophical Society. Up to this time she had always declared her theosophical writings to be inspired by an adept known to her and to other members of English lodges, but not an Oriental adept."[179]

The derivation of Mabel's works and whether or not the Masters dictated them was to lead to a huge scandal immediately following Mabel's expulsion and is discussed in the next chapter. It's commonly assumed that this issue lay behind Mabel's expulsion. But by the time the question was raised Mabel had already been ejected. Several writers have speculated about the likelihood of a lesbian affair between Blavatsky and Annie, and so by implication a previous similar involvement with Mabel. Blavatsky certainly held a deep affection for Annie from the onset writing to her as "Dearest, My Dearest, 'Dearly Beloved One'" and signing herself "Very adoring". However, her main reaction towards Mabel often appears to have been that of irritation. The theory of such a shift in Blavatsky's affections seems unlikely in terms of a lesbian affair, although it is certainly true that she had a number of extremely close relationships with her women friends and colleagues, many of which ended in disaster.

Right from the first of Blavatsky's accusations Mabel had talked about taking legal action against her. And this turned to be no idle threat. An action for libel was lodged in July 1889, although it didn't reach court until July 1890. Blavatsky wrote to Judge, "Well, that's all. Choose ye this day etc. Here Bert & I have received writs from Mrs. Cook, who proposes to sue us for defamation & damages for our two libels in *Light*!! She begins[?] & I had no right to reply & contradict her libel. What next. I am sick, sick, sick of all. If you don't help, I give up all."[180]

The case was very short lived. Blavatsky asked that a letter written by Mabel be produced. This letter was shown to counsel who went into court and asked the judge to take the case off the list. The action was halted immediately although the contents of that letter have never been disclosed. "We do not as a rule care to make mention of things disagreeable to others, but so many have written to us about the suit brought last year against Mme. Blavatsky by Mabel Collins – Mrs Cook- we are constrained to say that the suit was called in July and the plaintiff was ready to proceed and had through her council demanded the production of a certain letter written before the suit to people in London. The case was expected on for some days and people were there for the sake of the expected scandal, but the defendant's attorney's showed the letter beforehand to the plaintiff's counsel, who then came into court and asked the judge to take the case off the docket, thus confessing the weakness of the charge and bringing the matter to a final conclusion. He is said to have done this against the plaintiff's desires, but acting on his legal judgment and his responsibility as a lawyer to the bench and bar."[181] Mabel's reaction to this outcome was apparently "sensational".[182] She collapsed when confronted with the letter.

The stress of the scandal could not fail to get to Mabel. She developed eczema and started to suffer from incessant headaches. She could only bear to be in subdued lighting, stopped eating and sank into a deep depression. Finally, she had a complete nervous breakdown and spent four months being cared for by her sister, Ellen Hopkins, incapable of the simplest of tasks.

On Blavatsky's death in 1891 Mabel wrote about her in *The Sunday World*[183] under the title *The Modern Witch is Dead*. She called her a charlatan and mystic pretender, running through the story of Blavatsky's life. "I had been smitten…with the fatal fascination of Esoteric Buddhism as exhibited, rather than explained in Mr Sinnett's book of that name…It was said to me that…one should never speculate with ones illusions or ones banking account. I have done both to my bitter cost…She was an impostor pure and simple; but of the first water…When she wanted anything done…her master…showed his displeasure. In this way she got her furniture rearranged, when she wished it, got personally vituperative paragraphs inserted in the journals her disciples launched upon the world, had her special dishes prepared for her meals and got her favourite Russian tobacco to smoke…I commenced by being interested in her professed knowledge of magic…I ended by arriving at a condition of wonder at her genius in Charlatanry…Her system of tutelage was largely that of intimidation, assisted by the lowering consequences of a reduced diet, by her constantly *(sic)* mesmeric passes and the use of her truly terrible, yet beautiful glittering eyes."

Mabel's fury with Blavatsky continued unabated. In the same paper she gave a statement that was to be reproduced again and again over the years in attacks on Blavatsky, most notably by John Maskelyne in his attack on theosophy, *Modern Spiritualism*.

> "She taught me one great lesson. I learned from her how foolish, how gullible; how easily flattered human beings are en masse. Her contempt for her kind was on the same gigantic scale as everything else about her, except her marvellously delicate taper fingers. In all else she was a big woman. She had a greater power over the weak and credulous, a greater capacity for making black appear white, a larger waist, a more voracious appetite, a more confirmed passion for tobacco, a more ceaseless and insatiable hatred of those whom she thought to be her enemies, a greater disrespect for les

convenances, a worse temper, a greater command of bad language, and a greater contempt for the intelligence of her fellow beings than I had ever supposed possible to be contained in one person. These, I suppose, must be reckoned as her vices, though whether a Creature so indifferent to all ordinary standards of right and wrong can be held to have virtues or vices I know not."

KIM FARNELL

CHAPTER SEVEN

Watch the birdie

As far as people in general were concerned, whatever had been going on behind the scenes was destined to stay there for a while. But while Mabel was seething with resentment, a whole new theosophical crisis took wing. On 11th May 1889, there appeared a letter in the *Religio-Philosophical Journal* from Elliott Coues, including a letter to him from Mabel Collins.

Elliot Coues was an American ornithologist and naturalist, born in Portsmouth, New Hampshire. After studying at Columbian College, he served as a surgeon in the US Army for seventeen years. His most notable work was in natural history. Coues introduced into zoology the key system used in botanical manuals, issuing in 1872 his famous *Key to North American Birds,* with short descriptions that enabled observers to identify birds accurately and quickly. From 1873 to 1880 he took part in government surveys of new territories: he drew on his experiences to edit many accounts of the earlier explorations in America, notably the Lewis and Clark expedition.

After Coues returned to the United States from Europe, where he had met Olcott and Blavatsky in 1884, he founded the Theosophical Society in Washington DC, and became president of the American Board of Control of the Society. Both Blavatsky and Olcott wrote him chatty letters into 1889, airing their grievances against one another. Taking advantage of his insight and the strained relations between Olcott and Blavatsky was irresistible to Coues. He demanded to be appointed President for Life of the American Section, asking Blavatsky to send a cable to the convention gathering in Chicago in April 1888, ordering the delegates to elect him as president.

> "You know whom the majority of the F.T.S. have desired to put forward as their representative theosophist in America. It is only necessary for you to cable the Chicago Convention, to elect him president. Weigh these words well; pause, consider, reflect and ACT. 'If 'twere well done, 'twere well done quickly."[184]

Unfortunately, he had severely misjudged the situation – Blavatsky would do no such thing. In fact he was to finally be expelled from the Society. But that comes a little later.

Along with other members of the Board of Control, Coues wasn't happy about the theosophical attachment to their Mahatmas. He was gathering a solid power base in the US and it wasn't long before Olcott and Judge became worried about Coues' activities. Letters flew back and forth between Coues, Judge, Olcott and Blavatsky about matters of policy in American theosophy.

At the Chicago Convention Coues was present as a delegate and President of the Gnostic branch of the TS. He was elected Chairman of the Convention and presided over its sessions. The newspapers of the city reported on the proceedings and reporters were present at all of the open meetings. Following the Convention the *Chicago Tribune* published, without disclosing the source from which it had received them, a letter and facsimile of an alleged "message from a Mahatma" to Dr. Coues. Blavatsky and Judge decided to ignore this – at least publicly. Anyone who wanted to be a real theosophist hoped for a Mahatma letter. And some speeded the process along a little by their own efforts. Coues had for some time hinted at his own occult relations with the Mahatmas and his psychic powers. But his campaign to take over American theosophy was doomed to failure. He had simply marked himself as a traitor to the cause.

In what appears to be a fit of pique with Blavatsky, Coues hit on the idea of joining forces with other dissatisfied theosophists. It had become common knowledge that Mabel was embroiled in a major row with Blavatsky, and that she had been unceremoniously ousted from the

Society in April. The precise reasons for Mabel's fall from grace weren't clear at this time. But that mattered little to Coues. The point was that he had access to a prominent ex-theosophist who might be more than prepared to help him in seeing to Blavatsky's downfall.

Sometime in 1885, Coues had written to Mabel praising *Light on the Path* and asking about its real source. This was because it was supposedly dictated by one of the theosophical Masters. Mabel promptly replied to his letter saying that *Light* "was inspired or dictated from the source above indicated."[185] In other words she agreed with the view that the work was inspired by one of the Masters, specifically the Master Hilarion.

As this was the accepted view Coues accepted Mabel's answer and let the matter alone. However, at the beginning of May 1889 he received a letter from Mabel dated 18th April 1889, immediately after she had been ejected from the Theosophical Society.

" In 1885 appeared a strange little book entitled: *Light on the Path: A treatise written for the personal use of those who are ignorant of the Eastern Wisdom, and who desire to enter within its influence. Written down by M. C. Fellow of the Theosophical Society.* The author is Mabel Collins, until lately one of the editors of *Lucifer*. The book is a gem of pure spirituality, and appears to me, as to many others, to symbolize much mystic truth. It has gone through numberless editions, and is used by faithful theosophists much as orthodox sinners use their prayer book. This happened mainly because *Light on the Path* was supposed to have been dictated to Mrs. Collins by "Koot Hoomi," or some other Hindu adept who held the Theosophical Society in the hollow of his masterly hand."

"I liked the little book so much that I wrote Ms. Collins a letter, praising it and asking her about its real source. She promptly replied, in her own handwriting, to the effect that "Light on the Path" was inspired or dictated from the source above indicated. This was about four years ago; since which time nothing passed between Mrs. Collins and myself until yesterday, when I unexpectedly received the following letter. I was not surprised at the new light it threw on the pathway of the Theosophical Society, for late developments respecting that singular result of Madame Blavatsky's now famous hoax left me nothing to wonder at. I cabled Mrs. Collins yesterday for permission to use her letter at my discretion. Her cablegram from London reached me this morning, saying, "Use my letter as you please. Mabel Collins." So here is the letter.

"Dear Sir: - I feel I have a duty to write to you on a difficult and (to me) painful subject, and that I must not delay it any longer. "You will remember writing to me to ask me who was the inspirer of *Light on the Path*." If you had not yourself been acquainted with Madame Blavatsky I should despair of making you even understand my conduct. Of course I ought to have answered the letter without showing it to any one else; but at that time I was both studying Madame Blavatsky and studying under her. I knew nothing then of the mysteries of the Theosophical Society, and I was puzzled why you should write to me in such a way. I took the letter to her; the result was that I wrote the answer at her dictation. I did not do this by her orders; I have never been under her orders. But I have done one or two things because she begged and implored me to; and this I did for that reason. So far as I can remember I wrote you that I had received *Light on the Path* from one of the Masters who guide Madame Blavatsky."

"I wish to ease my conscience now by saying that I wrote this from no knowledge of my own, and merely to please her; and that I now see I was very wrong in doing so. I ought further to state that *Light on the Path* was not to my knowledge inspired by any one; but that I saw it written on the walls of a place I visit spiritually, (which is described in the *Blossom and the Fruit*) – there I read it and I wrote it down. I have myself never received proof of the existence of any Master; though I believe (as always) that the mahatmic force must exist."[186]

So Mabel was saying that Blavatsky had persuaded her to lie about the source of her work for the benefit of the Theosophical Society. If she and Coues had simply discussed this amongst themselves then the matter may have ended with two disgruntled ex theosophists having a good moan. But this was not how Coues operated. He was looking for a reason to bring Blavatsky down and here was Mabel handing him one on a plate.

The *Religio-Philosophical Journal* was an old established and leading Spiritualist publication printed in Chicago and edited by Colonel Bundy, a life-long Spiritualist and a friend of Coues. Colonel Bundy had joined the Theosophical Society in 1885, on the recommendation of Prof. Coues and was a member of the Gnostic Branch founded by Coues. *The Religio-Philosophical Journal* had previously given publicity to attacks upon Blavatsky by W. Emmette Coleman.[187] The letters appeared in the *Journal* on 11th May and 1st June 1889. Immediately, Blavatsky and her followers leaped into the ring to complete their demolition of Mabel, and defend the Theosophical Society and Blavatsky.

As *Light* was published in March 1885, it was claimed that with Blavatsky leaving for India in November 1884, and not returning to England until 1st May 1887, it was impossible for Mabel to have taken Coues letter to her. However, Mabel's original letter to Coues was undated and it was only from memory that he stated it to be from 1885.

The original letter was headed from Clarendon Road. Mabel was not living there until February 1885 and therefore it was claimed that this proved that it was impossible for Blavatsky to beg and implore her, as she was not in England. In fact, it only proves that the letter was written after February 1885.

Mabel had told Arch that *The Idyll of the White Lotus* arose from inspiration from a Being who she described to Madame Blavatsky. Madame Blavatsky said that, from the description and the tone of the thought, she believed this to be an old friend of her own among the Occult Brotherhood. Mabel said that this same Being urged her to endeavour to reach a higher state of consciousness, as there was work for her to do. This effort resulted in *Light on the Path*.[188]

Subsequent issues of the *Journal* carried letters from Colonel Bundy, W. Emmette Coleman and others, in addition to Prof. Coues. Other Spiritualist and sectarian publications, as well as the secular press followed suit. An attack on everything theosophical, including Blavatsky and Judge, raged in many quarters.

Mistakes Coues had made in his writing were pointed out again and again. His calling her "Mrs Collins", her penname, instead of Cook, her legal name, was taken to be a sign that he was lying.

However, Coues knew that he had a bomb in his hand and wrote to the *Religio-Philosophical Journal* in glee.

> "If your mail resembles mine in quantity and quality of theosophical correspondence since 'Mabel Collins' disavowal of inspiration

from Madame Blavatsky's Hindu 'controls,' it must be curious reading. ... At this revelation through the *Journal* some people are pleased; others sorry; others angry; some applaud; some condemn; many are curious, and most of them want to argue about it. My mail has a sort of shivery, gooseflesh quality, as if a panic in mahatmic stock were imminent and there is a tendency of the hair of the faithful to stand on end...."

"First, a good many persons are surprised that I seem to have only now found out that 'Light on the Path' was not dictated by our friend Koot Hoomi or any other Eastern adept. Such have always known all about its source and my discovery is discounted as a theosophical chestnut. Let me say to all such that I do not always tell all I know, and that I might have continued silent on the authorship of 'Light on the Path,' had I not had reasons for publishing Mrs. Cooke's letter just then and there — reasons I reserve for the present." [189]

In England the spiritualist journal *Light* repeated the material published in America. *Light* did allow space for a heated defence from theosophists in Britain though. On the 12th June, Mabel's sister, Ellen Hopkins, wrote a letter to *Light* a letter published 15th June 1889."... Will you allow me to state that my sister, Mabel Collins, is too ill at the moment to be able to speak for herself, but I trust that she will be well enough in a few days to furnish you with a reply which will put a very different aspect on the whole affair?"

In its issue of 29th June *Light* published the following reply to a correspondent's enquiry: "We have no intention of publishing anything further on the Coues-Collins case, unless a rejoinder is made by Mrs. Cook. That would command attention; no other letters or comments will be printed. Our single desire in noticing a matter that does not immediately concern us, was to act with strict impartiality and fairness to all persons concerned. That we have done, purveying news without expressing any opinion on its merits or demerits." The few days spoken of went by and rolled into months with no statement from Mabel.

Mabel's previous work was ignored. She was painted as an inexperienced theosophist, one who had previously been simply a journalist and novelist and so could know nothing of the matters under discussion.

Again and again the point was made that Mabel was not the most respectable, and so reliable, of correspondents. "As regards Miss Collins, I also state that this lady received in London during March and April, a serious official rebuke for grave cause, in the Theosophical Society. Up to this time she had always declared her theosophical writings to be inspired by an adept known to her and to other members of English lodges, but not an Oriental adept."[190]

The theosophical urge to issue pamphlets in times of crisis was adhered to as strongly as ever. Arch and Bert were dragged into the furore to make statements. They had little choice: to ally themselves with Mabel at this stage would have risked their own status, certainly their involvement in theosophy.

The charter of the Gnostic Branch was revoked and Coues expelled from the Society. Months later, while preparing a further attack, he wrote to *Light* saying that he had been mistaken in fixing the date of his first letter to Mabel Collins as 1885, when it should have been 1887. As proof he told the editor that on 1st June of that year, Mabel cabled him news of his mistake and he sent a card from Mabel Collins, which *Light* accepted as an explanation because *The Gates of Gold* was not published until 1887.

Mabel's illness was called into question. If she was so ill what was she doing cabling Coues about his mistakes with dates? We know now that Mabel was in the throes of a nervous breakdown, and it was perfectly possible that she arranged for a cable to be sent.

Claims that Mabel had no close contact with Blavatsky until September of 1887 conveniently ignored the few months Blavatsky had spent at *Maycot*. At this stage the less said about that, the better.

The story of the Coues attack and Mabel's role is much more complicated than the above account describes. Endless letters were written and published and every small error pounced upon and analysed. The culmination of the whole affair was a full page exposé of Blavatsky in the *New York Sun* on 20th July 1890. This prompted Blavatsky to take legal action against Coues and the *Sun*. Blavatsky's death in 1891 terminated the suit, but on 26th September 1892 *The Sun* published a biographical sketch of her written by Judge with their apologies.

The episode has passed into theosophical history, termed the Coues-Collins affair. Mabel is given credit, along with Coues, for attempting to bring about Blavatsky's downfall. Her testimony was claimed to be untrustworthy and valueless.

Blavatsky claimed "A *curious prophecy was made to me in 1879,* in India…"Beware of the letter C…I see three capital C's shining ominously over your head…They are the initials of three persons who will belong to the Theosophical body, only to turn its greatest enemies." I had forgotten the warning till 1884, when the Coulombs appeared on the stage. Are Dr Coues and Miss (Mabel) Collins (Cook) preparing to close the list – I wonder?"[191] The Coulombs were involved in the theosophical scandal of 1884, when the Society for Psychical Research undertook an investigation into phenomena produced by Blavatsky.

However, once the volumes of correspondence and the numerous analyses of the affair are sifted through, what stands out is that Mabel wrote a letter to Coues saying that she had been persuaded by Blavatsky to attribute her writings to the Masters, and that she subsequently gave Coues permission to use that letter as he saw fit. The original letter was dated 18th April 1889, immediately after she was ejected from the Theosophical Society, before she began legal proceedings against Blavatsky and became ill with depression. Her role went no further and no additional correspondence between her and Coues appears to exist.

In legend Mabel withdrew from the public eye and it wasn't until 1910 that she would talk about the breakdown she had suffered.

While theosophists everywhere were arguing between themselves of the rights and wrongs of Coues' actions, and pouring torrents of indignation into the press, Mabel was visiting WH Edwards for magnetic healing. Animal magnetism is mentioned regularly in nineteenth century texts, and we may be forgiven for believing that Mabel simply engaged in some outmoded, alternative form of healing. We may have images of magnets being placed on or around the body, passes of hands being made, a type of Victorian faith healing. And it is not impossible that this is what Mabel meant – at least in part - but it is highly unlikely. What we are actually talking about is an early form of psychotherapy, involving hypnotism, and the forerunner to psychoanalysis.

British medical attitudes towards hypnotism went through two distinct phases. In its early stages, from the 1830s through the 1850s, when it was called animal magnetism or mesmerism, it was linked to the ideas of the Viennese Doctor, Franz Mesmer, who claimed to have command over the curative powers of a universal, invisible magnetic fluid. His theory was that a force analogous to the effect produced by magnets coursed through the human body, causing illness when unequally distributed or blocked from flowing freely. This fluid could be returned to its proper state by touching the afflicted person or making passes with the hands over their body.

The conventional medical establishment scoffed at the idea. But when James Braid, a Scottish surgeon, sought other ways to interpret the process that cast the subject into a trance he developed neurohypnotism, later to be shortened to hypnotism. Although hypnotism lacked scientific credibility it was eagerly embraced by a number of unorthodox medical practitioners and flourished among a range of alternative health therapies. Although in Britain little was written about the therapeutic effects of hypnotism, on the continent it was used to treat hysterical and epileptic patients.

Interest renewed in hypnotism during the 1880s. It was stimulated by the inquiries undertaken by members of the Society for Psychical Research and during the next decade attitudes towards hypnotism changed drastically. Only a few practitioners used the technique in the 1880s, even though it had gained in respectability.

A taint of quackery and the occult clung to hypnotism and there were great fears of unscrupulous practitioners. There were worries that the power of hypnotism could be abused all too easily, a hypnotised patient might reveal secrets that jeopardised the doctor's ability to retain the role of confidante and counsellor. Or she - the patient was often female - might be subject to sexual advantages of which she was subsequently unaware. Would you send your wife or servant to a hypnotist? It was considered that susceptibility to hypnotism was an indication of instability, if not outright disease. And the subject would become a mental slave of the hypnotist. There was a genuine fear that hypnotism would become exceedingly harmful to those most likely to be exposed to it.

However, it was used, and by conventional medical practitioners on an unsystematic basis. It offered an alternative to drugs of a doubtful efficacy and potential danger. Many of Freud's early ideas were stimulated and clarified by the use of hypnotic suggestion with hysterical patients. And it is rarely mentioned today that this work was first publicised by the Society for Psychical Research.

At the time Mabel was reputedly instrumental in attempting to bring about the downfall of Blavatsky she was suffering from depression and spending time with her therapist; "I consulted Mr Edwards and after the first magnetic treatment had a sense of well being…"[192]

Mabel had lost many friends, some of them her closest, her reputation had been sullied and she had suffered financially. She began to write again and consider what was to come next. Surely life was to improve now? There is no possibility that Mabel could have foreseen the disasters lying ahead.

CHAPTER EIGHT

Love and the Ripper

Mabel's interests had always been a little wider than theosophy alone. She had been part of the Esoteric Section of the Theosophical Society. From early 1884 theosophists had petitioned the Masters for permission to establish an inner sanctum. Two of its earliest activists, Ralph Palmer Thomas and Isabelle de Steiger were later to join the Golden Dawn.[193] It was the growing appeal of groups such as the Golden Dawn that lead to the announcement being made that an Esoteric Section of the Theosophical Society was to be established. Blavatsky's intention was to stop would-be practical occultists from defecting to other groups. It was conditional on joining the Esoteric Section that members didn't join any other occult order.

Blavatsky claimed that Mabel had only been allowed to join the Esoteric Section after she begged and implored. She was placed on probation when the scandal broke and after Blavatsky had decided that it was time for her to be rid of Mabel, was accused of having broken her vows and being treacherous.

Blavatsky's desire that theosophists didn't join other occult orders was doomed to failure. Many joined the Golden Dawn and other groups. During its early years from 1888 to 1891, the Golden Dawn was primarily a theoretical school, which performed the initiation ceremonies of the

Outer Order, and taught its members the basics of Qabalah, astrology, alchemical symbolism, geomancy, and tarot, but no practical magic other than the Lesser Banishing Ritual of the Pentagram. Three hundred and fifty initiations took place between 1888 and 1896 – was Mabel amongst them?

The case for Mabel having been active in the Golden Dawn arises mainly because of her tendency to use terms in her writings that were common in that circle. For example, she refers to "neophytes" rather than using Blavatsky's favourite "chelas". Yeats told William Horton in a letter in 1896 that Sinnett was in charge of the Golden Dawn neophytes, the equivalent of a novice master. However, the names of Sinnett and Mabel appear nowhere in Golden Dawn records, and their association with the order appears to be mythical.

In 1888, when Mabel was still active at theosophical headquarters, the discussions of Jack the Ripper and his activities were grabbing as much attention there as anywhere else. Jack the Ripper is the popular name given to a serial killer who killed a number of prostitutes in the East End of London during 1888. The name originates from a letter written by someone who claimed to be the killer published at the time of the murders. The killings took place within a mile area and involved the districts of Whitechapel, Spitalfields, Aldgate, and the City of London proper. Although he was not the first serial killer, the Ripper was the first to appear in London since the general population had become literate and the press had become a force for social change. There was tremendous political turmoil in the late 1880s and liberals and social reformers tried to use the crimes for their own ends. The activities of the Ripper, along with news of police activities, were chronicled in the newspapers on a daily basis.

No-one knows exactly how many women the Ripper killed. It is generally accepted that he killed five, although some estimate seven or more. However, everyone agrees that he was responsible for the deaths of Mary Ann Nichols in August 1888, Annie Chapman, Elizabeth Stride and Catherine Eddows in September 1888 and Mary Jane Kelly in November 1888. They were all prostitutes and unknown to each other.

The Ripper's method of killing his victims was unclear at the time. However, it has now been established that he stood facing his victim until she raised her skirts and then seized her by the throat and strangled her. He then lowered her to the ground, their heads to his left. He then cut her throat and avoided being covered in blood by the position in which he placed her head. When he had succeeded in killing her, he mutilated the body. Usually he took a piece of the victim's viscera, in one case he removed a kidney and in another removed the sexual organs with a knife. Considering the speed at which he worked, often in near total darkness, it was assumed that he had some experience in using a knife, which led to speculations that he was a doctor or butcher.

A number of letters were written to the press, supposedly from the murderer, one signed "Jack the Ripper", followed by a postcard, to the Central News Agency which was responsible for the name he was to be known by through history. Because the postcard referred to a double event and came from the same source as the letter, the police believed that they were indeed from the murderer. The letter has also been attributed to a Central News Agency journalist however.

In mid October a small parcel was sent to George Lusk, who was head of a vigilance committee in Whitechapel. Inside was half a human kidney and a letter from someone claiming to be the killer, saying that it was part of the kidney he removed from Eddowes.

During this period the only way to prove someone committed a murder was to catch them in the act, or get them to confess. Two police forces were responsible for carrying out investigations. The Metropolitan Police, known as Scotland Yard, was responsible for crimes committed in all the boroughs of London except the City of London proper. The City of London had their own police force. When Eddowes was killed, it was in their territory and this brought them into the case.

It is believed that the rank and file of the two forces got along and worked well together, but there is evidence that the seniors in each force did not. To what degree, if any, their failure to cooperate fully interfered with solving the case is not known. The Metropolitan Police Force confined their activities to performing autopsies and taking statements. People in general believed the police to be incompetent and the Commissioner, Sir Charles Warren, was seen as only good for policing crowds and keeping order. The City of London Police made crime scene drawings, took photographs of Eddowes, and even though she was not in their jurisdiction, they took photographs of Kelly. She is the only victim who was photographed at the crime scene.

After Eddowes' murder a piece of graffiti reading "The Juwes are the men That Will not be blamed for nothing", was found by a constable near a doorway. The City Police officers wanted to photograph it. Warren felt that leaving it until it was light enough to be photographed might cause riots against the Jews living in Whitechapel, and ordered it removed.

The Ripper was never found, and to this day there is no certainty about who he was, although numerous theories abound. Those accused over the years include: M.J. Druitt, a barrister turned teacher who committed suicide in December 1888; multiple wife poisoner Severin Klosowski, alias George Chapman; Aaron Kosminiski a Polish Jew who was put away in an insane asylum after the crimes; Michael Ostrog, a con man; Dr. Francis Tumblety, an American doctor interviewed at the time who fled to America, Prince Albert Victor, Duke of Clarence - many others have been suggested.

And what does all this have to do with Mabel? Along with everyone else she read news reports and speculated on who it could be, and why the murders took place. What was exceptional is that she was soon to believe that she was sharing her home with the Ripper himself.

In December of 1888 an article in the *Pall Mall Gazette* appeared, suggesting that the Ripper was a black magician. In January 1889, two articles appeared in the *Pall Mall Gazette* about Rider Haggard's incredibly popular novel *She*. Entitled *The Real Original of She. By one who knew her*, the articles examined the theory that *She* was based on practices of the Obeeyah[194] in Cameroon, West Africa. The writer believed that Ayesha, the main character in *She*, was a young, white version of an Obeeyah woman. According to him, Obeeyah women made human sacrifices to Satan, whom they believed inhabited the body of a man eating spider, invoked evil spirits and possessed great magical powers. He recalled travelling through Africa and meeting one of these women himself, while involved with slave traders there. "Sube stood close on 6 ft. and was supposed by the natives to be many hundreds of years of age. Erect as a dart, and with a stately walk, she yet *looked* 2,000 years old. Her wrinkled, mummified, gorilla-like face, full of iniquity, hate and uncleanliness (moral and physical), might have existed since the Creation, while her superb form and full limbs might have been those of a woman of twenty four...her dress was very simple, consisting of a headdress made of shark's teeth, brass bosses and tails of some species of lynx. Across her bare bosom was a wide scarf or baldric made of scarlet cloth, on which were fashioned four rows of what appeared like large Roman pearls, of the size of a large walnut. These apparent pearls however, were actually human intestines, bleached to a pearly whiteness, inflated and constricted at short intervals, so as to make a series of little bladders. On the top of her head appeared the head of a large spotted serpent..."[195]

Someone dressed like this was doubtless possessed of great powers and so the author requested a demonstration. "*I was* astonished though, to find this six foot of humanity...standing on my outstretched hand when I opened my eyes (previously closed by her command) and when I could not feel the slightest weight thereon...While I looked round for her a stone fell near me; and looking upwards saw her calmly standing on the top of a cliff nearly 500 ft in height. I naturally thought it was a double...Without more ado she walked – not jumped - over the side of the cliff, and with a gentle motion...gradually dropped downwards till she alighted at my feet."[196]

Sube continued to perform miracles, replacing a cut off arm, changing toads into deadly snakes, causing a warrior to turn into an almost fleshless skeleton and turning another woman to stone as well as producing images in a pool of water. Unfortunately, the first article signed by RD, was too short to contain all the miracles the writer saw. Which is doubtless why a second article followed on 15th February.

(And things don't seem to have changed that much - in February 2002 *Anova* reported that a soccer coach had been banned in Cameroon after allegations of black magic![197])

Apparently numerous readers had written in requesting more. "RD" obliged by happily launching into an account of devil worship, horror, blasphemy and obscenity. Disappointingly he begins with a description of Indian conjuring tricks. He soon launches into an account of the tribe's worship on a man eating spider— mentioning his forthcoming book on the side, containing a terrible death, which seems never to have appeared. As a by the way the writer tells how he was kept prisoner and fattened up for sacrifice to the spider god while watching a series of miracles. Fortunately, he wore a talisman, given to him by Bulwer Lytton that protected him from her spells, and, in fact, annihilated Sube in the end. This tantalising piece was signed Roslyn D'Onston. Stephenson left the London Hospital on 7th December 1888. He was admitted again on 13th May 1889, suffering from "chloralism", brought on by the use of chloral hydrate. At the time he was living in the London Cottage Mission in the East End of London. It was during his second stay that he received a letter from Mabel. Mabel was one of many who wrote to the author care of the *Gazette*. After a few weeks she received a reply – Dr Roslyn D'Onston wrote to say that he was ill in hospital but as soon as he recovered he would arrange to meet Mabel. He did so and Mabel began her association with a man she believed to be a great magician.

D'Onston was actually Robert Donston Stephenson. He was the son of a Yorkshire seed mill owner and had studied chemistry in Munich and medicine in Paris. He fought for Garibaldi in the Italian Wars of Independence in the 1860s, working as a battlefield medic, and retired as a Lieutenant of the Southern Army of Italy in 1861. He was also reputed to have studied the occult under Bulwer Lytton.[198]

In 1863, under family pressure, he took a post with Customs in Hull; eventually he was fired and came to London. In 1867 he was forced to end a three year affair with a servant in order to marry an heiress. Having said their goodbyes, the couple swore to meet the following year at midnight. They arranged to meet one more time and shortly before their meeting Stephenson was involved in a shooting accident and so had to be wheeled in a bath chair to his rendezvous. Although the girl turned up, Stephenson found that his arms went straight through her and once he visited her family found out that she had died that night. The ghost is rumoured to appear each year and was sighted as recently as 1995.[199]

Married in 1876,[200] (a little unfortunately for the story above), he was separated from his wife – it is unknown what happened to her. He was a heavy drinker and reputed to use other drugs. It is possible that he was the same Robert Stephenson charged with assault in June 1887 and indecent assault on 30th October 1888. By the time Mabel was to make contact with him, Stephenson had already begun to build a mythology around himself.

Stephenson had a nervous breakdown and after going to Brighton for a cure was transferred to the London Hospital in July of 1888, diagnosed with neurasthenia.[201] Precisely what was wrong with Stephenson in today's terms is unknown. As a heavy drinker, he carried drugs with him to stave off delirium tremens. Stephenson was a patient there again in November 1888, in a private ward. It was here that he became convinced that Dr Morgan Davies was the Ripper, after he saw what he believed to be a re-enactment. Davies had performed a pantomime to demonstrate his own theory of how the Ripper brought down his prey. Stephenson deemed the simulation so convincing that he assumed that Davies had special insight into the killings.

Stephenson was in fact a patient in the London Hospital for 134 days from July 1888 through December 1888 covering the whole time span of the murders. He inserted himself into the investigation at various points, writing to the City of London Police on 16th October about the Goulston Street graffito.

> "Having read Sir Charles Warren's circular in yesterday's papers that 'It is not known that there is any dialect or language in which the word Jews is spelt Juwes' I beg to inform you that the word written by the murderer <u>does</u> exist in a European language, though it was not Juwes. Try it in script – Thus, The Juives. &c. now place a dot over the third upstroke (which dot was naturally overlooked by lantern light) and we get plainly The Juives, which I need not tell you is the French. The murderer unconsciously reverted, for a moment, to his native language."

In the same letter, Stephenson described a reference in a French book to the use of the removed uterus that had not so far been considered, and offered to give more information to the Police on this.

Stephenson later told his story about Davies to an unemployed ironmongery assistant called George Marsh who he met in the Prince Albert pub, in St Martin's Lane. The two of them passed themselves off as private detectives, investigating Dr Davies. They signed agreements to share any money gained and, on Christmas Eve 1888 Marsh went to Scotland Yard and told them that he believed Stephenson to be the murderer. Marsh told his story to Inspector Roots, who had known Stephenson for twenty years and held him in high regard. However, Roots was also aware that Stephenson was a heavy drinker and carried drugs with him to stave off the effects of the delirium tremens. By Boxing Day Stephenson was there to offer his version. The Police investigated Stephenson but it appears that the Police never entertained serious suspicions against either Stephenson or Dr. Davies.

In 1889 Vittoria Cremers left England for America, not returning until February 1890. Breaking her journey in Paris, she wrote to Mabel inviting her to stay and perhaps attend a few fashion shows. As she got no answer to her letter, Vittoria decided to visit Mabel as soon as she returned to England. Aleister Crowley fictionalised Vittoria in his novel *Moonchild*.[202]

"Her squat stubborn figure was clad in rusty-black clothes, a man's except for the skirt; it was surmounted by a head of unusual size, and still more unusual shape, for the back of the skull was entirely flat, and the left frontal lobe much more developed than the right; one could have thought that it had been deliberately knocked out of shape, since nature, fond, as it may be, of freaks, rarely pushes asymmetry to such a point. There would have been more than idle speculation in such a theory; for she was the child of hate, and her mother had in vain attempted every violence against her before her birth. The face was wrinkled parchment, yellow and hard; it was framed in short, thick hair, dirty white in colour; and her expression denoted that the utmost cunning and capacity were at the command of her rapacious instincts. But her poverty was no indication that they had served her and those primitive qualities had in fact been swallowed up in the results of their disappointment. For in her eye raved bitter a hate of all things, born of the selfish envy which regarded the happiness of any other person as an outrage and affront upon her. Every thought in her mind was a curse - against God, against man, against love, or beauty, against life itself. She was a combination of the witch-burner with the witch; an incarnation of the spirit of Puritanism, from its sourness to its sexual degeneracy."

Perhaps it was because of the earlier sex scandals that surrounded Mabel that her relationship with Vittoria was seen as questionable. Aleister Crowley for one assumed that Vittoria and Mabel had more than a friendship, "She did not go quite as far as the girl made famous by Mr. Harry Price upon the Brocken a few years ago, whose terror of losing her jewel of maidenhood was such that she thought it unsafe to go to bed without the protection of a man, but Mabel Collins had considerable experience of this form of chastity a deux; at the same time, reflecting that one of the points of HPB's mission was to proclaim the Age of the Woman, she occasionally chose a female for her bed fellow.."[203]

In early March Vittoria arrived back in England and almost immediately called at Mabel's home in York Terrace, behind Marylebone Road. Mabel's maid told her that Mabel was away in Southsea, writing a new novel. The next day Vittoria took a train to visit her.

She found Mabel lodging in a shabby, dingy house. On knocking at the door she was led to a poorly furnished room on the first floor. "It was a comfortless-looking place containing an unmade single bed, a dressing-table with a few cheap china ornaments upon it; and with the cinders of a previous fire still in the grate, it presented an utterly cheerless appearance."[204]

Vittoria waited for Mabel to return and heard the sound of her speaking to a man. Shortly afterwards Mabel came into her room and greeted Vittoria. She mentioned the letter she had written to Stephenson and explained what a great magician he was, possessed of numerous magical secrets. Mabel explained that she was caring for him and planned to return to London where the three of them would be able to set up in business. While Vittoria and Mabel were having tea and chatting about Vittoria's visit to Paris, and her meeting with Sarah Bernhardt, Stephenson returned. Vittoria describes him as a man who moved silently, fair haired, of unassuming appearance, carrying a cap and short cane. He was tall, with a military bearing and extremely pale. Vittoria noted that he was super clean and although wearing old and worn clothes had brushed them to within an inch of their life.

Vittoria decided that Mabel was infatuated with Stephenson. Two weeks later Mabel and Stephenson joined Vittoria in London. Vittoria arranged for Stephenson to take lodgings where she was staying. Her landlady complained about his rarely eating and took against him but eventually their difficulties were sorted and he was able to stay.

Mabel followed up on her suggestion that the three of them should go into business together and they began discussing the project. Stephenson had a number of recipes for beauty creams and potions, and with Vittoria and Mabel jointly putting up the money the three formed the Pompadour Cosmetique Company and took premises in Baker Street on the site where Baker Street tube station now stands. They had offices on the first floor, comprising one large room where the business was conducted and treatments made up, and a small room immediately behind it. Vittoria took the flat on the third floor and Stephenson moved into the room adjacent to the office. Vittoria took her maid who also performed tasks for Stephenson.

As both Vittoria and Mabel were still closely tied in with *Lucifer* they commissioned an article from Stephenson that appeared in November 1890. The article, "African Magic" by Tau-Triadelta was attributed to Blavatsky, and although the content is similar to that in the *Pall Mall* articles, her editorial hand can clearly be seen. It begins by explaining what the term "magic" means, something that follows as yet unknown scientific laws. After describing various schools of magic, and the difference between white and black magic, it explains how whereas in other schools the spectator only thinks they see a magical act, in Obeeyah magic it actually takes place. "...the necromancer must outrage and degrade human nature in every way conceivable. The very least of the crimes necessary for him (or her) to commit to attain the power sought is actual murder, by which the human victim essential to the sacrifice is provided. The human mind can scarcely realise or even imagine one tithe of the horrors and atrocities actually performed by the Obeeyah women. Yet, though the price is awful, horrible, unutterable, the power is real...I remember well my first experience of these wizards..." [205] A description of rainmakers followed along with that of a number of magical feats.

> "A most impressive feat, which they on a subsequent occasion performed, was the old custom of the priests of Baal. Commencing a lugubrious chant they slowly began circling around the fire...keeping a certain amount of rhythm in both their movements and cadences. Presently, the movement grew faster and faster till they whirled round like dancing dervishes... With the rapidity of their revolutions their voices were raised higher and higher until the din was terrific. Then, by a simultaneous movement, each began slashing his naked body on arms, chest, and thighs, until they were streaming with blood and covered with deep gashes...In a few minutes time the young man arose, and there was not the slightest trace of wound or scar in his ebony skin...In this performance there were many invocations, gestures, the circular fire, and other things which satisfied me that some portion, at all events, of the magical processes of West Africa had been handed down from the days when Baal was an actual God, and mighty in the land."

The name Tau-triadelta represented the triple triangle of Pythagoras, an occult symbol. It means Cross Three Triangles. The same name was used to by-line an article in the *Pall Mall Gazette* under the title *Who Is The Whitechapel Demon?*[206] In this Stephenson explained that a necromancer needed "a certain portion of the body of a harlot" and that the Ripper murders marked the points of a profaned cross over London.

Vittoria doesn't appear to have thought highly of Stephenson but it is difficult to ascertain whether that was due to jealousy of his relationship with Mabel. Vittoria said that Mabel would talk of little else but Stephenson and that he was a regular visitor to her flat that was only a few minutes' walk away. Mabel spent many hours discussing Stephenson's background and talents with Vittoria. Vittoria grew less and less impressed - or more and more jealous depending on your point of view.

Vittoria had initially found Stephenson inoffensive. But they worked closely together, and in retrospect she said that she became more and more uncomfortable in his company. On one occasion Vittoria saw Stephenson drawing an upside down triangle on his door. He told her that he'd done so to keep out an evil presence.

Stephenson delighted in telling Vittoria numerous colourful stories. He described how he had avenged a girl who had been seduced and left pregnant; how his friend had "accidentally" killed a Chinese prospector during the Californian gold rush; the amputations he had performed while fighting for Garibaldi… Vittoria herself mentioned that she didn't ask questions or interject, allowing the speaker to continue until the end. One cannot help but wonder if Stephenson was desperate to get some sort of reaction from her.

It was clear to Vittoria however that Mabel was closer to Stephenson than she would ever be to either of them. She would constantly talk about him, and he was a regular visitor to Mabel's flat. Mabel was happy to care for Stephenson; she had provided him with a home and supplied him with money. Mabel repeated to Vittoria stories that Stephenson had told her about a past love, how he had to give up that love to marry an heiress. Substantially, this was the same story as that of the ghost that haunted Liverpool. The difference being that in this version his lover drowned herself and the haunting took place in London. On balance though, Stephenson liked to retain an air of mystery and spoke little about his past.

Mabel and Vittoria's attentions were diverted for some time by the outcome of the libel case Mabel had brought against Blavatsky. Any credibility Mabel may have retained amongst theosophists was finally ended. "I could not imagine any earthly treasure which would tempt me to degrade myself for a mean pitiful revenge as Mabel Collins has done…I feel the wrong and suffer with her ..the whole weight of wrong effected by MC and her co-workers."[207]

About a month after the case was thrown out of court, Mabel entered the office in Baker Street looking nervous and questioned Vittoria as to the whereabouts of Stephenson. Once she found he wasn't there

Mabel told Vittoria that something Stephenson had shown her convinced her that he was Jack the Ripper. It was clear that Mabel was afraid. Vittoria, who had shown little interest in the murders, was rather taken aback at this sudden declaration. True, she didn't find Stephenson overly appealing, and she had many reasons to be jealous of the relationship he had with Mabel. But there was no reason for her to assume that he was a serial murderer.

Mabel admitted that she and Stephenson had quarrelled at times, mainly about his unrequited affair. But she refused to say why she had come to the conclusion that he was the Ripper. Vittoria's suspicions were awakened when Stephenson mentioned his wife for the first time to her and on being asked what had happened to her drew his finger across his throat. Vittoria decided that meant he must have killed her and after interrogating him about other family details became determined to find out more. Mabel was surprisingly accepting of the idea that Stephenson had murdered his wife once Vittoria relayed this theory to her.

Mabel had become more and more frightened of Stephenson but was afraid to leave him. She credited him with great powers and was clearly worried that they would be turned against her. More than anything, though, she wanted to be free of him.

A short time later, Mabel visited Vittoria at her flat. She had been weeping and, swollen eyed, told Vittoria that she was so afraid that she had to get away. Mabel had made arrangements to stay in Scarborough for a few months. She hadn't told anyone where she was going to be and swore Vittoria to secrecy. They arranged that Mabel would write to a post box so that mail couldn't be intercepted and after bidding Vittoria goodbye, Mabel repeated that she was convinced that Stephenson was Jack the Ripper. Precisely why Mabel was so frightened and what she had discovered is unknown.

Mabel left, though she occasionally wrote to Vittoria. Stephenson seemed to be remarkably unbothered by her departure. With the collapse of the threesome as a team, the Pompadour Cosmetique Company was floundering. Vittoria decided that it would be a good idea to wind the business up and get out of town herself for a while. She told Stephenson of her plans and he launched into an account of the intimate details of the relationship between Vittoria and Mabel as told to him by Mabel. Vittoria was upset that secrets she thought safe with Mabel had been passed onto Stephenson. She immediately wrote to Mabel demanding an explanation and threatening to cease their relationship if that wasn't satisfactory. Mabel wasted no time in responding, simply saying that she understood. Vittoria was furious – Mabel had called her bluff. She took her temper out on Stephenson, calling him into the office and telling him that he was a swine to betray Mabel in such a fashion.

Vittoria now despised Stephenson and one day when he had gone out let herself into his room to see what she could find. She had noticed that he had a box in which he kept his private papers, and at the least wanted to discover his true identity. Both Vittoria and Mabel were convinced that he was using a false name.

It had taken a search of local second hand shops for Vittoria to find a key that would fit his room. As soon as she could, she found the box and opened it to find a number of books on magic – no papers, no documents. However, there were several ties in the box, and on close inspection Vittoria found one to be stained underneath. Her curiosity was insatiable. On further examination she found a number of the ties to carry the same stain. She had no idea what this meant.[208]

Shortly afterwards Vittoria was chatting to Stephenson when he told her that he knew Jack the Ripper. He told her about Dr Davies and why he believed him to have committed the murders. In giving her the details he said that the organs taken from the bodies had been tucked behind the murderer's tie. When she asked Stephenson what happened to the parts of the women he carried away, Stephenson said that he ate them. In answer to her protest that his collar, tie and shirt would be stained with blood and he could not escape from the scene without being detected he put on his great coat and turned up the collar, demonstrating that when it was buttoned nothing showed underneath.[209]

It was fairly obvious what conclusion Vittoria was to leap to. She decided that the story of the doctor was a fabrication and the details Stephenson knew proved him to be the Ripper. Of course, as Vittoria had not followed the stories in the press, she had no idea how much of what Stephenson told her was public knowledge.

Although she claimed to be convinced it didn't occur to her to contact the Police herself. Vittoria claimed that as a theosophist she believed that each would receive their just desserts in the next incarnation and so she did not need to interfere. Hardly a typical theosophical attitude considering recent litigious activities. However, lest these thoughts be designated as delusions by hysterical women, it's worth recalling that the

Police twice interviewed Stephenson and WT Stead himself believed him to be the Ripper. "He has been known to me for many years. He is one of the most remarkable persons I ever met. For more than a year I was under the impression that he was the veritable Jack the Ripper; an impression which I believe was shared by the police, who at least once had him under arrest; although, as he completely satisfied them, they liberated him without bringing him into court."

Vittoria and Mabel were to meet for the last time in the summer of 1891. It was a brief meeting, a little under an hour. Mabel needed a favour from Vittoria. Stephenson held a collection of letters from Mabel, which were explicit enough for her to be worried about the possibility of blackmail. She knew where they were kept and even had a key to the trunk that contained them. But she was too scared to rifle through the trunk herself and so begged Vittoria to retrieve the letters for her. Vittoria did as she was asked and sent the letters onto Mabel. It was another three weeks before Stephenson discovered their disappearance but as Mabel had written to him saying that he no longer had a hold over her, assumed that she had come and taken them herself.

Now that she felt safer, Mabel wrote to Stephenson ordering him out of his room and telling him that his furniture was to be taken away during the next few days. The Pompadour Company was taken over by a West End consortium, Mabel returned to live in York Terrace in London and Vittoria returned to the lodgings she had stayed in when she originally returned to London. Stephenson took out a summons against Mabel asking for the return of the letters. The case was heard at Marylebone Court and Vittoria went along. When it came to the crunch Stephenson was unable to substantiate his allegation that Mabel had taken the letters from a locked trunk, in fact, he was unable to speak. Had the great magician finally had his powers turned against him? And if so, by whom? After his solicitor spoke to him the case was dismissed. Mabel was present but Vittoria left without speaking to either Mabel or Stephenson.

After a number of begging letters Vittoria agreed to give Stephenson some money. She left England shortly afterwards, returning four years later. On her return she found a bundle of letters waiting for her in Stephenson's handwriting. She burnt them unread. There was no contact between Mabel and Vittoria again and as far as anyone knows, none between Stephenson and Mabel.

Although Mabel's story continues no one knows what became of Stephenson. His movements are obscure from 1891 to 1896.[210] He was converted to Christianity in 1893 by Victoria Woodhull,[211] who once ran for office as President of the United States. In 1901 he was living back in his home town. At some stage he had adopted Harman Wheas as his son, who was then aged six. As he is recorded in the 1901 census as a widower, it seems likely he married again. In 1904, after publishing a book called *The Patristic Gospels*,[212] he vanished without trace. Despite repeated searches by numerous Ripper researchers, most notably Melvin Harris, no death certificate can be found within Britain or elsewhere. Vittoria continued to tell friends that she had met Jack the Ripper. "I always remember Cremers saying she knew Jack the Ripper quite well through her dear friend Mabel Collins."[213]

Aleister Crowley met Vittoria in 1912, long after this episode was over. He described her as a lesbian lady in her fifties, who had been Mabel's lover. Vittoria also claimed to have betrayed Blavatsky alongside Mabel.

"…one of the most remarkable characters I have ever known and for the influence of her intervention on my affairs. Her name was Vittoria Cremers…She was an intimate friend of Mabel Collins, authoress of *The Blossom and the Fruit*, the novel which has left so deep a mark upon my early ideas about Magick…Her face was stern and square, with terribly intense eyes from which glared an expression of indescribable pain and hopeless horror. Her hair was bobbed and dirty white, her dress severely masculine save the single concession of a short straight skirt. Her figure was sturdy and her gait determined though awkward."[214]

"She boasted of her virginity and of the intimacy of her relations with Mabel Collins, with whom she lived a long time. Mabel had however divided her favours with a very strange man whose career had been extraordinary. He had been an officer in a cavalry regiment, a doctor, and I know not how many other things in his time. He was now in desperate poverty and depended entirely on Mabel Collins for his daily bread. This man claimed to be an advanced Magician, boasting of many mysterious powers and even occasionally demonstrating the same. At this time London was agog with the exploits of Jack the Ripper. One theory of the motive of the murderer was that he was performing an Operation to obtain the Supreme Black Magical Power. The seven women had to be killed so that their seven bodies formed a "Calvary cross of seven points" with its head to the west. The theory was that after killing the third or the fourth, I forget which, the murderer acquired the power of invisibility, and this was confirmed by the fact that in one case a policeman heard the shrieks of the dying woman and reached her before life was extinct, yet she lay in a cul-de-sac, with no possible exit save to the street; and the policeman saw no signs of the assassin, though he was patrolling outside, expressly on the lookout. Miss Collins' friend took great interest in these murders. He discussed them with her and Cremers on several occasions. He gave them imitations of how the murderer might have accomplished his task without arousing the suspicion of his victims until the last moment. Cremers objected that his escape must have been a risky matter, because of his habit of devouring certain portions of the ladies before leaving them. What about the blood on his collar and shirt? The lecturer demonstrated that any gentleman in evening dress had merely to turn up the collar of a light overcoat to conceal any traces of his supper. Time passed! Mabel tired of her friend, but did not dare to get rid of him because he had a packet of compromising letters written by her. Cremers offered to steal these from him. In the man's bedroom was a tin uniform case which he kept under the bed to which he attached it by cords. Neither of the women had ever seen this open and Cremers suspected that he kept these letters in it. She got him out of the way for a day by a forged telegram, entered the room, untied the cords and drew the box from under the bed. To her surprise it was very light, as if empty. She proceeded nevertheless to pick the lock and open it. There were no letters; there was nothing in the box, but seven white evening dress ties, all stiff and black with clotted blood!" [215]

Unfortunately, this never actually happened. Crowley's account arose from two events. In 1925 the journalist Bernard O'Connell acted as ghostwriter for the autobiographical memoirs of Betty May. She told O'Donnell the story. However, her version simply says that they were stiff and stained. The story first appeared in a series in *World's Pictorial News* throughout 1925, and later was published in 1929 in Betty May's book *Tiger Woman*.[216] It has made an appearance in several later accounts of the murders.

However, in Crowley's unpublished diaries dated Monday 23rd August 1943 there is a note, "Jack the Ripper," in which he accuses Blavatsky of being the Ripper. At least some of Crowley's writings on this episode must have been tongue in cheek.[217] Vittoria spent the remainder of her life in Wales and London, dying in 1936.

Was Stephenson Jack the Ripper? It appears that Mabel believed he was. Recent theories suggest an occult association with the Ripper crimes. The pattern of the killings forms a geometric pattern that is highly suggestive of the perpetrator being versed in occult geometry at the least.

Whether Mabel was simultaneously the lover of Vittoria and Stephenson is also open to question. But she certainly had an intimate relationship with both of them. And the theory goes a long way towards explaining Vittoria's antagonism towards Stephenson.

Whatever the truth of the matter Mabel had felt it wise to retreat. After investing her money in supporting a doomed business venture and Stephenson she had no choice but to declare bankruptcy in 1892. Another episode over, Mabel had little time to lick her wounds before the next stage in her life was to begin.

View of Crown Hill early 20th century.

CHAPTER NINE

Ink stains lingering

Although in theosophical terms Mabel may seem to have disappeared, there is no doubt that she kept herself busy in the early 1890s. In 1890 *The Confession of A Woman* and *A Debt of Honour* were published; 1891 *Ida: An Adventure in Morocco* and *The Story of An Heiress*. Also in 1892 *Morial The Mahatma or, The Black Master of Tibet* was published. This was a fictionalised account of activities in and around the Theosophical Society and created a small scandal in itself. It was Mabel's final contribution to the Coues episode and contained a portrait of a woman - part fanatic and part con artist - and black magicians posing as white magicians. The Theosophical Society wasn't slow to realise that this was a fictionalised account of Blavatsky and the Masters M and Koot Hoomi. This book also contains the theme of a lost race, and was a direct precursor of James Hilton's *Lost Horizons* about hidden immortals in Tibet.
218

Suggestion or The Modern Hypnotist, taken from one of Mabel's short stories, was written in collaboration with W Heron Brown as a play, and performed at a matinee at the Lyric Hammersmith Theatre, in King Street London on 21st November 1891. Mabel had never learned to type, and had to employ a typist from the Typewriter Writing Offices on the Strand to finish her manuscript. In 1892 it was published as a novel.

119

As a play *Suggestion* passed almost unnoticed. Theatre magazines ignored it in general, and as far as can be ascertained it was only performed once for copyright purposes. *The Era*,[219] which did review the play, was unimpressed. "To shoot folly as it flies is one of the purposes of the drama, and that we expect was the aim of Mabel Collins and Helen (*sic*) Brown when they went to work upon their new three act comedy…"

On 22nd February 1894 the first performance of her second play *A Modern Hypatia: A Drama of Today* took place at the Bijou theatre, a hall in Archer Street, Bayswater, London.[220] Hypatia is described as a Roman scholar and philosopher who lived in Alexandria. She was the basis of much literature during the eighteenth century and many authors and historians resurrected Hypatia's story. During the nineteenth century Hypatia inspired French poets, Italian writers, and English historians. By the late nineteenth century and into the twentieth Hypatia was a feminist symbol.[221] Mabel's play clearly uses Hypatia in this way: "Having committed the folly of leaving my husband I have lost all power, all hope of mercy."[222] It is aimed at women, showing Mabel's views on the life of a woman without a husband in late nineteenth century England more clearly than many of her writings: "Be a woman…who love you as neither husband or child nor lover can do – for the bonds that hold us to you are spiritual ones…we women will free you."[223]

It also played at Terry's Theatre on the 17th June 1895. Terry's was a relatively new theatre built in 1887 on the site of the old Coal Hole public house and music hall by the actor Edward Terry. It held 800 people and was highly popular.[224] Far more popular than *Hypatia* turned out to be. Plays were performed at Terry's matinées as a testing ground to see whether or not they would be programmed for evening production. *Hypatia* was announced in *The Stage* on the 6th and 13th of June. A Mr C St. John Denton was attributed with organising business arrangements, and he ensured that this play would be reviewed.

> "After an experience of many years in writing on plays, and from that experience being generally able to unravel a plot, we must confess that the play under notice completely baffled us. The whole of that company did their best to put some vitality into a play, which really had no life in it and we can only complement them on their efforts to make bricks without straw."[225]

This was not to turn out to be one of Mabel's more popular ventures. The review in *The Stage* was one of the kindest she received. Mabel had chosen not to announce herself as the author of this play and so none of the reviewers were aware who was responsible for it. Again, *Hypatia* was played at a matinée, this time on a Monday afternoon, and there is no record of it playing a second time. It was a theatrical disaster.

"It is hard to conceive what induced the author or authoress of "A Modern Hypatia" to choose such a title. What conceivable resemblance can there be between the unhappy virgin of Alexandria who was scraped to death by wild monks with oyster shells, and the middle aged matron who made herself champion of her sex and stump-orator under the name of Marcia Royal? Really, the trial matinées of pieces by unknown authors are curiously interesting. In the case of "A Modern Hypatia" it may be said that, during two-thirds of the first act, the critics were unable to determine whether it was a curious, audaciously, unconventional play ill acted, or merely a piece utterly crude, bereft of merit. Unfortunately, when the first curtain fell, there was no room for doubt, and though they stayed on in hope of better things, or of the strange humours that enliven inept pieces, all the professional playtasters felt that the unnamed author had been wise in choosing anonymity."[226]

"The author of "A Modern Hypatia" has modestly withheld his or her name. Possibly there were doubts and fears with regard to the success of the production. If so, these forebodings of disaster were realised…when the new play was tried before an audience, which received the novelty with a good tempered tolerance, which was quite as significant in its way as the most pronounced condemnation. The principal characters in "A Modern Hypatia" were supposed to be types of modern society, but there was about them an air of unreality, which precluded any great interest being taken in their doings. The play, as a whole, betrayed a crudeness in the workmanship and a palpable lack of knowledge of stage effect that were fatal to its success."[227]

It would be some years before Mabel would attempt playwriting again. Her third play *Sensa* was first performed at the court Theatre on 20th

April 1914. This was adapted from *The Idyll of the White Lotus*, published in 1907, and co written with the actress and theosophist Maud Hoffman. Maud was a long time friend of Mabel's who was a follower of Gurdjieff and the executrix of A. P. Sinnett's estate after his death in 1921. The Mahatma as well as the Blavatsky letters had been bequeathed by Mr. Sinnett "solely and unconditionally" to Maud and were published in 1923 with the originals given to the British Museum.[228]

Money had become a serious problem for Mabel and she was obliged to work as hard as she could. By 1892 she was splitting her time between Wandsworth in London and Ostend. Her finances were so low that she was obliged to declare bankruptcy in 1892.

She certainly worked hard during this period. At least fourteen of her books were published during the 1890s. One of her best known, *The Blossom and the Fruit,* had first appeared in serial form in *Lucifer*. The story of a black magician it was intended to show the struggle of the magician to learn to practice good instead of evil, and to become part of the "White Brotherhood". Mabel claimed "This strange story has come from a far country and was brought in a mysterious manner; we claim only to be the scribes and the editors. In this capacity, however, it is we who are answerable to the Public and the critics. We therefore ask in advance, per favour only of the reader; that he will accept (while reading this story) the theory of the re-incarnation of souls as a living fact." This is one of the last works Mabel produced while still within the Theosophical Society. Blavatsky wrote the last six chapters, as she believed that Mabel had lost control of the story.

Mabel was an extremely prolific writer. She published at least forty six books in her lifetime, wrote a number of articles, some of which were to later form the basis for her books and was also a fashion correspondent for *The World*, writing a regular column. Most of Mabel's novels are romantic sensation fiction. In later years her experiences in the occult and theosophy were used as a basis for her fiction writing.

Current literary theory considers that meanings are created by influences beyond the control of the reader or writer. In other words, our interpretation of any written work is created by our knowledge and experience separate to the work. Obviously that needn't be a bad thing, the more angles we can take in studying such works, the more understanding we are likely to gain. These theories assume that literature is constructed by environmental influences and that neither readers nor authors can transcend these influences. Unfortunately these theories do not explain exceptional texts which emerge and are especially inapplicable to spiritual works. Does that mean that such works transcend normal literary theory? Do authors really know their own intentions? Doesn't the meaning of a text change over time? How can we be sure that the meaning we find in a text is the same one that the author intended? The constant attempts of theosophists to prove that Blavatsky led a chaste life shows that they believed that her writings did not transcend their knowledge. What was known of Mabel's lifestyle was equally damning to reception of her future works.

There are parts of Mabel's writings that are much easier to read with knowledge of her life. Consider the opening of *Through the Gates of Gold*.

> " We are all acquainted with that stern thing called misery, which pursues man, and strangely enough, as it seems at first, pursues him with no vague or uncertain method, but with a positive and unbroken pertinacity. Its presence is not absolutely continuous, else man must cease to live; but its pertinacity is without any break. There is always the shadowy form of despair standing behind man ready to touch him with its terrible finger if for too long he finds himself content. What has given this ghastly shape the right to haunt us from the hour we are born until the hour we die? What has given it the right to stand always at our door, keeping that door ajar with its impalpable yet plainly horrible hand, ready to enter at the moment it sees fit? The greatest philosopher that ever lived succumbs before it at last; and he only is a philosopher, in any sane sense, who recognises the fact that it is irresistible, and knows that like all other men he must suffer soon or late. It is part of the heritage of men, this pain and distress; and he who determines that nothing shall make him suffer, does but cloak himself in a profound and chilly selfishness. This cloak may protect him from pain; it will also separate him from pleasure."[229]

We know that Mabel suffered at least one nervous breakdown. It seems more than likely that she suffered from depression. Although without that knowledge you can sense from this passage that she has a personal experience of the misery she talks of, knowing that she does makes it all the more meaningful.

Another passage – "There are certain pleasures which appeal to each individual; every man knows that in one layer or another of sensation he finds his chief delight. Naturally he turns to this systematically through life, just as the sunflower turns to the sun and the water-lily leans on the water. But he struggles throughout with an awful fact which oppresses him to the soul, - that no sooner has he obtained his pleasure than he loses it again and has once more to go in search of it."

Veiled criticisms of Mabel's sexuality permeate the writings about her life. She is often seen as a pleasure seeker. Seeking pleasure and sensuality resulted in Mabel simultaneously conducting close relationships with Stephenson and Vittoria Cremers. Obviously we cannot be sure of the exact nature of these relationships but it is certain that they were intimate on one level or another. And Mabel's trust was betrayed by Stephenson - the relationship ended in her being afraid of him. She also chose to disconnect herself from Vittoria. As we have only Vittoria's account of their relationship it is difficult to be clear about what happened but we can read between the lines. Vittoria appears to have been highly possessive and Mabel a person who was repelled by someone who would seek to control her.

One of the long running arguments about some of Mabel's books is whether or not they were written by her, perhaps in an exceptional state of mind or being, or whether they were inspired by one or more of the Masters. Some consider this question to be irrelevant nit picking as whoever the true author is makes no difference to the value of the work. Others place a higher value on her work if it is seen as written by one of the Masters with Mabel acting as their conduit. It is almost impossible for us at this distance in time to have a certain view of this question. Anyone's answer to this question must be at least partially based on their belief or otherwise in the Masters and the way that they work.[230] I will not, therefore, attempt to do more with this issue than apprise the reader of the fact that it is there.

Mabel also tried her hand at poetry in *At the shrine of Venus and the End of the Season* [231]

>   At the shrine of Venus
>   All some homage pay
>   Flora brings spring flowers
>   To strew the pleasant way;

Orpheus yields sweet music,
(His joy the sounding flute);
...And passport to this pleasure?
'Tis the love divine,
When the Sun of Righteousness
In our hearts doth shine

This booklet of two poems seems to be the only published verse written by Mabel. While today we can be impressed by the sheer volume of Mabel's written work, it is often forgotten how many writers emerged during this period. Everyone was a writer. Books were written and being published at a rate hitherto unknown.

"At no age, so far as we are aware, has there yet existed anything resembling the extraordinary flood of novels which is now pouring over this land — certainly with fertilising results, so far as the manufacture itself is concerned. There were days, halcyon days — as one still may ascertain from the gossip of the seniors of society — when an author was a natural curiosity, recognized and stared at as became the rarity of the phenomenon. No such thing is possible nowadays, when most people have been in print one way or other — when stains of ink linger on the prettiest of fingers, and to write novels is the normal condition of a large section of society."[232]

"No divine influence can be imagined as presiding over the birth of [the sensation writer's] work, beyond the market-law of demand and supply; no more immortality is dreamed of for it than for the fashions of the current season. A commercial atmosphere floats around works of this class, redolent of the manufactory and the shop. The public wants novels, and novels must be made — so many yards of printed stuff, sensation-pattern, to be ready by the beginning of the season."[233]

But out of all Mabel's works it is *Light on the Path* that remains remembered. "The Light on the Path will ever remain one of the jewels in the crown that adorns the Theosophical Society, for it is a treasure of profound knowledge that will help many to find his Self and lead him to that path by the Light that burns in its pages and shines through them."[234]

Mabel as a young woman, from a pastel portrait by Louise Jopling drawn 1891 and exhibited at The Grosvenor Gallery 1892.

CHAPTER TEN

A brilliant tangerine

Despite all that had been going on in her life, Mabel continued to work for Edmund Yates, writing for *The World,* now as a journalist, rather than simply a fashion columnist. Although she was primarily known as a fashion writer, and indeed continued with this work, Mabel also spent a lot of her time interviewing celebrities of the day. One of these was the painter James Abbot McNeil Whistler.[235] Mary Morris[236] introduced the two of them after Mabel wrote in 1888 in the hope of securing an interview.

> "The "Sorcerer", my dear Miss Collins, is always at your service - and when one of these days you do him the honour to breakfast in The [Tree?] Yellow, he will, though you say you are not "curious" - he knows you to be "dainty" - answer all your questions."[237]

Whistler's dining room was decorated in yellow and his Sunday 'breakfasts' were a famous meeting place for stars of the theatre, literature and the arts, as well as collectors and leaders of fashion. A further, undated letter, called Mabel "charming".

Whistler had long been a friend of Yates', and his letters frequently appeared in *The World*. What precisely transpired between Mabel and

Whistler remains unrecorded, except for a strangely defensive letter Whistler later wrote to Mary Morris. He insisted that he was indeed charming, and would not "seem to enter upon a tilt with a lady!...Men are pigmies, and I am born to collect their scalps, but think you I have not sufficient wit to know that one brilliant woman against me, and I am lost?" Whistler wasn't the only artist who Mabel met. She met Louise Jopling[238] around the same time, through an introduction made by Edmund Yates.

> "I did a pastel portrait about this time of a very brilliant woman, the daughter of the writer, Mortimer Collins. She was a journalist and interviewed people for "The World". It was in her capacity of interviewer that I met her, Edmund Yates having given her an introduction to me. Miss Collins introduced me to Madame Blavatski, who lived in St John's Wood. I was not impressed with the personality of that famous woman: although I could not help being struck with the pale frozen blue of her eyes, which were absolutely expressionless. I could imagine their stare hypnotizing anyone of a susceptible nature."[239]

It is commonly assumed that following Mabel's separation from the Theosophical Society, she had nothing further to do with Blavatsky. But although Mabel was no longer a theosophist, it is clear from this statement that she must have retained contact to be able to introduce Louise to Blavatsky.

Mabel spent a lot of time in South Kensington, where Louise lived, on her hunts for fashion news. And she used her trips as an excuse to drop by and visit while Louise was painting.

> "...I determined to visit South Kensington, and being there, to refresh my eyes by a visit to Mrs Joplin's studio; it really was a refreshment, for there I found her painting an idyllic scene of three girls dancing on the sands..."[240]

Mabel's portrait, drawn at some time in 1891, was exhibited at the Grosvenor Gallery in 1892. Louise Jopling was a regular exhibitor. The gallery would be open for the London season each year, and artists were offered space to exhibit by invitation of the owner, Sir Coutts Lyndsay. The works of a number of popular artists, such as Whistler and John

Varley, could be seen there. Varley was a theosophist and Louise Jopling signed a declaration in favour of women's suffrage in 1889, finally leaving her painting career to campaign for women's rights.

One of Mabel's most famous columns resulted from a trip she made to Tangier, Morroco in 1889, and was published as a series of letters in *The World*.

Located on the Atlantic side of the strait of Gibraltar, Tangier was conquered and occupied by the Portuguese in 1471. For nearly three hundred years it was passed back and forth between the Spanish, Portuguese and finally the English, when it was given to Charles II as part of the dowry from Catherine of Braganza. The English granted Tangier a charter, which made the city equal to English towns.

In the nineteenth century, as European investment poured in, the gravitation towards urban areas had sapped the rural agricultural economy on which Morocco had always depended.

The strategic importance and economic potential of Morocco had excited the interest of the European powers. France, Great Britain, Germany, and Spain, benefited from a series of trade agreements with that country. France became Morocco's major creditor; Britain built railroads; and Germany acquired the largest amount of foreign-held property. Spain held several coastal regions, including Ceuta, which it had acquired from the Portuguese in 1580, and a portion of the Western Sahara that had been placed under a Spanish protectorate in 1884. France, after beginning a war with Algeria, defeated Sultan Abd ar-Rahman, who had aided the Algerians, in 1844. Spain invaded in 1860. In 1880 the major European nations and the United States decided at the Madrid Conference to preserve the territorial integrity of Morocco and to maintain equal trade opportunities for all. Political and commercial rivalries soon disrupted this agreement and brought on several international crises. By the early twentieth century Morocco had fallen under French control.

The Sultan Mulay Hasan I was born in 1836, and succeeded on the death of his father, 16th September 1873. He reorganised the Moroccan army, enacted a series of reforms, and secured European guarantees for Morocco's independence at the Madrid Conference of 1880.

Tangier began to revive from the mid-19th century when European colonial governments fought for influence over Morocco. France, Spain, England and Germany jockeyed for position in Tangier where most diplomatic missions were located. Although Tangier was only six days sail away from England, it was largely unknown to most of the British population. Tangier was a small city of the province of Hasbat, placed on the eastern slope of a hill, with the port at its west. Old Tangier lay four miles to the east, by the time of Mabel's visit a heap of ruins.

Among the highly mixed population of Tangier, resided the European diplomats. They lived in grand properties; so grand that the Swedish Consul's garden was open to European visitors. Along with the lieutenant governor of Tangier, who resided in a castle, eleven consuls were based in Tangier; the British, French, Spanish, Portuguese, American, Danish, Swedish, Sardinian, Neapolitan, Austrian, and Dutch. Each nation owned their house, although the land belonged to the Sultan.

In 1889, it was announced that the Sultan of Morocco planned to visit Tangier on 22nd September. There had been no royal visit to Tangier by the present Sultan. Mabel had decided to visit Tangier and see the Sultan's arrival for herself. She travelled to Liverpool and took a ship from the Albert Docks to Gibraltar, sailing for six days.

> "Happily, O happily indeed, has the steamship *Oriental*, one of the P & O's splendid fleet, brought me to Gibraltar. Not one misfortune attended the voyage; it was like a dream of the sea."[241]

Mabel had a pleasant trip, spending her days on deck and gazing at the stars at night. Her short stay in Gibraltar was enough to make her amazed.

> "The noise is simply amazing! Drivers yell at their mules and donkeys, which carry loads of gloriously coloured fruit and vegetables; troops of goats go by, each wearing a fearful clanging bell."[242]

She wandered the streets, peering into doorways and soaking up the atmosphere. As soon as she could, Mabel took the *Hercules* to Tangier. She stood on deck watching as they drew closer.

> "...what an attraction there is...in the dim-coloured hills of this mysterious country! There are no trees, nothing one could call beautiful; only the strangeness of the shape and the colouring of the earth and low growing plants. There is a long stretch before, at last, Tangier is sighted – standing most picturesque on a hillside, with a

lovely little bay that stretches some way to the left, with a long sandy ride at the edge of the water, while to the right is the open sea."[243]

The *Hercules* arrived and Mabel climbed into a small boat, which was rowed, to the pier. The landing stage was crowded with Moors, all shouting at once. Mabel was the first to get out of the boat. She began searching for the friend she had in Tangier, who she was expecting to meet her. Fortunately, he soon, along with another Englishman, arrived and helped Mabel to collect her luggage and sort out her passage through customs.

Mabel was full of resolve to gain all she could from her trip. She watched amazed as one donkey was burdened with her big trunk, cabin trunk, rugs and bags and then prepared to climb on a donkey herself.

"I had heard of this donkey riding as terrible, but was armed with determination."[244]

Riding down the stony streets, through noisy crowds, Mabel retained enough of her usual character to note – "…the shops are so wonderful…The strange dresses, the bewilderment of rich colours, the continual chattering and screaming, leave me no room for comment or speech…"[245]

Arriving at her friends' house, Mabel had supper, drank tea and then headed for her hotel. She was already making plans for the following day.

The Sultan of Morocco was due to visit the town of Tutuan, forty-three miles from Tangier. Mabel was sure that the journey could be made in one day and hired a guide. She had been told that the journey was impossible in one day and that she would likely die on the way. In response, Mabel simply didn't consult anyone before she left, and estimated that she was probably the only white woman to have made such a journey.

Mohammed, who Mabel described as being adept at a number of languages, and Mabel, set off at 6 am. They travelled on horseback with a mule carrying their luggage. Riding all day, they passed mountain camps filled with animals and soldiers' camps. After watching the sun set, the pair had a few more miles to go before reaching the city gates. The room they had hoped to take was already filled, but they were directed to a Spanish hotel, only opened for the Sultan's visit, which apparently had the last rooms left in town. The next morning they watched the Sultan enter the town from his morning ride.

> "A wild clashing sound from the Sultan's palace announces his approach and instantly from every entrance come the extraordinary, bizarre, half-mad-looking beings who crowd the town."[246]

As he approached, crimson jacketed men ran into the square; the people began a cry as the Sultan came into sight, followed by fifty men all clothed in white. Women covered the rooftops and as the Sultan went by they removed their veils. Once the festivities were over, Mabel had a little time to explore. She compared the filth and squalor of the back streets to the notorious London slums. No women were to be seen on the street, so Mabel was an unknown quantity to the locals.

She was invited to the home of Sid Labidyad, where she met his wife and drank mint tea, served by a Negro dressed in a striped loincloth. The family spoke nothing but Arabic, so conversation was hardly possible. They simply talked amongst themselves while Mabel happily sipped her tea.

There was less of a hurry for the return journey, so Mabel and Mohammed broke their travels halfway to spend the night in a donkey driver's hut. Soon, she was back at Onetto House, her luxurious hotel in Tangier, to await the Sultan's visit there.

On the day, the whole of the city was awake and moving by 6 am, as no one was sure what time he would arrive. Mabel had foregone her sunshade – being told that it was against etiquette when the Sultan was in town – and was dressed in a skirt made from a large piece of white cloth along with fringed, cream woven material, and a cream matinee jacket. Other European ladies wore afternoon dresses, but Mabel could always be relied on so far as clothes were concerned.

By 6:30 am, Mabel was seated on the old grey charger she had grown fond of, and was waiting to catch sight of the Sultan. As soon as Mohammed had brought her horse from the stable he had disappeared, so Mabel was left to wait alone. She rode to the market and ran into a group of Europeans who wasted their time telling Mabel that if she chose to be so foolish as to stay it was her responsibility. Mabel had a problem being worried when she was no more than a quarter of a mile from an anticipated English breakfast. Most Europeans had climbed onto the roof of the German Legation; a couple of ladies sat on their mules. Mabel was the only woman on horseback and sat proudly behind a line of handsome men.

The parade began at 8 am. The first arrival was a Circassian[247] slave, the mother of the heir apparent. She was wrapped totally in what appeared to be white gauze and was soon followed by horsemen, cavalry, artillery… finally the Sultan, followed by about twenty thousand men. As he reached the palace, seventy-five guns were fired to announce his arrival. Mabel decided it was time for breakfast. Later, fireworks were let off in celebration.

Tangier remained chaotic for some days. The Sultan visited the mosque with his Imperial Guard five days later and the crowds again covered the rooftops, waving their handkerchiefs and taking off their hats. In the excitement a European foolishly attempted to take a photograph but was stoned by soldiers and his equipment destroyed.

With the European residents throwing dances and parties, Mabel whimsically decided that the Sultan had been wandering incognito around town. She was certain he did so on at least one occasion. She fervently hoped that he would appear at a party, but if he did so, it goes unrecorded by history.

Mabel soon returned to England and resumed her life of writing. She continued to contribute letters, serials and short stories to as many society and fashion papers as were willing to take them. One of these was *The Sword and Chatelaine*,[248] which she wrote a column in for four months of its six month life in 1892.

Her column, *The Ladies Mirror and Review*, was similar to the fashion column she had contributed to *The World*. Concerned mainly with beauty treatments and clothes, the column also gave Mabel space to offer her opinions on a number of subjects.

> "The attainment of beauty has always been one of the occult sciences – one allowed to have an existence but practiced only by a few."[249]

Mabel insisted that two hours a day were necessary for a woman to attain beauty. The details she goes into when discussing treatments and clothes makes it clear that so far as she was concerned, two hours a day was the bare minimum. The unreality of all but the very young being able to attain the ideal of an eighteen inch waist, the obligation to curl your hair to keep up with the fashion and the importance of protecting your skin from the sun were the types of issues that worried Mabel for many column inches.

> "When you are angry, stamp if you want to, but keep your face smooth."[250]

It was still not the done thing for a lady to wear make up. When Mabel recommended the use of cosmetics she was talking about quality soaps and creams.

> "Exercise, air, good sleep in the early hours of the night, bathing in softened and perfumed water, and the use of restorative cosmetics…Avoid rouge…except a little at night; with diamonds and the light of wax candles…"[251]

It was fashion that persuaded Mabel to make a number of visits to Brussels to buy lace and fine linen. Unfortunately, the outbreak of typhus in Belgium in the summer of 1892 forced her to postpone her trip that year. It wasn't only women's dress that preoccupied Mabel.

> "Many officers, I am told, always wear corsets under their uniform but never in mufti. To do so is surely a lamentable sign of pandering to the effeminate tone of modern society. Many a stalwart young officer has a waist so small and well shaped that any pretty girl would enjoy it; but while men are held to be the strong ones, surely it cannot be good form to show off an essentially feminine beauty. However, among the gilded youth of Piccadilly it is regarded as the right thing to do this year."[252]

Mabel's advice can appear almost surreal in today's terms. But the columns she wrote describe the life and preoccupations of a lady far more clearly than any history book could. Taking your own hammock when you go boating, as she advises, may not be a priority today. But we can all recognise the sense of making sure that you wear a flexible corset. She pointed out that tea dances were becoming fashionable partially because it was cheaper than throwing a dinner party. And pragmatically suggested that if you can't afford a new dress, then you should simply turn down invitations until you can. We can almost imagine the parties that Mabel attended. Whispering in corners that Mrs So and So wasn't really indisposed but her husband had frittered away that month's dress budget. Things were changing though. A few years before it would have been outrageous to suggest using an outside caterer for your dinner parties as Mabel does. Major news events do occasionally creep into Mabel's writings. For example, she mentions the notorious Maybrick case in her column.[253] She also mentions her own activities from time to time.

> "I once travelled for three months with a star actress who had made two tours through America and had learned to live in the train…never took off hat, veil or gloves."[254]

As Mabel developed a close friendship with the American actress Maud, (or Maude), Hoffman, it seems likely that this is who she is referring to here. Maud Hoffman was Washington born, but frequently visited England. She was first seen on the English stage in *The Cardinal*, acting alongside the renowned actor Edward Smith Willard at St James's Theatre in 1901. This was directly after her successful stint on Broadway, where she had appeared in *The Cipher Code, New England Folks, Colorado* and *David Garrick* from the end of September through to the end of December of that year. In later years Maud shared a house in Harley Street with doctors Henry Maurice Dunlop Nicoll and James Carruthers Young. She became a follower of Gurdjieff after being a pupil of Ouspensky and moved to the Chateau du Prieuré, in Fontainebleau, France, in 1922. Maud was also a theosophist in the early days. She became the executrix of the estate of AP Sinnett, after caring for him during his final illness. When he died in 1921 he bequeathed the famous *Mahatma Letters* to her. After being involved in their publication she presented the entire collection of letters and Blavatsky papers to the Department of Manuscripts in the British Museum, (now British Library), where they can still be seen. And this is a pilgrimage made by many theosophists today.

Mabel's spiritual writings were taking over her time. *Green Leaves*, published in 1895, received positive reviews as another devotional classic.[255]

"After a silence of many years the gifted scribe of *Light on the Path* speaks once more to the mystics of the day. In her new devotional treatise *Green Leaves*, Mabel Collins follows closely the teachings outlined in her previous work, though the new textbook seems to aim to some extent at popularising the formers sublimated and often veiled teachings."[256]

Despite Mabel's good connections, her work was no longer selling as it had, primarily because she was beginning to write less fiction and more spiritual works. She was most popular in the US, but the copyright laws then applying made it almost impossible for her to profit financially from her books. Copyright of author's works had been based on the 1710 Statute of Anne, which established the principles of ownership and a fixed term of protection for copyrighted works. This provided the model for copyright provision in the US, implemented in 1790. Great Britain was one of the signatories to the Berne Convention of 1886, which gave copyright protection to citizens of the European state signatories. However, the US remained governed by the 1790 Act and longstanding piracy of works by Europeans continued to be an accepted way of life for American publishers. Because American copyright law applied only to American publications, European authors were unable to profit from the publication and sale of their works (often at extremely low prices) during the nineteenth century. The cheap books movement, spread rapidly by small publishers after the Civil War, threatened the courtesy principle of price fixing adhered to by the large established publishers. By the 1880s cheap books flooded the American market. Although later changes in the law meant that European authors could begin to profit from their works published in the US, most of Mabel's novels appeared before the changes were made. So although she was extremely popular in the US, the chances of her earning any money from this were extremely slim. Things came to a head in November 1892 when she was obliged to file for bankruptcy.

In an age that lacked almost all forms of social security, bankruptcy was extremely serious, and undertaken as a last resort. For Mabel to declare herself bankrupt, at a time when the stigma attached to it was worse than today, she must have been truly desperate. She had to attend an open court hearing where her finances were examined and the grant of bankruptcy was reported in *The London Gazette*, as required by law. The announcement of Mabel's hearing on 5th November at Wandsworth

MYSTICAL VAMPIRE

Court appeared in the *Gazette* on 8th November 1892. Mabel was listed as a widow of no occupation living in Wandsworth Southwest London, having previously lived in West Drayton, Middlesex. She had a rented room in Wandsworth, at 65 Alma Road.[257]

KIM FARNELL

CHAPTER ELEVEN

Rose scented vows

The town of West Hartlepool, where Mabel was to spend the next few years, was a relatively new town, founded in the mid 19th century by a group of entrepreneurs. It grew as the result of a battle between rival railway companies, and had a new harbour in competition to the old harbour at Hartlepool. The new town was placed with good access to the sea, to the coal mines of County Durham and to the iron ore mines of North Yorkshire.

West Hartlepool grew around a centre just north of the ancient village of Stranton and quickly enveloped it. Other villages were subsumed into the town. During its rapid growth, West Hartlepool was a rough and ready place. Huge numbers of labourers flooded into the town, and the atmosphere of the town then has been compared to the wild west of America. The new town soon boomed, growing rapidly and becoming rich. By 1900 it had a population of 63,000. It no longer exists, as in 1967 Hartlepool and West Hartlepool were amalgamated under the name Hartlepool.

Although she still spent much of her time in London, Mabel now made her home with her mother in law, Ellen, and sister in law, the unmarried Agnes. Ellen and Agnes had moved to Hartlepool some time after the death of Robert Keningale Cook the elder. They shared their home at Saxon Villas, Hutton Avenue, with a fifteen year old general domestic servant, Mary Place.

It was in and around Hartlepool that Mabel became the "... well-known worker in anti-vivisection cause" *(sic)*, described by Alan Leo in his book *1001 Notable Nativities*.[258] Rather than becoming involved in the anti-vivisection movement after she had moved north, it seems more likely, from later reports, that Mabel moved north to spread the word.

Vivisection had long been a concern of those in Mabel's circle. Mabel herself became a vegetarian and along with many theosophists would discuss the likelihood or not of animals having souls and the morality of vivisection. The theosophical press published a number of articles damning the practice. "Look at that other disgrace of our cultured age – the scientific slaughter-houses called "vivisection rooms"...For verily when the world feels convinced – and it cannot avoid coming one day to such a conviction – that animals are creatures as eternal as we ourselves, vivisection and other permanent tortures, daily inflicted on the poor brutes, will, after calling forth an outburst of maledictions and threats from society generally, force all Governments to put an end to those barbarous and shameful practices."[259] Theosophists weren't required to become vegetarians, but a great number of them were.

But concern over the treatment of animals in modern medicine wasn't restricted to theosophists. There had long been objectors to the vivisectionists and momentum against them was gathering in the late nineteenth century.

In the eighteenth century scant attention had been paid to the rights and sufferings of animals. A paper published by Jeremy Bentham in 1780, argued, *"The question is not – Can they reason? nor Can they talk ? but Can they suffer?"* This helped propel the agitation for anti-cruelty laws.

In 1822 Martin's Act, which is widely regarded as the first anti-cruelty legislation, was made law. This made it an offence to wantonly abuse, beat or ill-treat any animal if it was the property of any other person or persons. It had taken a long time to achieve this small success and it was another thirteen years before legislation was passed which gave similar protection to animals being cruelly treated by their owners.

Physiologists had been the first to express reservations about vivisection. From the seventeenth century onwards, eminent physiologists expressed concern for the welfare of their subjects but, generally, remained convinced that the costs to the animals were justified by the results of their research.

The other catalyst for the foundation of the anti-vivisection movement was a series of public lectures given in London by the French physiologist Francois Magendie, (1783-1855), in 1824. Magendie gave several public demonstrations of his method of the experimental section of cranial nerves of living dogs. Magendie also campaigned passionately against the use of anaesthesia induced by using ether. There followed an outcry against unnecessary cruelty in animal experimentation. The physiologist and neurologist Marshall Hall (1790-1857) began to pioneer welfare issues. In 1831 he suggested five guiding principles to ensure that vivisection took into account the suffering of animals and these guiding principles formed the basis of the subsequent Cruelty to Animals Act.

The Society for the Prevention of Cruelty to Animals was founded in 1824 and it became the Royal Society for the Prevention of Cruelty to Animals in 1840. But it was not until the advent of anaesthesia in the 1850s that the RSPCA began to oppose vivisection. When Queen Victoria herself expressed concern about animal experimentation in 1874, a Bill aimed at regulating vivisection was presented in the House of Lords and a Royal Commission of Inquiry was set up.

In response, Frances Power-Cobbe (1822-1904)[260] set up a lobby group, The Victoria Street Society for the Protection of Animals from Vivisection on 21st December 1875. The society, which argued for legal restriction of vivisection, rapidly gained popular support. It argued that anaesthesia should be compulsory in all experiments involving surgery and that animals should be euthanased before recovering. They also sought to prohibit the use of cats, dogs and horses for vivisection. Cobbe served as secretary of the VSS for eighteen years.

The protests led the Government to appoint the First Royal Commission on Vivisection in July 1875. It reported its findings on 8th January 1876, recommending that special legislation be enacted to control vivisection. This led to the Cruelty to Animals Act on 15 August 1876. The new act placed restrictions on the practice of experiments on animals. A license was required, as well as certificates setting forth the conditions under which the experiment was to be made. The Home Secretary was empowered by the Act to issue such additional regulations as he saw fit. Many saw the Act as legalising vivisection as well as providing total secrecy to the vivisectors and to the laboratories, with no public accountability. The Home Office awarded licences to vivisectors in secret; the locations of laboratories were secret.

The Society was disappointed with what it saw as inadequate legislation, and changed its name to The Victoria Street Society for the Protection of Animals from Vivisection with the aim of abolishing vivisection. On 6th October 1897 it was renamed the National Anti-Vivisection Society. At a meeting on 9th February 1898 the following resolution was passed: - *"The Council affirms that, while the demand for the total abolition of vivisection will ever remain the ultimate object of the National Anti-Vivisection Society, the Society is not thereby precluded from making efforts in Parliament for lesser measures, having for its object the saving of animals from scientific torture."*[261] The resolution was carried by twenty-nine votes to twenty-three. Frances Power-Cobbe didn't want the Society to promote any measure short of abolition. As a result she left the NAVS, and on 14th June founded the British Union for the Abolition of Vivisection.

The BUAV began initially in Bristol, yet through an extensive programme of tours, meetings and lectures they sought support throughout England and Wales. By the end of June 1898 the first branch, Wales, had been established claiming 253 members. The first half-yearly report also stated the intention to engage the services of a Medical Doctor, so they could meet medical opponents on their own ground when either the cruelty or the inadequacy of vivisection was disputed. The organisation was structured upon a regional basis and by 1899 had eight sections.

Its journal, *The Abolitionist*, first appeared on 15th April 1899 and continued as a monthly publication until December 1949. It was in this publication that Mabel first appears as a staunch anti-vivisectionist. In fact, it was Mabel's idea to start the magazine, which was to prove a key publication of the movement. Mabel had been an honorary member of the Victoria Street Society since 1895 and was Hon. Secretary of the North of England branch of the BUAV before 1899. She first met Frances Power-Cobbe in February 1899. "I first heard Miss Cobbe's wonderful laugh in February 1899…she lost it soon after I met her; and it is one of the things I prize among my store of recollections that I was permitted to hear it before age and illness finally took it from her. She told me herself how much it had always cost her to enter a sick room. I still have some sweet scented rose petals gathered in that wonderful garden of Miss Cobbe's with the rushing stream passing between it and the mountain she lived among the beauty that was her delight. She bade me never to let a day of my life pass without doing something in the cause. I took a vow, and the scent of roses reminds me always of it."[262] Mabel clearly took her vow seriously.

The anti-vivisection movement was gaining serious momentum during this period. Mabel was interviewed by the *Newcastle Daily Leader* in May 1899, about experiments on monkeys. The publicity in Newcastle led to a new branch of the BUAV being established. She also established the first women's only anti-vivisectionist meeting the same month, "...the Hon Sec. of the North of England branch, Mrs K Cook, (Mabel Collins), then said that her hope was to see a local committee formed to carry on the work in the town, and asked any ladies who were willing to give her their names before the meeting dispersed. Several ladies responded to this request..."[263] However, at a later meeting the idea of a women's only group was abandoned as it was made clear by a number of vocal men that they wanted the chance to serve on the committee.

It made little difference. The anti-vivisection movement was primarily made up of women, who were often dismissed as much for their gender as their beliefs. They were accused of being "irrational" and anti intellectual". Men who opposed vivisection were regarded as effeminate. Elie De Cyon, a prominent male physiologist of the day wrote: "...women—or rather, old maids, form the most numerous contingent of this group (referring to anti-vivisectionists). Let my adversaries contradict me, if they can show among the leaders of the agitation, one girl, rich, beautiful, and loved or some young wife who has found in her home the full satisfactions of her affections." Despite such opposition the anti-vivisection movement continued to grow and become more aligned to the early feminist movement.

Mabel was on a number of committees with a variety of political and aristocratic figures including Lady Helen Shewar, Sir Thomas Richardson and the MPs JM Paylton, AE Pease, Joseph Pease and Robert Cameron fighting for the anti vivisection movement. She wrote an abolitionist pamphlet and her letters were published frequently in the press championing the cause.

There was to be no stopping Mabel. She published the correspondence that had resulted from the *Newcastle Daily Leader* article in pamphlet form to distribute to interested parties. In July of 1899 she took part in a procession through Hartlepool. A lifeboat was used as a temporary centre and members leafleted the gathering crowds and carried the anti vivisection poster, *Have Pity*, on boards as they marched.

Her campaigning wasn't restricted to animal causes. In December 1899 Mabel had a letter published in the *South London Press* about the refusal by the drug board to provide for pauper patients, "Sir – a Metropolitan board of guardians has refused to supply anti toxin for pauper patients although requested to do so by one of the district medical officers."

Vaccination was frequently given as the reason why vivisection was necessary. A number of anti vivisectionists were opposed to vaccination, believing it to actually increase mortality rather than save lives. In the late 19th and early 20th century, government sponsored vaccination programmes caused tens of thousands of deaths. Japan suffered 48,000 deaths from smallpox vaccination and England and Wales experienced 45,800 smallpox deaths in a population that was 97% vaccinated against smallpox. Three million people died in Europe from the smallpox they had been vaccinated against.

Before the law was amended in 1898 to include a conscientious exemption clause, an average of 2,000 parents per year were jailed and prosecuted in England for resisting vaccination. Large numbers went to prison in default of paying fines. Hundreds had their homes and possessions seized.

The worst smallpox epidemic in recorded history occurred in England during 1871-1873 at a time when there was almost universal coverage under the government's vaccination programme. A Royal Commission was appointed in 1889 to investigate the history of vaccination in the United Kingdom. The evidence mounted that smallpox epidemics increased dramatically after 1854, the year the compulsory vaccination law went into effect. The Commission sat for seven years gathering evidence. In 1907, the Vaccination Acts of England were repealed. By 1919, England and Wales had become one of the least vaccinated countries, and had only twenty-eight deaths from smallpox, out of a population of 37.8 million people.

And so the campaign against vivisection wasn't simply about the love of animals. Many campaigners were opposed to vaccination, and were members of other reform movements. A large number of women were involved in the anti-vivisection movement, including those who would be remembered for their suffragist activities, such as Charlotte Despard.

Mabel was a tireless campaigner. As the Honourable Secretary of the North of England Branch she used her influence to write letters to the press. With the BUAV she joined in protests against the government enforced vaccination programme in South Africa, where she said the troops were "…very ill from vaccination – being inoculated is far worse than any flesh wound and causes a great deal more pain."[264] As well as vaccination research, much of the work carried out in medical laboratories at this time related to anaesthesia. Curare was commonly used by animal experimenters as it kept the animal conscious and aware, but didn't allow them to move, "The Reviewer of the British Medical Journal asserts that to cut up a dog alive under curare is not to torture it…full freedom to use the hellish drug."[265] It was clear from Mabel's writing at the time that she was an avid reader of medical literature.

Although Mabel spent a great deal of her time in West Hartlepool, she still kept a home in at 172 Wandsworth Road, in south west London. Just down the road from where she lived was the Brown Institute, ostensibly a hospital for sick animals, and a place where a large amount of animal experimentation took place. Brown's was to become renowned for its research into rabies, and numerous eminent medical practitioners of the late nineteenth century worked there for a time. It wasn't long before Mabel's attention was drawn to the activities taking place behind closed doors at Brown's.

Always the writer, Mabel produced a pamphlet detailing what she had found. She was convinced that many doctors had no idea of the sort of work that was being carried on in the name of medical research and that something needed to be done. At this time, Charlotte Despard,[266] known for her support of a variety of reform movements, was living in Wandsworth. She had moved there in 1890, following the death of her husband, to dedicate the rest of her life to helping the poor. Horrified at what she saw as the torture of animals on her doorstep, Mabel wrote to the Poor Law Guardians and Charlotte responded. "Mrs Cook has been fortunate in enlisting the sympathies of Mrs Despard, a sister of General French, who is very highly esteemed for all her noble work among the poor…she has lent a room at the Despard Club 95 Wandsworth Road, to be used as an office."[267]

With premises made available Mabel could now establish the South London Branch of the BUAV. She paid for 1,000 copies of her pamphlet to be made and together with May Woodridge and Helen Pierrepoint, she distributed copies of the pamphlet throughout Wandsworth, Vauxhall and Kensington. The North of England Branch, at Mabel's behest, took on the costs of setting up this new branch. Its first meeting took place on 23rd June 1900 and was reported in the *South London Press*. Charlotte was appointed as secretary with Helen Pierrepoint, with whom she shared her home, as Honorary Assistant. Callers were invited to visit on Tuesday and Friday afternoons to collect a copy of Mabel's pamphlet and find out more about the campaign.

Mabel travelled the country speaking about the horrors she had found at Brown's. She talked of a dying man who lived on Wandsworth Road who could gain no rest as he was constantly awoken by the cries of animals. "I have seen the helpless creatures being taken in, and I am sure that anyone who heard and saw these things would feel as I feel now-that the only joy to be found anywhere in the world is that of ceaselessly working to try and rescue Gods creatures from the torturers."[268] Ceaseless working was precisely what Mabel had in mind. Mabel attended meetings wherever she could, at times speaking alongside Frances Power-Cobbe.

The campaign began to hot up. Mabel described to anyone who would listen how rabbits would have their spleen removed while still alive; how puppies would have their spinal cords severed and how puppies operated on would be kept alive for days in agony. She described how dogs could be kept alive for up to one hundred and forty-nine days in a state of paralysis. And she quoted publications such as the *Journal of Physiology* to back up her statements.

While Charlotte formed a new branch of the BUAV in Surrey, and became its president, Mabel travelled to Bangor in Wales to speak against vivisectors being appointed to hospitals and to aid the campaign there. By January of 1901, Mabel had persuaded the *South London Press* to carry a story about the animal experiments going on at the Brown Institute. The *Journal of Pathology and Bacteriology* described how in one experiment parts of the kidney were removed from forty-nine dogs to see how long they could be kept alive without it. Later in the year she would talk about how a dog was kept alive without a brain for eighteen months.

In between her travels, Mabel was often at the newly formed Surrey branch. "We have two secretaries here, Miss Pierrepoint, the secretary of the branch and Mrs Mabel Cook, who helps us here and in many other parts of the kingdom and is most devoted to the cause we are serving."[269] Although Mabel was doubtless in a position to claim presidency of a branch of the BUAV, she never appears to have been interested, instead keeping her title of secretary and visiting as many groups as possible.

Throughout 1902 Mabel's work continued. In *The Morning Leader* of 24 January an article was carried about Mabel's newest novel – *The Star Sapphire*. "A cheap popular edition of *The Star Sapphire* by Mabel Collins (Mrs Cook)…The book contains a vivid character sketch of the great surgeon Professor Lawson Tait, well known as a powerful opponent of vivisection and a description of him at work, which he good humouredly accepted as very true to life. Another character in the novel is readily recognized as that of an eminent church dignitary, whose personal popularity has enabled him to champion more than one humanitarian cause in the face of strong opposition." Reprinted in *The Abolitionist* 15th February, the review makes it clear that not only had Mabel's novel writing continued, but that she still used her own life experiences as the basis of her work. *The Star Sapphire* enabled Mabel to reach a whole new audience, which could have done the anti vivisection campaign no harm at all.

The campaign against the Brown Institute remained Mabel's main focus. She had organised a petition of protest and after she had gathered 53,000 signatures,[270] the petition was handed to the University of London Senate, who bore responsibility for the Brown Institute. It was presented by Mabel along with Atherley-Jones[271] and Col. Sandys, both MPs and contained signatures of support from such leading figures as George Gissing, Marie Corelli and Alfred Russell Wallace.

By 1903 Mabel was no longer secretary of the North of England branch of the BUAV. However, this doesn't indicate that her work slowed down. Llewellyn Atherly-Jones wrote to Mabel on 6th August 1903 asking her what they should do next. Charlotte Despard suggested that they approach London University as the Trustees of the Brown Institute. Mabel then wrote a letter to the London University Senate along with Helen Pierrepoint, asking for its support against the misapplication of the Brown bequest. (The Brown Institute was funded through the Senate by a research bequest). The response from the Senate denied that animals were in torment and said that the Institute was being run in accordance with the terms of the bequest. It accused Mabel and Helen Pierrepoint of misapplying the facts. Another letter swiftly followed. This time there was no response.

There were now twenty federated societies and a Parliamentary Association, formulated to speak on behalf of the abolition cause in the House of Commons. In August the BUAV were invited to send a delegate to the second meeting of the International Congress of the World League for the Protection of Animals against Vivisection, held in Frankfurt. Propaganda work was undertaken in the form of correspondence through the newspapers and attacks upon universities with licenses to practice vivisection. Charlotte retired as President of the Surrey branch, but continued to be involved.

Mabel came up with a bright idea to capture public attention. Members searched for vacant shops in town centres. They were then rented by the BUAV on a short term lease, often for only a few weeks. The shop was filled with leaflets and posters displayed in the windows to attract passers by. The first shop was opened as an experiment in Wrexham, with Mabel overseeing it. Anti vivisection literature was handed to passers by along with tickets for a meeting the following month. One thousand people turned up at that meeting to hear Dr Hadwen[272] and a local MP speak against vivisection.

Its success meant that shortly afterwards shops were opened in Bangor and Bournemouth, followed by Liverpool. In short order they sprang up all over the country. Mabel was usually present, especially at the opening of the shop, and she, along with other members of the BUAV, sat in the shop ready to answer any questions that were put to them as well as discussing the issues with whoever decided to call in. The project was such a success in attracting new people to the cause that other branches were urged to do the same. Practically all of Mabel's time was now spent on campaigning. When the shop opened in Manchester, she spent a week there and gave two drawing room talks to attract more support. Mabel was ready to go anywhere and talk to anyone who would listen – as well as many who refused to.

1903 was also the year that Mark Twain wrote *The Dog's Tale*,[273] for the National Anti-Vivisection Society. The story describes the life of a college dog and its puppy. The owner of the dogs, a doctor, experiments on the eyes of the puppy. His experiments are successful in that he proves that damage to the brain causes the puppy to go blind. The puppy subsequently dies in this "successful" experiment. Anti-vivisection had grabbed public attention and was mentioned everywhere.

On 5th April 1904 Frances Power-Cobbe died. On her death, the plans to move the headquarters of the BUAV to London finally came to fruition. New premises were opened at Charing Cross, London. Mabel's book, jointly written with Dr Helen Bouchier, was published this year. It had first appeared in *The Abolitionist* in March 1903.

In 1906 the Government appointed the Second Royal Commission on Vivisection. This Commission heard a great deal of evidence from the NAVS and other interested parties. It published its findings in 1912, recommending an increase in the numbers of Home Office Inspectors; further limitations with regard to the use of curare; stricter provisions as to the definition and practice of pithing;[274] additional restrictions regulating the painless destruction of animals which showed signs of suffering after experimentation; a change in the method of selecting, and in the constitution of, the advisory body of the Secretary of State; and keeping of special records by vivisectors. Mabel had spent much of her time studying scientific journals, and becoming one of the most well informed people in the country, when it came to vivisection. She gave evidence to the Commission, mainly comprising her collection of accounts of animal experiments gleaned from journals.

There were now twenty-one societies federated to the BUAV and its involvement with other abolitionist societies continued to grow. In March 1906 Dr Hadwen represented the BUAV at a meeting of the International Anti-Vivisection Council, which called for the adoption of one parliamentary bill for the abolition party. Although the BUAV was at this time advocating its own abolition bill to supporters in the Houses of Parliament it co-operated with the joint proposals.

Mabel was spending less time up north and was now based in Southall, Middlesex. On 22nd July 1907 she applied to rejoin the Theosophical Society, now under Annie Besant's presidency. Her certificate was sent to her on 24th August 1907 and on Mabel's request she was readmitted on the basis of her old diploma.

By now national and international anti vivisection conferences had begun to take place. On Wednesday 6th July 1909, 500 delegates at the Westminster Palace Hotel received bouquets representing their countries. Mabel had clearly not forgotten her fashionable roots!

Mabel was now given the title of "Honorary Parliamentary Secretary". In this role she spoke to delegates and journalists at the congress. The *Forbidden Banner* was placed on view. This was a photograph of an emaciated and miserable dog that had been used as a campaign image. Many had objected to the picture, including vivisectors, and Mabel told her audience that it had been taken from *The Journal of Pathology*.

The Animal Protection Congress took place at Caxton Hall, London and continued for several days. The crowded reception on the opening night discussed humane killing methods and humane fishing, along with other issues. Photos of private slaughter, abattoirs and animals stretched on operating boards were shown to attendees. The congress continued through Thursday and Friday with a number of public meetings. Annie Besant and Charlotte Despard attended as speakers and thirty five of the more prominent anti-vivisectionists took time out to attend a garden party at Battersea Hospital. On Saturday the talks continued, culminating in a half mile long march of protest. A special church service protesting against vivisection was held in Saint John's church on Sunday morning, and the congress finally closed on Monday afternoon, following more talks. Not only was the congress a success, but also Mabel was its star.

She was never to be a theosophical star again however. On 1st April 1909 Mabel tendered her resignation to the Theosophical Society.

CHAPTER TWELVE

One Life, One Law

> "I know that I am an exceptional woman in some respects; but am convinced that the great tides of emotion which govern my life control the lives of others also."[275]

Mabel didn't find life easy at the start of the twentieth century. She was again active on the occult scene, writing regular letters to *The Occult Review*. The health problems that she had borne through her life now began to worsen. The breakdown that she suffered from in 1889 was more serious than people knew. She had spent fourteen months suffering from incessant headaches, an inability to bear anything but the most subdued of light, a loss of appetite and general malaise. This was now far enough in Mabel's past for her to talk about the episode as a way of praising the skills of WH Edwards. In 1910 she suffered badly from a bout of influenza and again sought treatment from Edwards. He was also given credit for curing the eczema she had suffered with for so long.

By this time Mabel had moved south again and was living at 74 Abbot Street, Ardat[276] in Southall, Middlesex. An inheritance of a few hundred pounds enabled her to buy a small cottage and invest the remainder of the money to live off. Things looked as if they would be comfortable for the next few years until in 1913 disaster struck.

Mabel was no longer able to sell her novels and all her savings she had at the Charing Cross Bank were lost when the bank collapsed. The bank declared bankruptcy in April 1913, when 16,000 creditors were left bereft of their funds. Mabel wrote to John Lovell,[277] her New York publishing agent on 13th June 1913, pleading for help.

> "I have to thank you so much for all your kindness I know it must have added greatly to your difficulty in finding our American publishers for "The Locked Room" that I have not found an English one – but it is useless at present for me to go round the circle having tried the main two friendly ones in vain. You see I have written no novels for so long that I am forgotten as a novelist and the publishers who bring out the theosophical books here cannot touch novels. I am working at the second and longer novel in the hope of better luck next year – in the meantime hoping to get a play out in (*illegible*) which would alter my position with the general public entirely now I am compelled to apply to the Royal Literary Fund for help, as I have nothing to go on with. They are friendly to me as my literary career is well known – and helped me last year or I must have been in the poorhouse now! – I have done a great deal of work since the failure of the Charing Cross Bank took all my little savings – but none of the work published so far will bring me any profit until after the next stocktaking – and I am at a moment of great difficulty. I want you to write me a letter to send to the Secretary of the Fund emphasising a hope that they will help me – and putting into plain words for their information the fact that my theosophical works have had great sales in America but have brought me nothing the copyright being too difficult to obtain under the old law between the countries. I know that this from an American publisher would have great effect and I beg you for the sake of old friendship to let me have it before the end of June – as I must send in one or two letters of this kind this month in order to get some help in July. The fund is very rich and some of my friends think I ought to get aid not only to the writing of the play but to the development of the project.
>
> This is a very egotistical letter but I fear I cannot help that under

the circumstances. I wish you were coming over this summer so that we might talk over many things of more interest than this base struggle of writing!"

John Lovell immediately set up a fund to help Mabel meet her most pressing needs. As Mabel received no payment from some of her works, he also devised a scheme whereby the publishers of those books could buy sheets of stamps, a hundred at a time, to a value of five cents each. These stamps were to be attached to every copy of her books that were sold and the proceeds sent direct to Mabel. Lovell also hoped that European and other publishers of Mabel's works would join the scheme, but it remains unrecorded whether or not he was successful. Mabel had little option. She agreed to the scheme and gave Lovell the authority to act on her behalf.

> "I am securing for her a fund to relieve her immediate necessities, but if I can obtain the co-operation of the publishers, like yourselves, who are publishing some of her books, in securing a permanent income in this way, it will be the most valuable work I can do for her."[278]

Mabel was probably drawn to apply to the Royal Literary Fund for help by the knowledge that her father had done the same on more than one occasion in the past. She had to supply details of her finances and copies of her work to the Fund, in the hope of receiving financial aid on several occasions. Mabel herself didn't even possess copies of her earlier books by this time and had to borrow copies to send to the Fund.

> "I am the daughter of Mortimer Collins and I appear myself in Who's Who and the Literary Year book as an author and journalist. A few hundred pounds left to me by a friend was deposited in the Charing Cross bank and the failure of the bank has placed me in a difficult position."[279]

Mabel's books were read by W Stebbing on behalf of the Fund. Although his reviews of her work were less than flattering, the Fund made a number of grants to support Mabel.

Top: The Priory, Woodchester. Catherine Metcalfe's family home.
Bottom: Cintra Lawns, now the Brent House Hotel. Catherine Metcalfe's town house in Gloucester Road, Cheltenham where Mabel died.

"*The Star Sapphire.* A disagreeable book, with a grand purpose. It has been a trial to read it; and I do not wonder that the author is unable to suppport herself by her work. *The Blossom and the Fruit,* thee same. Too much blossom for the fruit. A philosophic romance, in which the theme is that of the reincarnation of souls – is beyond the writer's power. But I find force of expression and description beyond anything in *The Star Sapphire,* though with the same inability to interest in the story."[280]

Unfortunately, Mabel's life was not to improve in the near future. Somehow, she dealt with her financial difficulties and although no longer so prolific as her earlier days continued writing in the hope of making a living. She had little option. She made deals with publishers in America and Germany and expected to get her first payment by cheque in mid August 1914. Then, on 4th August 1914, Britain declared war on Germany. Mabel was unable to think of anything else.

"I cannot write at length just now as my whole time is absorbed in the question of war. At eleven o'clock last night England declared War against Germany. Will Germany end by taking us as the Kaiser has long intended? I can think of nothing else."[281]

As Mabel wrote in *The Crucible,* many believed that the war would be over in three weeks, that it wouldn't be the Great War that others feared. She was unconvinced.

"…this is a great war, the nations are to be plunged into a seething pot…I was laughed at as an alarmist…I had been shown …I am writing now on the 52nd day…the allies must win…but let none think the darkest hour has passed."[282]

Was this war caused by the Masters to accelerate evolution as many theosophists believed? Mabel had enough theosophy left in her to at least acknowledge the possibility. She said that the previous Christmas she had been taken by her spirit guide to Egypt and had visions that forewarned her of "War! War! The War of the world!"[283] She was led in the same way as she had been when shown the visions of *Light on the Path.* After years of campaigning with politicians and rubbing shoulders with suffragettes, Mabel was returning to her spiritualist roots.

Mabel sought involvement in the Great War in the same way as most ladies of her class. A class that was soon to disappear as the war progressed. In October she went to visit wounded soldiers at a smart London hospital. The next day she took a trip to Epsom to watch new soldiers perform their drill. She could not quite forget all the campaigning she had done for animal rights. Mabel wrote to king Leopold of Belgium at the start of November, complaining about the way she had seen horses treated while in Ostend. King Leopold must have had other things on his mind, as he doesn't appear to have replied.

Surely Mabel's life wasn't only doom and gloom? She must have had something good going on during this period? Fortunately, yes. She had a Pekinese dog.

> "Those of us who have any part in the cult of recent years of Pekinese dogs and who love their Pekinese as they never loved any other dogs…"[284]

When the British overran the Chinese Imperial Palace in 1860, they discovered several Pugs and Pekinese, and brought the dogs back to England with them. A Pekinese dog named "Lootie", previously belonging to the Chinese Empress was the first to appear in England when presented to Queen Victoria. The Pekinese immediately captured the hearts of dog-lovers, and became the most eminently fashionable toy dogs. By the second half of the nineteenth century their popularity was established. Mabel sat for studio photographs in 1911 with her Pekinese, these are the only photographs that are commonly known of her, and one of them has been reproduced numerous times. Pekinese were the ultimate fashion accessory, and Mabel was long concerned with carrying the correct accessories. So many ladies with a certain reputation carried these dogs that rumours spread about the use they were actually put to.

But Mabel was destined to fall on her feet again. Catherine Metcalfe was a well heeled widow who inherited her family home in Woodchester, Gloucestershire. The village of Woodchester lies on the west side of the Nailsworth Valley the land rising steeply to Selsley Common and the village of Selsley which wraps itself around the scarp face overlooking both the Severn valley and the Frome valley. The depths of the valley was filled with signs of the woollen industry, mills and housing for the workers. Catherine lived at The Priory, a manor house that dated from the sixteenth century. Next to the house was the remains of the Norman Church of Saint Mary, several feet under which lay the remains of a grand Roman Villa. Catherine had first made contact with Mabel after returning from a trip to Vancouver. When in 1915 Mabel told her of her loneliness, and how she had pleaded with her Master Hilarion to send her a friend near her own age, many of her contemporaries now being dead, Catherine invited her to stay at her home. While there Mabel wrote *Our Glorious Future,* dedicating it to Catherine, and a short visit led to Mabel spending much of the last twelve years of her life with Catherine. Being able to spend time at Catherine's home saved Mabel from the worst effects of her financial problems.

> "I am staying with one of my readers Mrs Metcalfe who has been most kind to me and who owns this old house in the Cotswolds and I have been able to be of use in cooking and laundering, servants being unobtainable. But this will not continue as other uses will be probably be made of the house and I am much perplexed as to the future."[285]

Throughout the war years Mabel moved between her home in Southall, and Catherine's home in Gloucestershire. She still hoped to make money from her writing and agreed to write *Letters from England* to be syndicated in the American press. Unfortunately, she had no response for the first two letters she sent, and the third was returned by the censor. It was clearly impossible for Mabel to make money from overseas publications while the war continued.

> "I am past the age limit for paid war work otherwise I would go as an army cook. I have got through the last eight months by doing voluntary war work acting as cook in the house of a friend who takes convalescent Australian officers as guests and where I have myself stayed as a guest…the new arrangement about bringing over the wounded seems to affect the arrangements for convalescents and at the moment that work is not required and I have returned to my own home. I aim to return there if the officers begin to come again."[286]

Catherine and Mabel had a lot in common. They were both vegetarians and great lovers of animals. Although not such a political issue at this time, hunting was still guaranteed to anger those who shared Catherine's and Mabel's beliefs that animals had souls. In writing in *The Occult Review* of September 1918, Catherine quoted Mabel's *One Life, One Law* to make this point.[287]

"I do not eat the flesh of bird, beast or fish."[288]

She felt the suggestion that humanity needed to kill to live, as a previous writer suggested, not only absurd, but also an insult. Walter Winnans gleefully fell into debate with Mabel. He clearly believed her to be a feather headed idiot who was adopting vegetarianism as a fashion.[289] He apologised for suggesting that she would eat flesh and then went on to ask why she wore boots made from leather, described how kids were killed almost from birth to supply society ladies with gloves, described felt as originating from murdered rabbits and triumphantly ended with stating that an egg robbed a hen and milk robbed a calf. It seems strange that Mabel's years of campaigning had somehow passed by those in occult circles.

> "I really think Mr Winnans has got his knife in the wrong person. I didn't shake in my shoes, as I should have done when I read his letter because they happened to be velvet…long ago I took an interest in the humane substitute for leather which I believe now to be paper…as for furs and kid gloves my personal sins in respect to them ceased some 30 years ago."[290]

Just in case the point hadn't been made, Mabel pointed out that she preferred not to eat eggs and that eiderdowns were unnecessary. She was tempted to start keeping goats though.

Although Winnans had lost the argument, he did offer his opinion that Mabel may not enjoy keeping goats, as she would have to get rid of the kids. But if she insisted, well, he could personally recommend a cross between a goat and an ibex.[291]

Life was fairly quiet for Mabel now. She lived in the countryside with Catherine, spent her days working on novels and plays she hoped to sell,

Mabel's grave. Cheltenham Cemetery and Crematorium, Bouncers Lane, Cheltenham.

and exchanged correspondence with other writers. She was ending her life as it had begun, writing like her father. Not that Mabel spent all her time alone. On 17th February 1925, on hearing that the writer Grace Seton[292] was in England, Mabel wrote to her.

"Your name is beloved by me. *The Lives of the Hunted*[293] is one of my most precious books. I should dearly like to meet you – but I don't know how it is possible unless you are going about in England and would come and stay with us. I am a fixture here as I am 73 and have angina pectoris so that travelling is too difficult for me – and I have not been to London for years."[294]

Grace Seton immediately decided to visit, and arrived three days later.[295] She travelled down from Paddington by train to Cheltenham, a trip of three and a half hours at that time, compared with a little over two hours today.

The visit delighted Mabel. On leaving, Grace took away with her copies of Mabel's books to take to American publishers. Mabel had long wanted to make her books available again in America and was taken aback by the offer from someone she barely knew.

Grace and Mabel spent much of the afternoon chatting about Ouspenky's[296] teachings. In her letter of thanks to Grace Mabel wrote,

"…it isn't that we are three dimensional beings but that we are beings in three dimensional space – men. Plants, animals, all are in this space – I have been looking at the book written by the originator of the fourth dimension[297] and he says beings in two dimensional space would be so narrow that they could not have two eyes side by side."

Grace clearly enjoyed her visit to Mabel. After she left, she sent a parcel of cigarettes as a gift.

Mabel had recently finished a novel about reincarnation at this time, although it never saw the light of day. She'd offered it to publishers with little success until sending it to Foster Bailey,[298] the husband of the theosophist, Alice Bailey.[299] Although Bailey signed a contract with Mabel, he later broke it so that he could go on printing his wife's works, as the demand for them had risen so much. Mabel hoped that it would appear sometime but history deemed otherwise.

Mabel never talked of her early life and experiences. She was approached by the American Theosophical Society to write a history of the rise of the Theosophical Society but refused. She warned Catherine that if she ever attempted a biography she would appear in wrath. Mabel told Catherine that she lived and worked under the guidance of the Master and often joined him and watched the world Masters weaving the karmic threads on her deathbed. Hilarion told her she must not think she was coming to rest, as she would have to join him in the Workshop.

For the last ten years of her life Mabel suffered badly from heart problems. She finally died from angina at Catherine's town house, Cintra Lawns, in Gloucester Road, Cheltenham on 31st March 1927 at the age of 76. Her niece, Alice Hodgson, who lived nearby was there at her death. In her will she left what little she had to her niece and her niece's husband, William Pickering Hodgson.

Mabel was buried two days later at Cheltenham Cemetery and Crematorium, Bouncers Lane, Cheltenham. A worn and weathered cross stands over her grave. Its inscription reads, "Minna Mabel Cook, Mabel Collins, Author of Light on the Path, Born 9 September 1851, Entered into life 31st March 1927. Her death was announced in the local press and *The Theosophist* published an obituary. And then she passed into the realm of obscure footnotes…

Endpiece – a personal note.

In July 1999 I wrote an email to Leslie Price saying, "As an aside do you know who is the best authority on Mabel Collins? I have the feeling that she will become relevant to what I am planning to do and warrants a look at. I suppose if there is no-one who has already taken a close look at her then that is another job to put on the list."

Leslie instantly responded with, "She would be worth a biography similar to the Old one,[300] and I should like to encourage you to write it."

I demurred. I had a novel I wanted to write first. And I wasn't at all sure that Mabel would be that easy to find information about, or even that interesting. And I'd never said anything about writing a BOOK. Though I was tempted. I kept coming across Mabel's name and yet there was nothing that really explained how she fitted into the scheme of things. By March of the following year I'd begun to pull together what information I could find easily. By June I was sending out calls to anyone and everyone for ideas. By September I was living and breathing Mabel. It did help that Leslie appears to know everyone, everywhere.

This led to long conversations with people from all over the world. My favourite still being a long phone conversation with the late Melvin Harris about a man who got his kicks having jam tarts thrown at him. I'm not sure what relevance that had in the long run, but it kept things interesting. And as for what Victorian women reputedly did with their lap dogs…

It took a while. I had to work to bring in money to pay the bills and in the middle of Mabel started my Masters degree. But in the last four years I have created a group of people who have now become Mabel fans, although they'd never heard of her until I gave them no choice. I have discovered Mabel fans, sitting quietly in their own worlds, thinking they were the only ones. I have found out how helpful archivists can be if you ask them a strange question. Perhaps not enough people do that. And one of the biggest joys was being able to join the dots. The Theosophists knew their theosophy and the Ripperologists knew their murders – but the many groups I had contact with seemed to be completely unaware of each other's work.

I had plenty of information in a short time, but was making a complete pig's ear of putting it into some readable form. So for help with that, I am indebted to Russ Chandler, who read the first draft and told me the many things that were wrong with it. Although a bottle of wine down the line made us realise this wasn't going to be dealt with quickly. So, Russ wins the prize for having seen the most versions of this book over the last few years.

If we are awarding prizes here, which it seems I am, it needs to be recorded that Garry Phillipson knows his hyphens. Using a spurious excuse, I managed to persuade him to nitpick his way through the text and insert punctuation and zap gremlins with frightening efficiency. And it did help to have the occasional *Buffy* dialogue sent to me.

There was only one thing left to do. So, in June 2004, Garry Phillipson accompanied me on a pilgrimage to Mabel's grave in Cheltenham. Taking the train from London, I found a number of promotional packages for the Glastonbury festival, containing a small pencil along with a programme. I picked up a number of these. On a brilliantly sunny day, we finally arrived at the cemetery and found a grave that *should* have been Mabel's – it was certainly in the right location. But the stone was so weathered and worn that there was no chance of reading the inscription. Now I knew why I'd picked up the pencils earlier. I lay down on Mabel's grave and Garry positioned pieces of paper so that I could do what can only be described as a "grave rubbing" As the inscription slowly began to appear we knew we had the right grave. Despite Garry's fears, or perhaps an overdose of *Buffy,* no arm reached from within the grave to stop me. It was time to say goodbye.

I never did finish the novel. Not yet.

Kim Farnell, London, June 2004.

The Works of Mabel Collins

Mabel's theosophical and spiritual works have been translated into numerous languages and several English language editions have appeared. This list includes only the first English language appearance in book form of Mabel's works. Many of her novels appeared first in serialised form in periodicals such as *Short Cuts* and *Temple Bar*.

Books

A Cry from Afar. To students of "Light On The Path.". By the author of "Light On The Path". Theosophical Publishing Society, London, 1905.

A Debt of Honour, Eden Remington & Co, London, 1892.

An Innocent Sinner, Tinsley Brothers & Co. London, 1877.

As The Flower Grows. Some Visions and An Interpretation, Theosophical Publishing Society: London, 1915.

At The Shrine of Venus and The End of The Season, Simpkin, Marshal, Hamilton, Kent & Co. London, 1901.

Cobwebs, Tinsley Bros, London, 1882.

First Steps in Occultism, Being 1. Practical occultism / by H.P.B. [i.e. Elena Petrovna Blavatskaya]. 2. Occultism v. The occult arts, by H.P.B. [i.e. E.P. Blavatskaya]. 3. Comments on "Light on the Path", by M. C. [i.e. Mabel Collins]. Reprinted from Lucifer, Theosophical Publishing Society, London, 1895.

Fragments of Thought and Life. Being Seven Essays and Seven Fables in Illustration of The Essays. Theosophical Publishing Society, 1908.

Fragments of Thought and Life: Being Seven Essays, and Seven Fables in Illustration of The Essays. Theosophical Publishing Society, London, 1908.

Green Leaves, Kegan Paul & Co, London, 1895.

Ida - An Adventure in Morocco, Ward and Downey, London, 1890.

Illusions, Theosophical Publishing Society, London, 1905.

In the Flower of Her Youth, F. V. White & Co, London, 1883.

In The New Forest, English Illustrated Magazine, London, 1885.

In This World, Chapman & Hall, London, 1879.

Juliet's Lovers, Ward and Downey, London, 1893.

Light on The Path, A Treatise Written for The Personal Use of Those Who Are Ignorant of the Eastern Wisdom, and Who Desire to Enter Within Its Influence, Reeves & Turner: London, 1885.

Lord Vanecourt's Daughter, Ward & Downe, London, 1885.

Love's Chaplet, Theosophical Publishing Society, London, 1905.

One Life, One Law-"Thou Shalt Not Kill", Theosophical Publishing Society, London, 1909.

Our Bohemia, Tinsley Bros. London, 1879.

Our Glorious Future, The interpretation of "Light on the Path", Theosophical Bookshop, Edinburgh, 1917.

Outlawed: A Novel on The Women Suffrage Question, With Despard, Charlotte, Henry J Drane Limited, London, 1908.

Suggestion, Lovell, Gestefeld & Co, New York, 1892.

The Awakening, Theosophical Publishing Society, London, 1906.

The Blossom and The Fruit; a True Story of A Black Magician, Published by the Authors, London, 1888.

The Builders, Theosophical Publishing Society, London, 1910.

The Confessions of A Woman, (Anonymous), Griffith, Farrar & Co, London, 1893.

The Crucible, Theosophical Publishing Society, London, 1914.

The Idyll of The White Lotus, Reeves & Turner: London, 1884.

The Locked Room, Theosophical Publishing House, London, 1920.

The Mahatma: A Tale of Modern Theosophy, Downey & Co, London, 1895.

The Prettiest Woman in Warsaw, Ward and Downey, London 1885.

The Scroll of The Disembodied Man, John M Watkins, London, 1904.

The Star Sapphire, Downey & Co, London, 1896.

The Story of Helena Modjeska: Madame Chiapowska, WH Allen & Co, London, 1883.

The Story of Sensa. An interpretation of the Idyll of The White Lotus, etc, Theosophical Publishing Society, London, 1913.

The Story of The Year: A Record of Feasts and Ceremonies, George Redway, London, 1895.

The Torn Cloak, Brief Sketches of The History of Our Race, from King Solomon to The Present Day, etc, Covenant Publishing Co, London, 1928.

The Transparent Jewel, [On the Aphorisms of Yoga compiled by Patan~jali.] W. Rider & Son, London, 1912.

Through The Gates of Gold, Ward and Downey, London, 1887.

Too Red A Dawn, Tinsley Brothers, London, 1881.

Viola Fanshawe, FV White, London, 1884.

When Love Is True, Street and Smith, New York, 1892.

When The Sun Moves Northward, The Way of Initiation, Theosophical Publishing House, London, 1987.

Plays

A Modern Hypatia, 1894

Sensa, 1914.

Suggestion or the Hypnotist, 1891.

Periodicals

A full list of Mabel's contributions to periodicals is too long to list here and would be incomplete as I continue to find articles and letters. However, the following can be regarded as an indicative listing. The editors cited are those holding the office during the period that Mabel wrote for the publication.

Lucifer, A Theosophical monthly, London, 1887-1897. Eds. HP Blavatsky and Mabel Collins, Vol. 1-3.

Reply to "Interrogator", October 1887, p139.

The Demand of the Neophyte [continuation of Comments on *Light on the Path* by the author], November 1887, p170.

Correspondence, November 1887, p226.

Our Third Volume, Death, Reply to Anon Questioner, September 1888.

Lodges of Magic, Editors' Notes, Editors' Answer, with HP Blavatsky, October 1888.

Is Theosophy A Religion? with HP Blavatsky, November 1888.

Is Denunciation A Duty? Dialogues between the Two Editors, with HP Blavatasky, December 1888.

The Year Is Dead, Long Live The Year, with HP Blavatsky, December 1888 & January 1889.

Answer, A Paradoxical World, Review - Qabbalah, The Philosophical Writings of Solomon ben Yehudah ibn Gebirol (Avicebron) by Isaac Myer with HP Blavatsky, January 1889.

Broad Views, London, 1904-1907. Ed. AP Sinnett.

Psychic Development: The Inner Vision, February 1905.

Occult Review, London 1905-1933. Ed. Ralph Shirley.

The Reality of Dream Consciousness, May 1907.

A Rosicrucian Ideal, March 1912.

The Transparent Jewel, August, September and October 1912.

The Supreme Secret, April 1913.

Dr Rudolf Steiner on Human Evolution, May 1913.

As The Flower Grows - an interpretation of Light On The Path, June to September 1915.

Letters: The Morality of Killing, November 1918, March 1919, May 1919.

Letter: Is Killing Animals Cruelty? January 1919.

Letter: What is Spiritualism? March 1921.

The Astral & Ethereal Worlds, September 1922, October 1922, January 1923.

Letter: The Mystery of Sleep, March 1924.

Letter: Tolstoy & the Doctrine of Non-Resistance, April 1925.

Letter: The Doctrine of Non-Resistance & The Sermon On The Mount, June 1925.

Letter: The Path, August 1925.

Theosophical Siftings, London, 1889-1895. Ed. Constance Wachtmeister.

Astral Bodies, with HP Blavatsky, 1895.

The Theosophist, Adyar, India, 1879 onwards. Ed. Henry Steel Olcott.

The Angel Peacock, February 1888 to September 1888.

The Disciple, The Story of a White Magician, December 1907 to June 1908.

The Path, London, 1910-1814. Ed. DN Dunlop.

The First Step in Occultism, August 1912.

Temple Bar

With John Lillie, *Helena Modjeska*, September 1882.

Out of Our Sphere, July 1877.

Sources and references

Books

A History of English Drama 1660-1900, Cambridge University Press, Cambridge, 1959.

Houghton, Boston, p316, 1986.

Ackroyd, Peter, *London: The Biography*, Vintage, London, 2000.

AE, *Shadows of Life and Thought, The Autobiography of AE*, Selwyn & Blount, London 1938.

Arundale, Francesca, *My Guest – HP Blavatsky*, Theosophical Publishing House, Adyar, Madras, India 1932.

Bailey, Victor, "The Metropolitan Police, the Home Office and the Threat of Outcast London," in *Policing and Punishment in Nineteenth Century Britain*, London, p108, 1981.

Balleine, George Reginald, *Balleine's History of Jersey*, Phillimore, London, 1981.

Begg, Paul, Fido, Martin and Skinner Keith, *The Jack The Ripper A to Z*, Headline, London, 1991.

Besant, Annie, *An Autobiography*, T Fisher Unwin, London, 1893.

Blavatsky, Helena Petrovna, , Edited by A. Trevor Barker. *The Complete Works of H. P. Blavatsky*, Rider & Company, London, p427, 1933.

Blavatsky, Helena Petrovna, *Collected Writings, Vol 7, 1886-1887*, The Theosophical Publishing House, Adyar, India, 1958.

Bouchier, Helen and Collins, Mabel, *The Scroll of The Disembodied Man*, John M Atkins, London, 1904.

Bradlaugh, WR, (by a former associate of the SPR) *Theosophy: The History of a 19th Century Imposter The New Religion of Mrs Besant*, John Snow & Company, London 1891.

Braude, Ann, Radical Spirits *Spiritualism and Women's Rights in Nineteenth Century America*, Beacon Press, Boston, 1989.

Brooks, FT, *Neo Theosophy Exposed,* self published, Madras, India, 1914.

Brooks, FT, *The Theosophical Society and its Esoteric Bogeydom,* Vyasashrama Bookshop, Madras, 1914.

Buchnan, Robert, *Letters from Dante Gabriel Rossetti to Algernon Charles Swinburne, Regarding the attacks made upon the latter by Mortimer Collins and upon both,* London. Private circulation. Richard Clay & Sons. 1921.

Burtchaell, George Dames and Sadleir, Thomas Ulick, Alumni Dublinenses ... 1593-1860, Thom & Company, Dublin, 1935.

Caldwell, Daniel H, (Ed.), *The Occult World of Madame Blavatsky. Reminiscences and Impressions by those who knew her,* Impossible Dream Publications, Tucson, Arizona, 1991.

Caldwell, Daniel H, *The Esoteric World of Madame Blavatsky. Insights into the Life of a Modern Sphinx,* Theosophical Publishing House, Wheaton, Illinois, 2000.

Campbell, Bruce F, *Ancient Wisdom Revived. A History of the Theosophical Movement,* University of California Press, Berkeley, 1980.

Cavendish, Richard (Ed.). *Man, Myth & Magic: An Illustrated Encyclopedia of the Supernatural* (vol. 15), Marshall Cavendish Corporation, New York, p2039, 1970.

Christian Literature Society, *Madame Blavatsky: Her Tricks and Her Dupes,* Christian Literature Society, Madras, India, 1894.

Cleather, Alice Leighton, *HP Blavatsky as I Knew Her,* Thacker, Spink & Company, London, 1923

Cleather, Alice Leighton, *HP Blavatsky: A Great Betrayal,* Thatcher, Spink & Company, Calcutta, India, 1892.

Cleather, Alice Leighton, *HP Blavatsky: Her Life and Work for Humanity,* Thatcher, Spink & Company, Calcutta, India, 1922.

Cobbe, Life of Frances Power Cobbe as Told by Herself, Frances Power Cobbe, Swan Sonnenschein and Company, Limited, London, 1904.

Collins Edward Mortimer, *Summer Songs,* Saunders, Otley & Company, London 1875.

Collins, Edward James Mortimer and Mortimer and Frances, *Frances*, Frederick Warne & Company, London, Undated.

Collins, Edward James Mortimer, (Ed. Edmund Clarence Stedman),"The Ivory Gate". Wade, Alan, (Ed.), *The Letters of W. B. Yeats*, Rupert Hart-Davis: London, 1954.

Collins, Edward James Mortimer, *A Fight with Fortune*, Hurst & Blackett: London, 1876.

Collins, Edward James Mortimer, *Attic Salt*, B Robson & Company, London, 1880.

Collins, Edward James Mortimer, *Blacksmith and Scholar*, Hurst & Blackett, London, 1876.

Collins, Edward James Mortimer, *Comedy of Dreams*. Uncompleted work published in part in Ed. Miles, Alfred Henry, *The Poets and Poetry of the Century*, Vol. 5. Hutchinson & Company, London, 1892.

Collins, Edward James Mortimer, *Idylls and Rhymes*, J. McGlashan, Dublin, W. S. Orr & Company, London, Stephen Barbet, Guernsey, 1855.

Collins, Edward James Mortimer, *Pen Sketches by A Vanished Hand* Ed. Tom Taylor Richard Bentley & Son 1879.

Collins, Edward James Mortimer, *The Inn of Strange Meetings And Other Poems*, Henry S. King & Company, London, 1871.

Collins, Edward James Mortimer, *Selections from the Poetical Works of Mortimer Collins: Made by F. Percy Cotton*, Richard Bentley & Son, London, 1886.

Collins, Edward James Mortimer, *Summer Songs*, Saunders, Otley & Company, London, 1860.

Collins, Edward James Mortimer, *Thoughts in My Garden*, Richard Bentley & Son, London, 1880.

Collins, Frances (Ed.), *Mortimer Collins, His Letters and Friendships*. Sampson Low 1877.

Collins, Frances, *Mortimer Collins: His Letters and Friendships, with Some Account of His Life*, Sampson Low & Company, London, 1877.

Collins, Francis, *Spiritual Poems*, Plymouth, 1826.

Collins, Mabel, *A Debt of Honour*,, Eden, Demington & Company, London, 1892.

Colquhoun, Ithell, *Sword of Wisdom. MacGregor Mathers and 'The Golden Dawn'*, Spearman, London, 1975.

Cook, Keningale Robert, *Love in A Mist. A Romantic Drama in Familiar Blank Verse.* Pickering & Company, London, 1882.

Cook, Keningale Robert, *Purpose and Passion: Being Pygmalion, and Other Poems,* Virtue & Company, London, 1870.

Cook, Keningale Robert, *The Guitar Player, with Sundry Poems.* Pickering & Company. London, 1881.

Cook, Keningale Robert, *The King of Kent,* Pickering & Company. London, 1882.

Cook, Keningale, *The Fathers of Jesus, A Study in the Lineage of The Christian Doctrine and Traditions,* Kegan Paul, Trench & Company, London, 1886.

Cook, Louisa, *Geometrical Psychology, or, The Science of Representation. An Abstract of The Theories and Diagrams of B. W. Betts,* George Redway, London, 1887.

Cranston, Sylvia, *The Extraordinary Life and Influence of Helena Blavatsky: Founder of The Modern Theosophical Movement,* GP Putnam's Sons, New York, 1993.

Crowley, Aleister, *Jack The Ripper,* Anonymous, Cambridge, 1988.

Crowley, Aleister, *Jack The Ripper*, edited by J. Edward Cornelius, California, Thelema Lodge OTO, 1992.

Crowley, Aleister, *Moonchild*, Mandrake, London, 1929.

D'Onston, Roslyn, *The Patristic Gospels: An English Version of The Holy Gospels as They Existed in The Second Century,* Grant Richards: London, 1904.

Despard, Charlotte, *Theosophy and The Women's Movement,* Theosophical Publishing Society, London 1913.

Dictionary of National Biography, 1917-1973, Oxford University Press, Oxford.

Dictionary of Terms Used in Medicine and The Collateral Sciences, Richard D. Hoblyn, Whittaker & Company, London, 1892.

Dorland, WA Newman, *American Illustrated Medical Dictionary 1900.*

Dutton, *The Theosophical Movement - A History and A Survey,* Dutton and Company, London, 1925.

Eek, Sven, *Damodar and The Pioneers of The Theosophical Movement,* Theological Pub. House, Madras, 1965.

Endersby, Victor, *The Hall of Magic Mirrors. A Biography of HP Blavatsky,* Hearthstone, London, 1969.

Ephesian, (CE Bechofer), *The Mysterious Madam. A Life of Madame Blavatsky,* John Lane at the Bodley Head Limited, London 1931.

Evans, Stewart and Skinner Keith, *The Ultimate Jack The Ripper Sourcebook,* Constable and Robinson, London, 2000.

Evans, Stewart P and Skinner, Keith, *Jack The Ripper, Letters from Hell,* Sutton Publishing, Gloucestershire, 2002.

Farnell, Kim, *The Astral Tramp: A Biography of Sepharial,* Ascella Publications, Nottingham, 1998.

Fuller, Jean Overton, *The Magical Dilemma of Victor Neuburg,* Mandrake, Oxford, 1990.

Fuller, Jean Overton, *The Magical Dilemma of Victor Neuburg,* W.H. Allen, pp 166-168, 1965.

Fussell, Joseph H, *Incidents in The History of The Theosophical Movement, Founded in New York City in 1875 by H. P. Blavatsky, continued under William Q. Judge, and now under the direction of their successor Katherine Tingley,* Ayryan Theosophical Press, Point Loma, USA, 1910.

Gilbert, RA, *The Golden Dawn and The Esoteric Section,* Theosophical History Centre, London, 1987.

Godwin, Joscelyn, Chanel, Christian and Deveney, John P, (Eds.), Weiser, USA, 1995.

Goldsmith, Barbara, *Other Powers: The Age of Suffrage, Spiritualism and The Scandalous Victoria Woodhull*, Alfred Knopf, New York 1998.

Gomes, Michael, *Theosophy in The Nineteenth Century*, Garland, London, 1994.

Harris, Melvin, *The True Face of Jack The Ripper*, O'Mara, London, 1994.

Harris, Melvin, *Jack The Ripper, The Bloody Truth*, Columbus Books, London, 1987.

Harris, Melvin, *The True Face of Jack The Ripper*, Brockhampton Press, London, 1996.

Hartmann, Franz, *The Talking Image of Urur*, J. W. Lovell Company, New York, 1890.

Hopley, Emma, *Campaigning Against Cruelty*, London, BUAV.

Houghton, Esther Rhoods and Walter Edwards and Slingerland, Jean Harris, *The Wellesley Index to Victorian Periodicals, 1824-1900*, Routledge & Kegan Paul, London, 1966-1990.

Houghton, Walter E, *The Wellseley Index to Victorian Periodicals 1824-1900*, University of Toronto Press, Toronto, Canada, 1966.

Howell, Basil P, (Ed.), *The Theosophical Society, The First 50 Years*, Theosophical Publishing House, London 1925.

Jinarajadasa, C, *The Golden Book of The Theosophical Society. A brief history of the Society's growth from 1875-1925*, Theosophical Publishing House, Adyar, India, 1925.

Johnson, Paul K, *The Masters Revealed. Madam Blavatsky and The Myth of the Great White Lodge*, Albany State University of New York Press, New York, 1994.

Johnstone, Peter, *A Short History of Guernsey*, La Societe Jersaise, Jersey, 1976.

Jopling, Louise, *Twenty Years of My Life 1867-87*, John Lane: The Bodley Head Limited, London, 1925.

Kelly, John, (General Ed.) and Domville Eric, (Associate Ed.) *The Collected Letters of W.B. Yeats, Vol 1. 1865-1895*, Clarendon, Oxford, 1986.

Kingsland, William, *The Real H. P. Blavatsky. A Study in Theosophy, and A Memoir of A Great Soul,* JM. Watkins, London, 1928.

Knight, Stephen, *Jack The Ripper. The Final Solution,* Harrap, London, 1976.

Leadbeater, Charles Webster and Besant Annie, *Lives of Alcyone,* Theosophical Publishing House, Madras, 1894.

Leo, Alan, *Notable Nativities,* Modern Astrology, London, 1900.

Leslie-Smith, Leslie Horace, *100 Years of Modern Occultism. A Review of The Parent Theosophical Society,* Theosophical History Centre, London, 1987.

Lillie, Arthur, *Madame Blavatsky and Her Theosophy: A Study,* Swan Sonnschein & Company, London, 1895.

Maccormick, George Donald King, *The Identity of Jack the Ripper,* Jarrolds, London, 1959.

Marryat, Florence, "My Spirit Child" in *Researches Into The Phenomena of Modern Spiritualism,* Two Worlds Publishing Company, London, 1904.

Maskelyne, John Nevil, *The Fraud of Modern "Theosophy" Exposed ... A Brief History of the Greatest Imposture Ever Perpetrated Under The Cloak of Religion,* George Routledge & Sons, London, 1912.

Matters, Leonard W, *The Mystery of Jack The Ripper,* Hutchinson & Company, London, 1929.

May, Betty, *Tiger Woman: My Story,* Duckworth, London 1929.

McHugh, Roger, WB Yeats: Letters to Katharine Tynan, Clonmore & Reynolds, Dublin, 1953.

Meade, Marion, *Madame Blavatsky, The Woman Behind The Myth,* GP Putnams & Sons, New York, 1980.

Neff, Mary K, *Personal Memoirs of H. P. Blavatsky,* Rider & Company, London, 1935.

Olcott, Henry Steel, *Old Diary Leaves,* Vol.3, Putnam, USA, 1895.

Oppenheim, Janet, *"Shattered Nerves". Doctors, Patients, and Depression in Victorian England,* Oxford University Press, Oxford, 1991.

Oppenheim, Janet, *The Other World: Spiritualism and Psychical Research in England, 1850-1914*, Cambridge University Press, Cambridge, 1985.

Owen, Alex, *The Darkened Room,* Virago, London, 1989.

Praed, Rosa Campbell, *Affinities, A Romance of Today,* Bentley & Son, 1885.

Prothero, Stephen, *The White Buddhist*, Bloomington, Indiana, 1996.

R, AJ, *The Suffrage Annual and Women's Who's Who,* Stanley Paul & Company, London, 1913.

Ransom, Josephine, *A Short History of The Theosophical Society*, Theosophical Publishing House, Adyar, India, 1938.

Rubens, Morris, *Anti-Vivisection Exposed, including a disclosure of the recent attempt to introduce anti-semitism into England,* Education Society's Steam Press, Bombay, India, 1894.

Rule, Ann, *The Stranger Beside Me,* Norton, New York, 1980.

Ryan, Charles J, *H.P. Blavatsky and The Theosophical Movement. A Brief Historical Sketch*, Theosophical University Press, Pasadena, 1975.

Sadleir, Michael, *Dublin University Magazine: Its History, Contents and Bibliography: A paper read before the Bibliographical Society of Ireland, 26 April 1937,* Bibliographical Society of Ireland, Dublin, 1938.

Sinnett, Alfred Percy, *Autobiography of Alfred Percy Sinnett*, Theosophical History Centre, London, 1986.

Sinnett, Alfred Percy, *Incidents in The Life of Madame Blavatsky,* Theosophical Publishing Society, 1913.

Sinnett, Alfred Percy, *The Early Days of Theosophy in Europe,* Theosophical Publishing Society, London, 1922.

Smith, Warren Sylvester, *The London Heretics, 1870-1914,* Constable, London, 1967.

Steiger, Isabel de, *Memorabilia. Reminiscences of A Woman Artist and Writer,* Rider & Company, London, 1927.

Steiner, Rudolf, *Autobiography, Chapters in The Course of My Life - 1861-1907,* Anthroposophic Press, New York, 1999.

Sutherland, John, *The Longman Companion to Victorian Literature*, Longman, London, 1988.

Symonds, John and Grant, Kenneth, (Eds.), *The Confessions of Aleister Crowley: An Autohagiography* Arkana, London, 1989.

Symonds, John, *In The Astral Light*, (also known as *The Life of Madame Blavatasky Medium and Magician)*, Panther, London, 1965.

Symonds, John, *Madame Blavatsky, Medium and Magician. In The Astral Light. The life of Madame Blavatsky-Medium and Magician. [First published as Madame Blavatsky: Medium and Magician.]*, Panther Books, London, 1965.

Symonds, John, *The Great Beast: The Life and Magick of Aleister Crowley*, Macdonald and Company, London, 1971.

Tillett, Gregory, *The Elder Brother*, Routledge & Kegan Paul, London, 1982

Wachtmeister, Constance, *Reminiscences of HP Blavatsky and The Secret Doctrine*, Theosophical Publishing Society, London, 1893.

Wade, Alan and Hart-Davis, Rupert T, (Eds.) *The Letters of WB Yeats*, London, 1954.

Wade, Allan, (Ed.) *Some Letters from W. B. Yeats to John O'Leary and His Sister. From Originals in The Berg Collection. (Reprinted from the Bulletin of the New York Public Library.)* New York, 1953.

Waite, Arthur Edward, *Shadows of Life and Thought. A Retrospective Review in The Form of Memoirs*, Selwyn & Blount, London, 1938.

Washington, Peter, *Madame Blavatsky's Baboon*, Schocken Books, New York, 1993.

Watson, George and Willson, IR (Eds.), *The New Cambridge Bibliography of English Literature*, Cambridge University Press, Cambridge, 1972.

Wearing, JP, *The London Stage 1890-99: A Calendar of Plays and Players*, Scarecrow Press, New Jersey, 1976.

Who Was Who. A Companion to "Who's Who," containing the biographies of those who died during the period 1897-1916, A & C Black, London, 1920.

Whyte, George Herbert, *HP Blavatsky: An Outline of Her Life*, Theosophical Publishing House, Adyar, India, 1920.

Williams, Gertrude Marvin, *Priestess of The Occult,* Alfred A Knopf, New York 1946.

Wilson Colin and Odell, Robert, *Jack The Ripper: Summing Up and Verdict*, Bantam Press, London, 1987.

Yeats, William Butler, *Memoirs: Autobiography [and] First Draft Journal.* Transcribed and edited by Denis Donoghue, Macmillan, London, 1972.

Yeats, William Butler, *The Autobiography of William Butler Yeats, Consisting of Reveries Over Childhood and Youth, The Trembling of The Veil, and Dramatis Personae,* Macmillan Company, New York, 1938.

Zirkoff, Boris de, *Helene Petrovna Hahn Blavatsky, Collected Writings*, Theosophical Publishing House, volume 11 p 322.

Periodicals

Blackwood's, Oliphant, Margaret, 94 (August 1865): 168.

Blackwood's, Oliphant, Margaret 102 (September 1867) 257 - 280.

Borderland, Stephenson, Robert D'Onston, *A Modern Magician.* London, 1886.

Broad Views, Sinnett, Alfred Percy (Ed.), London, May 1904 and February 1905. 'Some Psychic Experiences, MC's Narrative", Volume 1 1904.

Daily Gazette and Bulletin, "Suits Suddenly ended", Williamsport, Pennsylvania, p3, 25th July 1890.

Dublin University Magazine, Cook, Keningale Robert, (Ed.) "Journalism and Poetry of Mortimer Collins", K.M.C. (Keningale Cook and Mabel Collins) November 1877.

Dublin University Magazine, Cook, Keningale Robert, (Ed.) London, 1877.

Dublin University Magazine, Cook, Keningale Robert, (Ed.), " Early Days of Mortimer Collins" K.M.C. (Keningale Cook and Mabel Collins) September 1877 and October 1877.

Five Years of Theosophy ... Essays, selected from "The Theosophist", Reeves & Turner, London, 1885.

Fraser's Magazine for Town and Country, London, 1870-2 and 1879.

Fraser's Magazine for Town and Country, Asgill, John, "The Cowardliness of Dying, London, 1871.

Herald of The Star, Krishnamurti, Jiddu, (Ed.), 1st March 1925, p74, 14th March 1925.

Light, 10th July 1886, 15th June 1889, 2nd November 1889.

London Gazette, London, 8th November 1892.

Lucifer, Stephenson, Robert Donston, *African Magic* By Tau-Triadelta *Lucifer* November 1890.

Newcastle Daily Leader, Newcastle, March 1899.

Occult Review, (Ed. Ralph Shirley), Rider & Co. London, 1906 to 1933, esp. Collins, Mabel, 10th March 1910, XI 3, p164, January 1913, April 1913, August 1918, September 1918, p173, February 1919, March 1919, April 1919, October 1922, March 1929, April 1929, November 1933.

Pall Mall Gazette, 1st December 1888, 3rd January 1889, 15th February 1889.

South London Press, London, 30th December 1900.

Sword and Chatelaine the Weekly Journal of the Services and Society, April 1892- December 1892.

Sword and Chatelaine: The Weekly Journal of the Services and Society, London, 9th April 1892 to 17 December 1892.

The Abolitionist, BUAV, Bristol, 1898-1902, esp, 15th May 1899, 15th May 1900, p156, 18th May 1900, p250, 15th September 1900 p212, 15th July 1901.

The Anathaeum, Journal of English and Foreign Literature, Science, Fine Arts, Music and The Drama, Francis, John (Ed.), London, p451, 2nd April 1870.

The Anti-Vivisectionist Review, No. 1, London, 1909.

The Berkshire Chronicle Saturday 5th August 1871.

The Era, London, p11, 22nd June 1895.

The Era, London, p16, 28th November 1891.

The Grail, Coryn, Herbert, (Ed.), The Book Company, London, 1897.

The Irish Book Lover, London and Dublin, Vol. X, No. 9, p10, April 1919.

The Lamp, Vol 1, Toronto, Canada, p44, 3rd October 1894.

The Northern Theosophist, Bulmer, WA, (Ed. reprint), Edmonton Theosophical Society, Edmonton, Canada, 1997.

The Path, Judge, William Quan, New York, July 1889, August 1890 p.154, "To All Theosophists", September 1890.

The Path, London, Vol 4, p97, July 1889.

The Sketch, London, p464, 26th June 1895.

The Stage, London, p10, 20th June 1895.

The Sunday World, Social Reform, Literature, Labour, Athletics, The Drama, Yates, Edmund, (Ed.), London, Vol.2, No. 34, 10th May 1891.

The Theosophical Movement, Theosophy Company, Bombay, India, p44, 1961.

The Theosophist, Olcott, Henry Steel, (Ed.) Theosophical Society, Adyar, India, April 1887, June 1887 p 576, July 1927 p390, May 1895, July 1927, October 1928, March 1929, Khandalvala, ND, "Madame H.P. Blavatsky As I Knew Her" June 1929, Keightley, Bertram, September 1931.

The Woman's Herald, London, 16th May 1891.

The World: A Journal for Men and Women, Yates, Edmund, (Ed.), 1874 and 1886-9, Collins, Mabel, (Flower O' the May), "Tea Table Talk", 1887-1888, "Tangerines", August and September 1889.

Theosophical History. An Independent Quarterly Journal, Price, Leslie, (Ed.) London, 1987 and Santucci, James 1992. Price, Leslie, Gomes, Michael "Light on Mabel Collins", October, 1987, Gomes, Michael, Mabel Collins, Romance of the White Lotus", July 1991, "LW Rogers meets Mabel Collins, v4, January, 1992.

Theosophical Review, Theosophical Society, Theosophical Publishing House, London 1927.

Theosophical Siftings, Theosophical Society, George Redway, London 1889.

Times, London, 17th April 1913.

Transactions of The Blavatsky Lodge, Theosophical Society, Theosophical Publishing Society, London 1890.

Transactions of The London Lodge of The Theosophical Society, Theosophical Society, Leadenhall Press, London, 1884, 1885, 1886.

Woman, Lewis, Amelia, (Ed.), London, 1871-1872. Mabel Keningale Cook, "Domestic Arrangements, Suburban Wives", *Woman,* London, 23rd March 1872.

Online Sources

About, *Alternative Religions, Obeah,* http://altreligion.miningco.com/library/glossary/bldefobeah.htm 2004

Adherents.com, http://www.adherents.com/ *Obeah,* http://www.adherents.com/Na_468.html#2888

Ananova, http://www.ananova.com/news/story/sm_517090.html. 6th March 2003.

Association of Research Libraries, A History of Copyright in the United States, Washington DC, 22 November 2002, http://www.arl.org/info/frn/copy/timeline.html

Barker, AT, *The Letters of HP Blavatsky to AP Sinnett,* Theosophical University Press Online Edition, Pasadena, California, http://www.theosociety.org/pasadena/hpb-aps/bl-hp.htm

Blavatsky Net, http://www.blavatsky.net,

Blavatsky Study Centre, Blavatsky Archives, http://www.blavatskyarchives.com/index.htm, especially the following: Helena Petrovna Blavatsky, by Vera Petrovna de Zhelihovsky, (Reprinted from Lucifer (London), Nov. 15, 1894 – 15th April 1895.) http://www.blavatskyarchives.com/zhelhpbl.htm; Archibald Keightley, *Reminiscences of H.P. Blavatsky* [First published in *The Theosophical Quarterly*, New York, October 1910, pp. 109-122; William Q Judge and Archibald Keightley, www.blavatskyarchives.com/keightle.htm; *Light on the Path and Mabel Collins*, Reprinted from an 8-page pamphlet issued in New York in June, 1889, available online at Blavatsky Study Centre, http://blavatskyarchives.com/judgelotpamc89.htm; Archibald Keightley, "From Ostende to London". *The Path*, New York 7th November 1892 pp 245–8, http://www.blavatskyarchives.com/keightleyafromostende.htm; Letters of H.P. Blavatsky to Her Family in Russia, http://blavatskyarchives.com/blavletc.htm; Letter to Vera Zhelihovsky, May 1887,*The Path*, New York, October 1895, http://www.blavatskyarchives.com/blavle11.htm; The Very Latest News From the World of Occultism – Blavatsky and her Mahatmas [An Interview with William Q. Judge] [Reprinted from *The New York Times*, 6th January, 1889, p. 10.], http://blavatskyarchives.com/judgebsli89.htm; Letter from Blavatsky to Judge 7th July 1889, http://www.blavatskyarchives.com/hpbwqj7789.htm; Letter of HP Blavatsky to Dr. Elliot Coues, http://www.blavatskyarchives.com/blacouesb.htm; The Esoteric Section of the Theosophical Society. http://www.blavatskyarchives.com/blav89ess.htm;

Blavatsky, HP, "Have animals Souls?" *Theosophist,* January, February, and March, 1886. http://theosophy.org/tlodocs/hpb/HaveAnimalsSouls.htm

Caldwell, Daniel, *The Esoteric World of Madame Blavatsky,* Theosophical Society in America, http://www.theosophical.org/theosophy/books/esotericworld/index.html, 2001

Cornell University Library, *About Historical Math Monographs,* 2004, http://historical.library.cornell.edu/math/about.html

Friends of West Norwood Cemetery, http://www.anoraque.demon.co.uk/cemetery/index.htm

Hall, William, *The Lost London Street Index,* 1999, http://members.aol.com/WHall95037/londonc.html

http://www.theosophy-nw.org/theosnw/books/wqj-all/j-arts.htm

http://www.victorianlondon.org/publications3/nightside-01.htm

Intellectual Property, *A History of Copyright,* http://www.intellectual-property.gov.uk/std/resources/copyright/history.htm

Jack the Ripper Casebook http://www.casebook.org/

Justice, Faith, Hypatia, http://pages.prodigy.net/fljustice/hypatia.html

Kessinger Publishing's Rare Reprints, http://www.kessinger-publishing.com/searchresults_subject.lasso?Category=Transcendental%20Physics&Submit=Query

Knoche, Grace F, *Combined Chronology for Use with The Mahatma Letters to A. P. Sinnett and The Letters of H. P. Blavatsky to A. P. Sinnett* by Margaret Conger, Theosophical University Press, http://www.theosociety.org/pasadena/mahatma/ml-ccfor.htm 1973.

Landow, George P, National University of Singapore, Victorian Web, http://www.victorianweb.org/, *Bankruptcy in Victorian England — Threat or Myth,* http://www.victorianweb.org/economics/bankrupt.html

London Borough of Lambeth, *Ideal Homes: Suburbia in Focus,* "West Norwood Station", http://www.ideal-homes.org.uk/lambeth/norwood/west-norwood-station-01.htm

Mater, Kirby Van, *The Writing of the Secret Doctrine,* Theosophical University Press, Archives, Theosophical Society, Pasadena, http://www.theosociety.org/pasadena/invit-sd/invsd-4.htm,1988

Mehdi, Sharifi, University of Sussex, *Sussex History of Art Research Publication,* http://www.sussex.ac.uk/Units/arthist/sharp/index.shtml, January 2002, "Florence Fenwick Miller", http://www.sussex.ac.uk/Units/arthist/sharp/issues/0002/pHTML/pFlorenceFenwickMiller05.shtml

Museum of London, http://www.museumoflondon.org.uk/frames.shtml?http://www.museumoflondon.org.uk/MOLsite/exhibits/creative/artistloc/1900/1900_ljopling.html *"Creative Quarters,*

"Louise Jopling", 2003, http://www.museumoflondon.org.uk/frames.shtml?http://www.museumoflondon.org.uk/MOLsite/exhibits/creative/artistloc/1900/1900_ljopling.html

Music Business Journal, *History of Copyright,* 2002-2002, http://www.musicjournal.org/01copyright.html

National Anti Vivisection Society, http://www.navs.org.uk/about/125/, 2003

New Advent, Catholic Encyclopedia, *Spritism,* http://www.newadvent.org/cathen/14221a.htm, *Florence Marryatt,* http://www.newadvent.org/cathen/09715a.htm

Noah's Ark Society, *DD Home, Physical Medium,* http://www.noahsarksoc.fsnet.co.uk/mediums/d_d_.htm

Pajares, Frank, Welcome to the Middle, http://www.emory.edu/EDUCATION/mfp/index.html, Biography, Chronology, and Photographs of William James, 2002, http://www.emory.edu/EDUCATION/mfp/jphotos.html

Pearson Education, infoplease, *Morocco, Early History to The Nineteenth Century,* 2000-2003, http://www.infoplease.com/ce6/world/A0859770.html

Pekingese Home Page, Colorado, Noah's Ark Society, *DD Home, Physical Medium,* http://www.noahsarksoc.fsnet.co.uk/mediums/d_d_.htm

Pioch, Nicolas, WebMuseum, Paris, *Whistler, James Abbott McNeill.* October 2002, http://www.ibiblio.org/wm/paint/auth/whistler/

Salmonson, Jessica, Violet Books, http://www.violetbooks.com/index.html

Slemen, Tom, *The Valentine Ghost of Sefton Park,* from *Haunted Liverpool,* Slemen, Tom, Bluecoat Press, Liverpool 1995 http://www.geocities.com/Area51/Shuttle/9089/haunted.html

Southern E-Group, *Crystal Palace,* 9th October 2003. http://www.semg.org.uk/location/cpalace_01.html

Spartacus Educational, http://www.spartacus.schoolnet.co.uk/, *The Secular Society,* http://www.spartacus.schoolnet.co.uk/Rsecular.htm

Spartacus International, http://www.spartacus.schoolnet.co.uk/index.html, UK, *Annie Besant*, http://www.spartacus.schoolnet.co.uk/b5.htm

Terry's Theatre, http://mysite.freeserve.com/arthurlloyd/Terrys.htm

The History of Economic Thought Website, http://cepa.newschool.edu/het/home.htm, *Robert Owen, 1771-1858*, http://cepa.newschool.edu/het/profiles/owen.htm.

The International Survivalist Society, 2003, http://www.survivalafterdeath.org/home.htm, Johann Zollner, http://www.survivalafterdeath.org/scientists/4.htm

The Theosophical Society, Pasadena, http://www.theosociety.org/pasadena/ The *Letters of H. P. Blavatsky to A. P. Sinnett*, Theosophical University Press Online Edition, Letter No. 85, http://www.theosociety.org/pasadena/hpb-aps/bl-85.htm and Foreword to the *Combined Chronology* of Margaret Conger

The Victorian Dictionary, http://www.victorianlondon.org/, Ritchie, J Ewing, *The Night Side of London*, 1858.

The Wardrobe, Home of the Royal Gloucestershire, Berkshire and Wiltshire Regiment (Salisbury) Museum, June 2004, http://www.thewardrobe.org.uk/historyto1881.php3

Theatres of New York, Toronto and London, http://members.tripod.com/~clairsedore/RazzleDazzle/my_cdnow_store.html 2002.

Theos-L, email List, http://www.theos-l.com/archives/199702/tl00073.html

Theosophy Northwest, http://www.theosophy-nw.org/ Judge, William Q, *Reply to the Attack on Madame Blavatsky*, 7th June 1889,

Thomas, Graham, "A Genealogical Guide to Woodchester, Selsley and the south Cotswolds", http://www.grahamthomas.com/history3.html at *A History of Woodchester and Selsley*, http://www.grahamthomas.com/history1.html 1999-2003.

Thorp, Nigel, Centre for Whistler Studies, http://www.whistler.arts.gla.ac.uk/, *The Correspondence,* April 2004, http://www.whistler.arts.gla.ac.uk/letters/08089.asp?target=2

Wardle 2000, http://wardle2000.homestead.com/index.html "Family History", http://wardle2000.homestead.com/Family_History.html

Wikipedia, The Free Encyclopedia, http://en.wikipedia.org/wiki/Main_Page, *Society for Psychical Research,* http://en.wikipedia.org/wiki/Society_for_Psychical_Research

Wisdom World, http://www.wisdomworld.org/index.html, *The Theosophical Movement,* http://www.wisdomworld.org/additional/TheTheosophicalMovement-Series/

Other documentary sources:

1881 census records.

1891 census records.

British Union for the Abolition of Vivisection, First Annual Report, BUAV, Bristol, 1st May 1899.

Death Certificate Keningale Robert Cook.

Marriage certificate Minna Collins and Keningale Robert Cook.

Post Office London directories 1870-1880.

Post Office London directory 1869-1886.

Post Office London Directory 1871.

Royal Literary Fund, Case file 2871.

Will, Keningale Robert Cook.

Notes

1   Jessica Rabbit in *Who Framed Roger Rabbit?* Dir. Robert Zemeckis, collaboration between Disney Studios and Steven Spielberg, 1988.

2   HPB to Vera Zhelihovsky May 1887, *The Path* New York, October 1895- via Meade p391 (in reference to Archibald and Bertram Keightley and Mabel Collins).

3   Mortimer Collins, *Summer Songs*, Saunders, Otley & Company, London 1875.

4   Mabel Collins was born in St Peters Port, Guernsey, Channel Islands (49n27/2w36), on 9 September 1851 at 8:30 Local Mean Time. Time taken from Alan Leo's *1001 Notable Nativities* Modern Astrology 1900 supplied by Mabel herself in answer to a letter from Leo.

5   Although the name Collings was used on official documents, Francis and his father would often sign their name as "Collins", though Mortimer was the first to consistently use this spelling.

6   *Spiritual Poems,* Plymouth, 1826.

7   Robert Hawker, (1753-1827), was for six years the curate and for forty-three years the vicar of Charles, Plymouth. He was born in Exeter, 13th April 1753. The son of a surgeon, he was originally trained for a career in medicine. After three years as an assistant surgeon in the Royal Marines, Hawker matriculated at Oxford University but left without taking a degree. Ordained in 1778, he served as Curate at Charles near Plymouth and later succeeded to the Living. He was appointed Deputy Chaplain to the Plymouth Garrison in 1797 and in 1802 founded the Great Western Society for Dispersing Religious Tracts. Hawker was one of the most prominent Calvinists in the Church of England. Known as a brilliant orator, for many years he paid an annual visit to London where he preached in crowded chapels. He also wrote extensively on theological matters and was a pioneer of Sunday Schools in Plymouth.

8   *The Poor Man's Commentary on The Bible,* 10 volumes, London

1822-1826.

9   John Nelson Darby was born in London of Irish parents on 18th November 1800. In 1819 he graduated from Trinity College Dublin with a degree in law. He became ordained in the Church of Ireland. Distressed by the rampant modernism among his fellow Anglican clergy, he left the Church of Ireland and joined himself to those who later became known as 'Plymouth Brethren' and from 1848 as the 'Exclusive Brethren'. John Nelson Darby died on the 29th of April, 1882.

10 Edward Cronin was born a Catholic in Cork, Eire, in 1801. He studied medicine at the Math Hospital, Dublin. During the earlier portion of his career, Cronin devoted himself to missionary work. His first wife having died in 1829 - a year after marriage - Dr. Cronin went to the East as a missionary. In 1838 he married again and settled in Brixton, London. He died 1st February 1882.

11 John Gifford Bellett was born in Dublin in 1795. He studied at Trinity College, Dublin, where he met John Nelson Darby and was a Classics prize-winner. He practised as a lawyer in Dublin. Bellett remained in Ireland until moving to Bath in 1846 and returned there in 1854.

12 Francis Hutchinson (1802-33), was the son of Sir Samuel Synge-Hutchinson, Archdeacon of Killala.

13 Remembered by many as "the wickedest man in the world", Aleister Crowley was born 12th October 1875 in Leamington, Warwickshire, Edward Alexander Crowley into a wealthy family. His father died when Aleister was eleven years old. Crowley went on to attend Cambridge University and later began working in the Diplomatic Service. In 1898 he began his involvement in magic joining the Hermetic Order of the Golden Dawn. Crowley advanced quickly through the ranks of the Golden Dawn, but his activities led to the fragmentation of the order. He was expelled in 1900 and began his travels throughout the world. He also married Rose Kelly. In 1905, he was part of an expedition to climb a Himalayan mountain peak, in which several members of the party died. He spent several years travelling through China, Canada and the United States, with

and without his wife and child. In 1907, Crowley formed the Order of The Silver Star. In 1909 he began publishing *The Equinox*. In 1909, Crowley divorced his wife. He became the head of the Ordo Templi Orientis in 1912. Crowley spent World War I in the USA. After the war, Crowley had a daughter, Poupée, with Leah Hirsig, and in 1920 set up the notorious Abbey of Thelema in Sicily, where Poupée died. In 1925 he was elected World Head of the O.T.O., and 1929 saw the publication of *Magick: In Theory and in Practice*. After his expulsion from Italy, he spent the remaining years as a wanderer, addicted to heroin, desperately in need of both disciples and money. Aleister Crowley died December 1st, 1947.

14 Alan Leo was born 7th August 1860. His given name was William Frederick Allan. He pursued various employments but found nothing satisfactory until he became a travelling salesman for a vending machine company. He stayed in that work until 1898. Leo taught himself astrology and in 1888 became acquainted with another astrologer, F.W. Lacey. Through Lacey he met W. Gorn Old, who belonged to the inner circle of the Theosophical Society. Leo joined the Society in 1890 and formed a partnership with Lacey to publish *Astrologer's Magazine*, later *Modern Astrology*. Lacey withdrew in 1894 to pursue other interests, and left Leo as the sole proprietor. Leo married Bessie Phillips in 1896. By 1898 Leo was able to abandon his sales job and devote himself to astrology. In the early 1900s, he wrote several substantial books as well as a number of short works on astrology. Leo founded the Astrological Lodge of the Theosophical Society in 1915. He was twice prosecuted for fortune telling. In the first case, in May 1914, he was acquitted on a technicality. In the second case, in July 1917, he was fined £25. Leo died 30th August 1917 and is remembered as the father of modern astrology.

15 Sir Robert Anderson, was born in Dublin 29th May 1841. His father, Matthew Anderson, was Crown Solicitor in the Irish capital, a distinguished elder in the Irish Presbyterian Church. In 1863 he was called to the Irish Bar. In 1865 he assisted the Irish

government in interrogating prisoners and preparing legal briefs. In 1873 he married Lady Agnes Moore, sister of the Earl of Drogheda. In 1877 he was appointed as Irish Agent at the Home Office, and, in 1888, when London was in the midst of the 'Jack the Ripper' scare, he moved into Scotland Yard as Assistant Commissioner of Metropolitan Police and Chief of the Criminal Investigation Department. He directed this work till 1901, when he was knighted upon retiring. He died 15th November 1918.

16   Mabel Collins *Our Bohemia: A Family Party* Tinsley Brothers, London 1879, *In the Flower of Her Youth* F.V. White & Company, London 1883.

17   Mabel Collins *Our Bohemia: A Family Party* Tinsley Brothers, London 1879.

18   Richard Harris Barham, (1788-1845), was a parodist best known for his humorous verse and fiction. He wrote under the name of Thomas Ingoldsby. Much of his work was published in *Bentley's Miscellany*, a popular weekly magazine. Bentley also published a collection of *Barham's Ingoldsby Legend*, which went through numerous editions being published as a book in 1840.

19   Now Lechdale on Thames.

20   Knowl Hill is thirty miles from London, three miles west of Maidenhead, and was originally part of Windsor Forest. Windsor Forest ceased to officially exist in 1813. The name of the village comes from 'The Knolle', which was a hill on the south side, crowned with a clump of trees. Berkshire acquired its railways early, and it was relatively straightforward to travel into London.

21   *The Lancaster Gazetteer, and General Advertiser for Lancashire, Westmorland, etc* 20 June 1801-30 June 1894.

22   Morecambe had become popular since the 1750s, crossings by coach and horses of the sands of Morecambe Bay was considered to be a prelude to a visit to the Lake District which was becoming fashionable. By this time it was highly fashionable.

23   The ancient gateway and capital of Cornwall, Launceston lies

close to the Devon border. At this time its main claim to fame was to have over forty pubs and several beer and cider houses.

24 John Edward Bromby was born in Hull, England, on 23rd May 1809. He was educated at St John's College, Cambridge and elected a fellow of the College, and ordained deacon in 1834 and priest in 1836. He was appointed second master at Bristol College and then ran a private school at Clifton, Bristol. From 1847 to 1854 he was principal of Elizabeth College, Guernsey, university preacher at Cambridge in 1850, when he obtained the degree of D.D., and after 1854 was curate for two or three years to his father at Hull. He was then appointed headmaster of the newly founded Church of England Grammar School at Melbourne, where he arrived in February 1858. He died at Melbourne 4th March 1889. He was married twice and was survived by his second wife and two sons and three daughters of the first marriage.

25 K.M.C. (Keningale Cook and Mabel Collins) "Early Days of Mortimer Collins" *Dublin University Magazine* October 1877.

26 Ibid.

27 Ed. Tom Taylor *Pen Sketches by A Vanished Hand* Richard Bentley and Son 1879 p. xvi

28 James Bertrand Payne published a book in the 19th century, *Containing The Chief Events in The Lives of Eminent Persons of All Ages and Nations Arranged Chronologically*, containing a number of highly dubious family "histories", taking eminent namesakes and claiming them as relatives to plump the family pride. He also wrote *The Gossiping Guide to Jersey* 1863 and *Armorial of Jersey*, London, 1865.

29 The poet, painter, and designer Dante Gabriel Rossetti, born Gabriel Charles Dante Rossetti, 12th May 1828, was a cofounder of the Pre Raphaelites, a group of English painters and poets who hoped to bring to their art the richness and purity of the medieval period. He was the son of the exiled Italian patriot and scholar Gabriele Rossetti and a brother of the poet Christina Rossetti. He died 9th April 1882.

30 Mortimer and Frances Collins *Frances* Frederick Warne &

Company, London, Undated.

31 Mortimer Collins *Attic Salt* London B Robson & Company, 1880 p17.

32 Frances Collins, *Mortimer Collins, His Letters and Friendships*. Sampson Low 1877 p33.

33 Mortimer Collins *Attic Salt* B Robson & Company, London 1880 px.

34 Edmund Hodgson Yates was born 31st July in Edinburgh, where his parents were acting at the time. In 1847 he began work in the general post office at London, and by 1862 had become the head of the Missing Letter Department. He remained in this position until 1872, although most of his time was devoted to literary work. He began writing in 1850, contributing to various periodicals. In 1853 he was married to Louise Wilkinson, by whom he had four sons. From 1854 to 1860 he was dramatic critic of the *Daily News*, and in 1855 conducted a column in the *Illustrated Times*. In 1858 he was editor of *Town Talk*, in 1860 of *Temple Bar*, and in 1867 of *Tinsley's Magazine*. From 1879 to 1884 he was editor of *Time*. In 1872-73 he made a lecture tour of the United States and later was special correspondent to the *New York Herald*. In 1874 he was assistant editor of *The World* and after 1875 its proprietor. He was a founder member of The Arts Club, and was on the council of The Society of Authors in 1893. He also wrote numerous novels. Yates died 20th May 1894.

35 Richard Dodderidge Blackmore (1825-1900), was trained in law and called to the bar. He gave up his legal career owing to ill health. His reputation rests chiefly on his romantic novel about the 17th-century outlaws of Exmoor, *Lorna Doone* (1869), but he wrote also 13 other novels - including *The Maid of Sker* (1872) and *Springhaven* (1887) - and several volumes of poetry.

36 John Francis Waller (1810-1894), born in Limerick, Eire, also wrote under the name of Jonathan Freke Slingsby. He qualified in law and became a permanent official in courts of Chancery; Registrar of Rolls Court in 1867. He was a frequent contributor to *Dublin University Magazine*, and became its editor. Waller was a popular poet, author and lyricist.

37 Frances Collins, *Mortimer Collins, His Letters and Friendships*. Sampson Low, 1877 p6.

38 Mortimer Collins, *Comedy of Dreams*. Uncompleted work published in part in *The Poets and Poetry of the Century* 5 Ed. Alfred H Miles Hutchinson & Company, no date.

39 Mabel Collins, *Our Bohemia: A Family Party* Tinsley Brothers, London 1879 p.69.

40 Mabel Collins *In the Flower of Her Youth* F.V. White & Company. London 1883.

41 Frances Collins, *Mortimer Collins, His Letters and Friendships*. Sampson Low, London 1877 p 73.

42 St. Peter's Church was consecrated in 1841 and enlarged in 1870. It was designed by J.C. Buckler of Oxford, runner-up to Sir Charles Barry in a competition concerning a design for the Houses of Parliament.

43 Frances Collins, *Mortimer Collins, His Letters and Friendships*. Sampson Low, London 1877 p78.

44 Mabel Collins, *In The Flower of Her Youth. A Novel.* F. V. White & Company, London, 1883.

45 Ibid.

46 Dr JEN Molesworth was Vicar of Rochdale for 38 years, from 1839 to 1877.When he came to the parish the church was in a state of collapse and stagnation. He achieved an appreciable upturn in its fortunes. Numerous new churches were consecrated in his time. He died on 21st April, 1877, aged 87. Molesworth was a Tory opponent of the Rochdale radicals. His son, the Rev W Nassau Molesworth, was a formative member of the co-operative movement.

47 A prominent Rochdale banker. He was immortalised by having a street named after him, Albert Royds Street, in Rochdale.

48 Founded in 1592, Trinity College, is Ireland's oldest university. A university had been founded in 1320 at St Patrick's Cathedral but closed at the end of the 15th century owing to lack of funds. Elizabeth I founded Trinity in 1592 so that students in Ireland could be 'free from papish influence'. The college has allowed Catholics to study there only since the nineteenth century but

the Roman Catholic Church continued to ban Catholic students from Trinity until 1971. John Charles McQuaid, Archbishop of Dublin from 1940 to 1972, deemed it a mortal sin to attend Trinity because of 'pagan' influences at the college. Trinity produced many of Ireland's leading revolutionaries such as Wolfe Tone and Robert Emmet. When Robert attended, the law school had been recently updated.

49 Victorian London - Publications - Social Investigation/ Journalism - The Night Side of London, by J. Ewing Ritchie, 1858 – Introduction www.victorianlondon.org/publications3/nightside-01.htm

50 Keningale Robert Cook, *Purpose and Passion: Being Pygmalion, and Other Poems, etc.* Virtue & Company, London, 1870.

51 Established by the Irish writer William Maginn in 1830, *Fraser's* was a general and literary Tory journal whose contributors included Samuel Taylor Coleridge and William Makepeace Thackeray.

52 Mabel Collins, *An Innocent Sinner. A Psychological Romance,* Tinsley Brothers, London, 1877.

53 Frances Collins, *Mortimer Collins: His Letters and Friendships, with Some Account of His Life,* Sampson Low & Company, London, 1877.

54 *Dublin University Magazine,* August 1877.

55 Aenon is where John the Baptist baptised Christ. Its precise location has long been the source of speculation, and its meaning is generally taken to be "springs, fountain or his eye", indicating a place near the Jordan river. However, some commentators have interpreted the word as "course of the world" or "time, eternity". The translation used affects the sequence of events around the crucifixion, and the validity of Biblical authority for baptism. I have been unable to locate the precise reference but it appears likely that Robert followed Max Muller's view that "aenon" refers to "time", rather than a precise location, and it is this that caused offence.

56 Letter dated 21st May 1877 published in *The Irish Book Lover,* April 1919.

57   Quoted on the cover of *An Innocent Sinner* from Anathaeum.

58   Quoted on the cover of *An Innocent Sinner* from Whitehall.

59   Quoted on the cover of *An Innocent Sinner* from Morning Post.

60   Quoted on the cover of *An Innocent Sinner* from *The World* newspaper.

61   For a time, Edward Bulwer-Lytton, (1803-1873), was regarded as England's most popular novelist. In Victorian times he was an important social and political figure. Edward produced poetry from the age of seven and was considered a prodigy by his family. Against his mother's wishes, he married Rosina Doyle Wheeler, in 1827. Bulwer became estranged from his mother for a period: she stopped his allowance because of his marriage, and he became an author and journalist to support himself and his wife in the style to which they had become accustomed. Although he later was reconciled with his mother, he chose to refuse the allowance she offered. Elected as MP for St Ives, Huntingdonshire in 1831, Bulwer was often derided for his writing. He separated from Rosina in 1836 and she made numerous accusations of infidelity and violence against him, resorting to lawsuits and finally ending up certified insane. Bulwer was knighted in 1837 and on his mother's death in 1843 he succeeded to Knebworth and took the name Bulwer-Lytton. He was elected MP for Hertfordshire in 1852, a position he held until his elevation to the peerage as Baron Lytton of Knebworth in 1866. Lytton died at Torquay, in the arms of his only son, Edward Bulwer Lytton, a poet and diplomat, on 18th January 1873. He is buried in Westminster Abbey. His thrillers and family sagas influenced Dickens, Wilkie Collins, Thackeray and Trollope. Although his work is often derided today, Lytton had a profound influence on the Theosophical movement. Recommended by Blavatsky, Lytton's novel *Zanoni* was highly popular amongst occultists and *The Coming Race* is held to have been influential in the occult ideas behind the Nazi movement.

62   Mabel Collins, *In This World. A Novel.* Chapman & Hall, London, 1879.

63   Mabel Collins, *Our Bohemia. [Tales.]* Tinsley Bros. London, 1879.

64 Mabel Collins, *Too Red A Dawn,* Tinsley Bros. London, 1881.

65 Mabel Collins, *Cobwebs,* Tinsley Bros. London, 1882.

66 Mabel Collins, *In The Flower of Her Youth,* F. V. White & Company, London, 1883.

67 Mabel Collins, *The Story of Helena Modjeska-Madame Chiapowska,* W. H. Allen & Company, London, 1883.

68 Mabel Collins, *Viola Fanshawe. A Novel.* F. V. White & Company, London, 1884.

69 MC, Fellow of the Theosophical Society, *The Idyll of The White Lotus,* Reeves & Turner: London, 1884.

70 Mabel Collins, *Lord Vanecourt's Daughter,* Ward & Downe, London, 1885.

71 Mabel Collins, *The Prettiest Woman in Warsaw,* Ward & Downey, London, 1885.

72 In Kensington, London, this district, included Holland Park and lay between Kensington Gardens and the West London Railway. It was a highly fashionable and relatively expensive area to live in and well served by railways.

73 Margaret Oliphant, *Blackwood's,* 94, (August 1865), 168,

74 Margaret Oliphant, *Blackwood's,* 102, (September 1867), 257 - 280.

75 Mabel Collins, *Illusions,* Theosophical Publishing Society, London, 1905,

76 John Sutherland, *The Longman Companion to Victorian Literature,* Longman, London 1988.

77 Keningale Robert Cook, *The Guitar Player, with Sundry Poems.* Pickering & Company, London, 1881.

78 Keningale Robert Cook, *The King of Kent, [A Drama in Verse.],* Pickering & Company, London, 1882.

79 Keningale Robert Cook, *Love in A Mist. A Romantic Drama in Familiar Blank Verse.* Pickering & Company, London, 1882 a second edition appeared in 1886.

80 Walt Whitman, America's greatest poet, was also a theosophist. *Leaves of Grass* drew on his own mystical experiences and his readings in Hindu scriptures and the writings of Western mystics

such as Swedenborg.

81 " *To Kenningale Cook* 328 Mickle street / Camden New Jersey U S America / Feb: 11 '86 My dear K C, I send you the two Volumes, same mail with this, (same address as this note) - The price is one pound two shillings, which please remit me." 1378. Henry W. and Albert A. Berg Collection, New York Public Library. Walt. The Correspondence. Volume IV: 1886-1889. *The Collected Writings of Walt Whitman.* Ed. by Edwin Haviland Miller. 6 vols. New York: New York University Press, 1969. March 21 *Keningale Cook* Shorter's Court Throgmorton St. London Eng sent by mail L of G & T R paid [in red pencil:] ? $20 recd "Check mark" X 17.

82 Kenningale Robert Cook, *The Fathers of Jesus. A Study of The Lineage of The Christian Doctrine and Traditions,* Kegan Paul, Trench & Company, London, 1886.

83 *Light* July 10th 1886. Arnewood is part of the village Sway, midway between Southampton and Bournemouth and about three miles north of Lymington.

84 *Light* is the magazine of the College of Psychic Studies, and has been published without a break since 1881. The College of Psychic Studies was founded in 1884 by a number of people who were engaged in psychical research and sought to proclaim that human personality survives bodily death and that this is open to demonstration. In 1883, the dissolution of the Central Association of Spiritualists and The London Spiritualist Alliance was formed. In 1925 The London Spiritualist Alliance acquired its own premises. Its name was changed to The College of Psychic Science on 31st January 1955 and The College of Psychic Studies in 1970.

85 Mabel Keningale Cook, 'Domestic Arrangements, Suburban Wives", *Woman,* London, 23 March 1872.

86 Ibid.

87 Catherine Maude Metcalfe, letter in *Occult Review* April 1929 XLIX.

88 Daniel Dunglas Home was born in Edinburgh on 20th March 1833. Adopted by his aunt, he was taken to Connecticut when

he was nine. As a child, he experienced visions and precognition. When physical phenomena began he was forced to leave home. Demonstrations of his abilities were sought, and he was welcomed by many living in New York and New England. Two Harvard researchers heard of him and found that physical phenomena occurred without there being any indication of a cause. By the early 1850s, he was levitating, and partial materialisations were being produced in his séances. By 1855, when Home came to Britain, the news of spiritualism had already reached this country. Home found a receptive audience when he arrived here. Home's séances often displayed extraordinary phenomena, levitation of tables and other objects, playing of musical instruments by unseen hands and the materialisation of spirit hands. Sitters would sometimes be aware of the room shaking, raps, touches, direct writing, spirit lights appearing and psychic breezes being felt. Communicators also spoke through Home when he was entranced. Unlike most other mediums, he was able to conduct his séances in a lighted environment. There were other abilities that distinguished Home from other mediums. One was the elongation of his body by up to a foot in length. Another was his handling of pieces of coal taken from the fire. For long periods of his life Home lived in England. The number of séances that Home gave is estimated to have been over fifteen hundred.

89 In 1869 the London Dialectical Society appointed a committee of thirty-three members "to investigate the phenomena alleged to be spiritual manifestations, and to report thereon". The committee's report (1871) declares that "motion may be produced in solid bodies without material contact, by some hitherto unrecognised force operating within an undefined distance from the human organism, and beyond the range of muscular action"; and that "this force is frequently directed by intelligence".

90 In the early 1850s groups called secular societies began forming all over Britain. Charles Bradlaugh, the leader of the Secular Society in Sheffield, believed that religion was blocking progress and could not be ignored. In 1860 Bradlaugh and Joseph Barker

formed a new journal called the *National Reformer*. Bradlaugh toured the country giving lectures on religion and politics and was soon acknowledged as the new leader of the Secular movement. In 1866 Bradlaugh announced plans for a new national freethought organisation with headquarters in London and branches in all the provincial towns. At the inaugural meeting in London in 1866, Bradlaugh was elected president.

91   The Society for Psychical Research was founded in 1882 by three Cambridge scholars because of their interest in spiritualism. Its purpose was to encourage scientific research into psychic or paranormal phenomena. Research was initially aimed at six areas: telepathy, mesmerism and similar phenomena, mediums, apparitions, physical phenomena associated with séances and, finally, the history of all these phenomena. The Society was especially active in the thirty years after it was founded, gaining fame for its investigation of Madame Blavatsky and the Theosophical Society in 1884.

92   William James was born in New York City on 11th January 1842. He studied medicine at Harvard receiving his MD in 1869. In 1872 Harvard's president, Charles Eliot, invited him to teach psychology at Harvard. He accepted, and remained there for the next thirty-five years. In 1879, he shifted to philosophy. The following year he was made assistant professor of philosophy and remained in that position until 1907 when he resigned from Harvard. James published a twelve-hundred page masterwork, *The Principles of Psychology* in 1890. William James is often recognised as the father of American pragmatism, as it became one of the prevailing philosophical movements of the 20th century under his leadership. He was criticised for his interest in psychical research, and he was known to have attended séances. He was the brother of the writer Henry James and died in 1910.

93   Robert Owen, (1771-1858), was a utopian socialist who founded the famous New Lanark Mills in Scotland as an example of the viability of co-operative factory communities. He attempted to extend these into agriculture - advocating collective farming. Although most of these efforts failed, he continued on his social work - becoming the head of one of the largest trade union

federations in Britain in 1843.

94 AP Sinnett 'Some Psychic Experiences, MC's Narrative" *Broad Views*, Volume 1 1904

95 Florence Marryat, (1838-1899), was the daughter of Captain Frederick Marryat, the novelist. In 1854 she married T. Ross Church, afterwards colonel of the Madras Staff Corps, with whom she travelled through India, and to whom she bore eight children. Her first books appeared in 1865. Before her death she produced ninety novels. She was also a frequent contributor to newspapers and magazines, and edited *London Society*, from 1872 to 1876. Florence was also a playwright, operatic singer, actress, lecturer, dramatic reader and public entertainer and conducted a school of journalism. She was involved in spiritualism for a number of years and during the latter part of her life converted to Catholicism.

96 Florence Marryat, "My Spirit Child" in *Researches into The Phenomena of Modern Spiritualism,* Two Worlds Publishing Company, 1904 reproduced at http://www.survivalafterdeath.org/books/crookes/researches/marryat.htm

97 Mabel Collins, *The Locked Room. A true story of experiences in spiritualism.* Theosophical Publishing House, London, 1920.

98 Mabel Collins, *The Awakening,* Theosophical Publishing Society, London, 1906.

99 'Cleopatra's Needle' is the name given to two Egyptian obelisks, formerly at Alexandria and now in New York and London. The 60 foot high and 187 ton granite obelisk dates from 1475 BCE. It was given to Britain by Turkey, then ruling Egypt, in 1819. It reached the UK in January 1878 and it was originally planned to erect it outside the Houses of Parliament. On September 13th 1878 it was raised on the Victoria Embankment in London.

100 AP Sinnett 'Some Psychic Experiences, MC's Narrative" *Broad Views*, Volume 1, 1904

101 Ibid.

102 Mabel Collins, *The Story of The Year,* George Redway, London, 1895.

103   Mabel Collins and Helen Bouchier *The Scroll of the Disembodied Man*. J. M. Watkins, London, 1904.

104   *Memorabilia – Reminiscences of a Woman Artist and Writer* – Isabelle de Steiger, Rider & Company, London 1927.

105   The quotation continues, "the rain fell in torrents—except at occasional intervals, when it was checked by a violent gust of wind which swept up the streets (for it is in London that our scene lies), rattling along the housetops, and fiercely agitating the scanty flame of the lamps that struggled against the darkness." Edward George Bulwer-Lytton, *Paul Clifford*, Colburn & R. Bentley: London, 1830. One of the most used literary quotations of this century, it is recognised for its continual appearance at the start of *Peanuts* cartoon strips. It is accepted by many to be one of the worst ever openings for a novel.

106   Ramsgate is a seaside town on the Isle of Thanet in East Kent. It was one of the great English seaside towns of the nineteenth century.

107   Constance Wachtmeister, *Reminiscences of H.P. Blavatsky and The Secret Doctrine,* Theosophical Publishing Society, Wheaton, Illinois, 1893.

108   Helena Petrovna Blavatsky was born on 12th August 1831, at Ekaterinoslav, Ukraine. In 1849 she married N. V. Blavatsky, and began more than twenty years of extensive travel. In 1873 Blavatsky arrived in New York from Paris. At first she attempted to interest the Spiritualists in the philosophy behind phenomena but they resented her refusal to accept their standard explanations. In July 1875 she was urged "to establish a philosophico-religious society," and in the autumn of that year she became the principal founder of the Theosophical Society. Her first major work, *Isis Unveiled*, was published in 1878 and following this she and H. S. Olcott left for India. There they worked to re establish Oriental philosophical and religious ideas, largely through the pages of *The Theosophist*, a magazine which Blavatsky founded and edited. In 1884, disgruntled TS employees in India went to the missionaries with forged documents, bringing charges of fraud against her. The Society for Psychical Research sent Richard Hodgson to investigate the

charges, and subsequently published an unfavourable report. Under the strain, Blavatsky's health broke down, and in 1885 she left India for Europe, where she wrote *The Secret Doctrine*. In 1888 *The Secret Doctrine* was published and she formed the Esoteric Section of The Theosophical Society. Shortly afterwards she wrote *The Key to Theosophy* and *The Voice of The Silence*. In 1890 she became head of a newly established European Section. She died in London on 8th May 1891.

109 There is a strict hierarchy amongst these beings. The Lord of the World is at the head of all. He is the agent on earth of the First Logos. Next there is the present Buddha, who is the first of our humanity to reach such an exalted position. The Mahachohan is the third being to hold such a high position. Below these beings are those known as the Masters – Manu Vaivasvata, who deals with world rulers; Bodhisavatta Maitreya, who is the head of all faiths and deals with religious leaders; Master Morya, responsible for guiding men and forming nations and one of the Masters responsible for forming the Theosophical Society; Koot Hoomi, a great linguist and magician and connected with religion, education and art; The Venetian Master, connected with adaptability and tact, Serapis, connected with harmony and beauty; Hilarion, connected with science; Jesus, in charge of the saints and mystics of every religion; Prince Rakoczi, connected with ceremonial magic. Other characters exist in the occult hierarchy. The Masters take physical form at times and have several places where they reside. They partake in a number of activities ranging from assisting the dead in the astral world to guiding humanity.

110 Henry Steel Olcott was born 2nd August 1832, in Orange, New Jersey. After an early career in agricultural science and journalism, he served during the Civil War as a military investigator of fraud and corruption. This was followed by a career in law, which he later combined with journalism, reporting on Spiritualistic phenomena. He remained President Co Founder of the Theosophical Society until his death Adyar, Madras, on 17th February 1907.

111 William Quan Judge was born in Dublin, Ireland, on 13th April

1851. His family emigrated in 1864 to New York where he became a lawyer. He later became General Secretary of the Theosophical Society's American Section and Vice President of the International Society. He organised and presided over the Theosophical Congress at the World's Parliament of Religions held in Chicago in 1893. An argument within the Society, relating to whether or not Judge had genuinely received letters from the Masters, led to the secession of the American Section of the Theosophical Society in 1895. Judge died in New York City on 21st March 1896.

112 Present at the first meeting of the Theosophical Society in 1875 while visiting New York, Massey became the first president of the British Theosophical Society. A barrister by profession, Massey had a long interest in spiritualism and was Vice President of the British National Association of Spiritualists in 1873. Massey was responsible for translating Johann Zollner's *Transcendental Physics* in 1880.

113 Alfred Percy Sinnett, (1840-1921), was the recipient of the controversial "Mahatma Letters". Sinnett was the author of *The Early Days of Theosophy in Europe* (published posthumously in 1922), a work denounced by other theosophists, including Alice Leighton Cleather and Basil Crump.

114 Anna Bonus Kingsford, (16th September 1846-1888) helped to establish theosophy in England. She was a medical practitioner, a campaigner for women's rights and for vegetarianism, an ardent opponent of vivisection, and writer. The youngest of twelve children, Anna suffered from ill health from childhood. After attending a finishing school, she devoted herself to writing. In 1867 she was introduced to spiritualism and began to attend séances. The same year she married Algernon Kingsford, a cousin. In 1870 she was received into the Roman Catholic Church. Anna commenced her medical studies in 1873 in England and went to Paris in 1874 for her main studies. She received her M.D. in 1880. Anna's life was intertwined with that of Edward Maitland (27th October 1824-2nd October 1897) from 1874. In 1882 *The Perfect Way* was published. In 1883 Anna became President, and Edward Vice-President, of the London

Lodge of the Theosophical Society. Although they were to later step down from their positions, they never severed connections with the Theosophical Society. They formed the Hermetic Society, grounded in Western esoteric traditions. In November 1887 in Paris, she caught pneumonia which developed into pulmonary consumption. She died at on 22nd February 1888.

115 Francesca Arundale joined the Theosophical Society in 1881 and served as Treasurer in 1884. She was the first English woman to be initiated into a co-masonic lodge in France in 1893. Francesca was the aunt of George Arundale, who became President of the Theosophical Society after Annie Besant's death.

116 Allan Kardec, (1804-1869), was the pseudonym adopted by Hippolyte Léon Denizard Rivail under which he published his books on Spiritism. Born in Lyon, Rivail held a doctorate in medicine. In 1824 he published his first book based on his own system for teaching mathematics. In 1825 he opened his own school, followed by a second in 1826. He taught chemistry, physics, mathematics, astronomy, comparative anatomy and rhetoric, and spoke nine languages. In 1854 he first came across spiritualism and decided to investigate the phenomenon further. Attending séances, he adopted the practice of arriving at every meeting armed with a list of penetrating questions. The communications he received were published under the title of *The Spirits Book* in 1857. It was so successful that a second edition was printed the following year. Kardecist Spiritism survives as one of the main established religions in Brazil. It considers itself a form of Christianity. Reincarnation is a central tenet of Kardecism, and plays a central role at its ceremonies, where the spirits of deceased persons are invoked, manifest themselves in various ways, and may be incorporated or chanelled by mediums.

117 Richard Hodgson, (1855-1905), was born in Melbourne, Australia. He graduated with an M.A., LL.D. from the University of Melbourne attended the University of Cambridge where he received a B.A in mental and moral sciences. During 1884-1885, he became increasingly active in the investigations

that the Society for Psychical Research were conducting in England. He became the secretary and treasurer for the Society for Psychical Research. He is probably most remembered for being one of the founding members of the American Anthropological Association. Amongst theosophists he is remembered for the "Hodgson Report" of 1885 which declared Blavatsky to be a fraud. The Society for Psychical Research published a report in 1986 which found the report to be inaccurate and untrustworthy.

118 Mabel Collins, *The Locked Room: A True Story of Experiences in Spiritualism*, Theosophical Publishing House, London, 1920, p115.

119 Mabel Collins, *The Locked Room: A True Story of Experiences in Spiritualism*, Theosophical Publishing House, London, 1920. p 175.

120 A member of the Theosophical Society in its early days in England, Isabelle de Steiger joined the Golden Dawn in 1888.

121 Alfred Percy Sinnett, *The Early Days of Theosophy in Europe*, Theosophical Publishing House, London, 1922.

122 Arthur Edward Waite, *Shadows of Life and Thought. A Retrospective Review in The Form of Memoirs*, Selwyn & Blount, London, 1938.

123 Mabel Collins, *The Mahatma: A Tale of Modern Theosophy*, Downey & Company, London, 1895. p136.

124 Alfred Percy Sinnett, *Autobiography of Alfred Percy Sinnett*, Theosophical History Centre, London, 1986, p122.

125 Started in 1856, *Banner of Light* was a popular spiritualist magazine, based in Boston, USA, with an international readership.

126 Finch was elected President of the London Lodge of the Theosophical Society on 7th April 1884 and was the first President of the Blavatsky Lodge in 1887.

127 The Master Hilarion influenced great scientists. He was cited as being behind Blavatsky's *The Voice of The Silence*. He was an ancient Greek, born in Crete or Greece and lived at times in Egypt. Blavatsky sometimes referred to him as the Cyprian Adept. Blavatsky stated that she saw him both in Egypt and

Greece and that he helped her to write some of her stories.

128 Helena Blavatsky, Edited by A. Trevor Barker. *The Complete Works of H. P. Blavatsky,* Rider & Company, London, 1933, p427.

129 Mabel Collins, *The Mahatma: A Tale of Modern Theosophy,* Downey & Company, London, 1895.

130 A lawyer, Bertram Keightley, along with his nephew, Dr Archibald Keightley, was a devoted follower of Blavatsky and an important theosophist by the time of her visit to England in 1887. They were often mistaken for brothers being about the same age and bearing a strong physical resemblance. Archibald was the older by a year. They came from a wealthy Liverpool family and both studied at Cambridge. After reading Sinnett's *Esoteric Buddhism* they gained an introduction to its author. They joined the Theosophical Society in 1884 and from then onwards Bertram trailed around Europe following Blavatsky. Archibald was engaged in his medical studies, but still appeared whenever able.

131 Mohini Mohun Chatterji was a young disciple of Blavatsky's from India and Assistant Secretary of the Bengal Theosophical Society. Originally a lawyer in Calcutta, Chatterji accompanied Blavatsky on her travels through Europe and became a major sex object. Although he had a wife in Madras, he had an affair with an English theosophist in Paris. He is often presented as equivalent to a servant of Blavatsky's.

132 Archibald Keightley, *Reminiscences of H.P. Blavatsky* [First published in *The Theosophical Quarterly,* New York, October 1910, pp. 109-122.

133 Marion Meade, *Madame Blavatsky. The Woman Behind The Myth,* G.P. Putnam's Sons. New York, 1980.

134 Alfred Percy Sinnett, *Autobiography of Alfred Percy Sinnett,* Theosophical History Centre, London, 1986.

135 George Herbert Whyte, *H. P. Blavatsky: An Outline of Her Life,* Lotus Journal; Percy Lund, Humphries & Company, London, 1909.

136 Elliot Coues, *Blavatsky Unveiled,* online at Blavatsky Study

Centre, http://www.blavatskyarchives.com/coues.htm

137 Michael Gomes, *Theosophical History. An Independent Quarterly Journal*, " Mabel Collins, Romance of the White Lotus", July 1991.

138 Mabel Collins, *The Mahatma: A Tale of Modern Theosophy*, Downey & Company, London, 1895. p21.

139 Victor Bailey, "The Metropolitan Police, the Home Office and the Threat of Outcast London," in *Policing and Punishment in Nineteenth Century Britain*, London, 1981, p108.

140 Constance Georgine Louise de Bourbel de Montjucon, or Countess Wachtmeister, of Sweden, was widely known as a companion and intimate friend of Blavatsky.

141 Archibald Keightley, "From Ostende to London". *The Path*, New York 7 November 1892 pp 245–8. Online at Blavatsky Study Centre, http://www.blavatskyarchives.com/keightleyafromostende.htm

142 Archives, TS, Pasadena. HPB describes her move in a card to William Q. Judge: Maycot, Crownhill. Upper Norwood. London C.S. May 7th.

143 Kirby Van Mater, *The Writing of the Secret Doctrine*, online at Theosophy Northwest, http://www.theosophy-nw.org/theosnw/theos/th-kvms.htm

144 *Religio-Philosophical Journal* 21 September 1890 quoted in Marion Meade, *Madame Blavatsky. The woman behind the myth*, G.P. Putnam's Sons. New York, 1980.

145 Mabel Collins, *The Mahatma: A Tale of Modern Theosophy*, Downey & Company, London, 1895. pp46 and 52.

146 A former Spiritualist, Francesca joined the Theosophical Society with her mother Mary, in 1881 and was treasurer of the Theosophical Society in 1884. Francesca's sister, was a very prominent feminist, and was the first Grand Secretary of the French Co-Masonic Order. Through her, Francesca was introduced to Co-Masonry, and she became a Master Mason on August 16, 1896, and received the 33rd degree on September 26, 1904. Francesca brought up her nephew, George from when his mother died in childbirth, who was to become president of the

Theosophical Society after Annie Besant's death.

147 Francesca Arundale, *My Guest: H.P. Blavatsky*. Adyar, Madras, India: Theosophical Publishing House, 1932.

148 Constance Wachtmeister, *Reminiscences of H. P. Blavatsky and "The Secret Doctrine,* Theosophical Publishing Society: London, 1893, p65.

149 West Norwood Station no longer exists. It originally opened as Lower Norwood Station in December 1856 and was part of the Crystal Palace to Wandsworth line. This area was previously known as Sydenham Hill and was developed for housing following the opening of the Crystal Palace in 1854.

150 Letter to Vera Zhelihovsky, May 1887, The *Path*, New York, October 1895 online at Blavatsky Study Centre, http://www.blavatskyarchives.com/blavle11.htm

151 Bertram Keightley, *The Theosophist* September 1931.

152 William Butler Yeats, (1865-1939), was an Irish poet, dramatist and prose writer and received the Nobel Prize for Literature in 1923. Born in Dublin, Yeats studied at the Metropolitan School of Art. In 1885 Yeats formed the Dublin Lodge of the Hermetic Society. He met Blavatsky for the first time at Maycot. Yeats ran into trouble with Blavatsky early on. He attended séances in 1888 and was impressed with the phenomena he saw. This placed him under severe criticism from Blavatsky. In Christmas of that year he formally joined the Theosophical Society. In December 1889, he began several experiments to satisfy himself that occult phenomena were real, without success. His experiments caused more problems and he last attended a meeting August 1890, after which he was asked to leave. Yeats was initiated into the Golden Dawn in 1890 and remained an active member for thirty-two years. In 1896 Yeats returned to live in Dublin.

153 Daniel Caldwell, *The Esoteric World of Madame Blavatsky*, Theosophical Society of America, online at http://www.theosophical.org/theosophy/books/esotericworld/chapter18/

154 Daniel Caldwell, *The Esoteric World of Madame Blavatsky*,

Theosophical Society of America, online at http://www.theosophical.org/theosophy/books/esotericworld/chapter18/

155 Isabel Cooper Oakley had met Blavatsky in 1884. She was married to Alfred Oakley, and the couple were friends of Archibald Keightley's. Blavatsky stayed at their home in autumn 1884.

156 The Letters of H. P. Blavatsky to A. P. Sinnett, Theosophical University Press Online Edition Letter 112, http://www.theosociety.org/pasadena/hpb-aps/bl-112.htm.

157 Ibid.

158 Ibid.

159 Alice Leighton Cleather was new to theosophy at this time, although she was later to become a member of Blavatsky's inner group.

160 Daniel Caldwell, *The Esoteric World of Madame Blavatsky*, Theosophical Society of America, online at http://www.theosophical.org/theosophy/books/esotericworld/chapter18/

161 Kim Farnell, *The Astral Tramp: A Biography of Sepharial*, Ascella Publications, Nottingham, 1998.

162 Archibald Keightley, *Reminiscences of H.P. Blavatsky* [First published in *The Theosophical Quarterly* (New York), October 1910, pp. 109-122.] available online at Blavatsky Archives online http://www.blavatskyarchives.com/keightle.htm

163 Archibald Keightley, *Reminiscences of H.P. Blavatsky* [First published in The Theosophical Quarterly (New York), October 1910, pp. 109-122.] online at Blavatsky Archives http://www.blavatskyarchives.com/keightle.htm

164 *Lucifer*, September 1887.

165 The Very Latest News From the World of Occultism – Blavatsky and her Mahatmas

[An Interview with William Q. Judge] [Reprinted from The New York Times, 6th January 1889, p10.] Online at The Blavatsky Study Centre http://blavatskyarchives.com/judgebsli89.htm

166 "Tea Table Talk", *The World* October 19 1887 p27.

167 Ibid.

168 William Stead, the son of a Congregational minister, was born in Embleton in 1849. In 1871 he became editor of the *Northern Echo* in Darlington. He moved to London in 1880 and began to work for *The Pall Mall Gazette*. In 1883 he became editor. Stead became famous for his articles on child prostitution. He served three months in prison for unlawfully kidnapping a minor, which he did to show how easy it was to procure young girls for prostitution. As a result of the publicity Parliament raised the age of consent from thirteen to sixteen in 1885. Stead supported the growth of the trade union movement and played an important role in the success of the match girl's strike, working with Annie Besant. He was the first editor to employ women on the same pay as men. In 1912, Stead was asked to speak at a international conference on world peace in New York. He decided to travel to America on the Titanic. It was later reported that he made no attempt to get into the final lifeboats and was last seen standing upright on the deck in prayer.

169 Known primarily as a poet and artist, Russell, (1867-1935), was a lifelong theosophist. He belonged to the Dublin group with Johnston and Yeats. Although he was not a member of any of the major theosophical societies, Russell maintained the Hermetic Society in Dublin until 1933. He was a frequent visitor to London headquarters. Today he is remembered as a major figure in the revival of Irish literature.

170 George Robert Stowe Mead became a member of the Theosophical Society in 1884. He abandoned his teaching profession in August 1889 to become Blavatsky's private secretary and served in this position until Blavatsky's death in 1891. He worked as assistant editor to *Lucifer*, after Mabel left and renamed it *The Theosophical Review*. Mead was appointed General Secretary of the European division of the society but resigned in 1897. He was offered the presidency following Olcott's death, but also turned this down as he wished to pursue his own studies. He is remembered for his scholarly translations of Gnostic and hermetic works.

171 Archibald Keightley, *Reminiscences of H.P. Blavatsky* [First published in The Theosophical Quarterly (New York), October 1910, pp. 109-122.] Available at Blavatsky Archives Online http://blavatskyarchives.com/keightle.htm

172 Ibid.

173 Allan Wade, editor, *Some Letters from W. B. Yeats to John O'Leary and His Sister. From Originals in The Berg Collection.* (Reprinted from the Bulletin of the New York Public Library.) New York, 1953.

174 William Butler Yeats, *The Autobiography of William Butler Yeats,* Macmillan, New York, 1938.

175 Ibid.

176 Aleister Crowley, informally edited from the typescript, most likely in some university archive, this literary joke was first "published" in a limited-circulation Thelemic magazine called Sothis 1:4 (1974), pages 61-67, and was almost immediately reprinted in a similar "publication" appropriating the title of the Oriflamme 1:3 (New York: March 1975), 38-40. (Neither of these publications had any legitimacy or permission from the OTO as owners of Crowley's copyright, but instead they constituted private exchanges between early Thelemic students and scholars, not intended to conflict with commercial publication rights.) The essay was reprinted as a pamphlet (Berkeley, CA: Thelema Lodge/Magick Theater, OTO, 1992), which constituted its first appearance with permission under OTO copyright.

177 Aleister Crowley, *Moonchild*, Mandrake, London 1929.

178 Annie Besant, *An Autobiography,* T. Fisher Unwin, London, 1893, p342/3.

179 Miscellaneous Letters Transcribed, Compiled, and with an Introduction by AT Barker http://www.theosociety.org/pasadena/hpb-aps/bl-hp.htm *Combined Chronology for Use with The Mahatma Letters to A. P. Sinnett and The Letters of H. P. Blavatsky to A. P. Sinnett* by Margaret Conger, Theosophical University Press1973; available in print edition "Reply to the Attack on Madame Blavatsky", by William Q. Judge, Editor of Golden Gate, William Q Judge, FTS, New York City, 7th June 1889,

[*The Golden Gate,* San Francisco, June 22, 1889] http://www.theosophy-nw.org/theosnw/books/wqj-all/j-arts.htm

180 Letter from Blavatsky to Judge, 7th July 1889. At Blavatsky Archives online http://www.blavatskyarchives.com/hpbwqj7789.htm

181 William Quan Judge, *The Path,* New York, August 1890 p.154.

182 "Suits Suddenly ended", *Daily Gazette and Bulletin,* Williamsport, Pennsylvania, 25 July 1890, p3.

183 *The Sunday World, Politics, Social Reform,Literature, Labour, Athletics, The Drama,* London, 10th May 1891, No. 34, Vol 2, p.1

184 *The Theosophical Movement,* Chapter 12, originally published in *Theosophy,* Vol. 9, No. 3, January, 1921 and as the book *The Theosophical Movement, 1875-1925, A History and A Survey.* E. P. Dutton & Company, New York, 1925, online at http://www.wisdomworld.org/additional/TheTheosophicalMovement-Series/Chapter-12.html

185 William Q. Judge and Archibald Keightley, *Light On The Path and Mabel Collins,* Reprinted from an 8-page pamphlet issued in New York in June, 1889, available online at Blavatsky Study Centre, http://blavatskyarchives.com/judgelotpamc89.htm

186 Ibid.

187 These dated back to 1877.

188 William Q Judge and Archibald Keightley, *Light On The Path and Mabel Collins,* Reprinted from an 8-page pamphlet issued in New York in June, 1889, available online at Blavatsky Study Centre, http://blavatskyarchives.com/judgelotpamc89.htm

189 *The Theosophical Movement,* Chapter 13, originally published in *Theosophy,* Vol. 9, No. 3, January, 1921 and as the book *The Theosophical Movement, 1875-1925, A History and A Survey.* E. P. Dutton & Company,: New York, 1925, online at http://www.wisdomworld.org/additional/TheTheosophicalMovement-Series/Chapter-13.html

190 William Q Judge, *The Golden Gate,* San Francisco, June 22, 1889, online at http://www.theosophy-nw.org/theosnw/books/wqj-all/j-reply.htm

191 Helene Petrovna Hahn Blavatsky, edited by Boris de Zirkoff, *Collected Writings*, Theosophical Publishing House, volume 11 p 322, available online at Blavatsky Net, www.blavatsky.net/

192 Mabel Collins, *Occult Review*, London, March 10 1910, XI 3, p164.

193 In 1887, when Dr. William Wynn Westcott, a London Coroner, Theosophist, Freemason, Rosicrucian and member of Anna Kingsford's Hermetic Society in 1885, obtained a Cipher Manuscript in which there were skeleton rituals of initiation, attributions of the Tarot Trumps to the letters of the Hebrew Alphabet, and the name and address of a Rosicrucian Adept located in Germany, Soror Sapiens Dominabitur Astris (Fräulein Sprengel). Westcott wrote to her and in November of 1887 she authorized him to found an English branch of the Golden Dawn. This led to the establishment of Isis-Urania, Temple No. 3, of the Order of the Golden Dawn in the Outer, in 1888. Westcott was a member of an Esoteric Society of Master Masons, called the Rosicrucian Society of England, founded in 1866 by Robert Wentworth Little. After the death of its founder in 1878, Dr. William Robert Woodman became its Chief or Supreme Magus and following his death in 1891, Westcott became the Supreme Magus of the Soc. Ros. Another member of this esoteric society was Samuel Liddell MacGregor Mathers, another member of the Hermetic Society, who eventually became the sole Chief of the Order. The most famous member of the Golden Dawn was Aleister Crowley.

194 "Obeeyah", Obi or Obiah is not the name of a tribe, as Stephenson appeared to believe, but is rather an African belief system; some say a religion, although it exists outside religions. Mainly associated with the Yoruba of West Africa, Obeeyah is a belief system, similar to Voodoo, that nowadays has adherents in Jamaica and the US, as well as Africa. (Other sources claim it is of Ashanti origin, e.g. in *Webster's International Dictionary*). Obeeyah is a system of beliefs grounded on spirituality and in an acknowledgement of the supernatural and involving aspects of witchcraft, sorcery, magic, spells, and healing. It has two components: one is the casting of spells and the use of magic

for diverse purposes such as to protect from harm and attain good fortune; and the second is for healing by using folk remedies and techniques. http://www.millennium-exhibit.org/sanchez1.htm The word is taken to mean sorcery, and refers to a number of folk magic traditions both within specific faiths, or practiced as a separate tradition combining aspects of African traditional religion with western ritual magic. http://altreligion.miningco.com/library/glossary/bldefobeah.htm When defined as a religion it is traditionally polytheistic and a largely secret religion of West African origin. It recognises that there are a multitude of gods and ghosts each having their own myths, rites, offerings, taboos, and magical forces. Within Obeeyah, a healer god can also be invoked to bring illness and other calamities to one's own enemy. http://www.adherents.com/Na_468.html#2888 It was, and is, often used as a general term to describe supernatural power; also applied to evil magic. Cavendish, Richard (ed.). *Man, Myth & Magic: An Illustrated Encyclopedia of The Supernatural* (vol. 15). New York: Marshall Cavendish Corporation, (1970); pg. 2039. Charms are commonly used and the term is also used to describe these charms or fetishes.

195 *Pall Mall Gazette* 3rd January 1889, front page.

196 Do.

197 http://www.ananova.com/news/story/sm_517090.html 6 March 2003.

198 Lytton was part of Francis Barrett's group of Magi Apprentices. After Barrett's death Lytton continued the group. Lytton initiated Stephenson into the Lodge of Alexandria, a Rosicrucian order, in 1860.

199 *The Valentine Ghost of Sefton Park, Liverpool, England* from *Haunted Liverpool*, Tom Slemen Bluecoat Press, Liverpool 1995 http://www.geocities.com/Area51/Shuttle/9089/haunted.html The original version of this story appeared in WT Stead's *Review of Reviews* 1892, New Year's Extra Number.

200 To Anne Deary, 14 February 1876, St James' Church, Holloway, London. This was also the first time that Stephenson used the forename "Roslyn". Anne was no heiress, but had previously

been Stephenson's mother's servant.

201 There has been much argument about whether there is a difference between neurosthenia, and the more commonly cited neurasthenia. The *Encyclopedia Britannica* and *Oxford English Dictionary* recognise only neurasthenia. Neurasthenia is credited with the symptoms of anxiety, headaches, neuralgias, a morbid hypersensitivity to weather, noise, light, the presence of other people, and any kind of sensory or mental stimuli, sleeplessness, loss of appetite, on and on. Neurosthenia has been defined as a state of over activity, where individuals had too much energy and needed to slow down and relax. A differing definition does appear in some sources, notably W. A. Newman Dorland's *American Illustrated Medical Dictionary 1900* and *Dictionary of Terms Used in Medicine and The Collateral Sciences*, Richard D. Hoblyn, Whittaker & Company, London, 1892 which gives the following definitions - Neurasthenia – (want of strength). Nervous exhaustion, characterized by over-sensitiveness, irritability, mutability, &c. Neurosthenia – (force). An excess of nervous irritation; an inflammatory affection of the nerves. Neurosthenia and neurasthenia have fallen out of use as medical terms, although associations are made with Fibromyalgia Syndrome, Chronic Fatigue Syndrome and other similar disorders. So many symptoms are associated with neurasthenia that it seems possible that although two differing conditions were intended by the different spellings, gradually neurosthenia became subsumed into neurasthenia. The two terms are often used interchangeably. In any event they both describe a nervous disorder and are associated with forms of depression.

202 *Moonchild. A Prologue,* Aleister Crowley, Mandrake Press, London, 1929.

203 Aleister Crowley, *Jack The Ripper,* edited by J. Edward Cornelius, California, Thelema Lodge OTO, 1992.

204 Melvin Harris, *The True Face of Jack The Ripper,* O'Mara, London, 1994.

205 *African Magic* By Tau-Triadelta *Lucifer* November 1890.

206 1st December 1888.

207 "Julius" (Mrs. Julia Verplanck, later Mrs. Archibald Keightley), *Religio Philosophical Journal* 1 June 1889.

208 The version given of this story is substantially from Vittoria's own memory as quoted to journalist Bernard O'Donnell in the 1920s and related in Melvin Harris' book *The True Face of Jack The Ripper*, Brockhampton, London 1999. There are a number of variant stories about the ties. Crowley mentions them in his *Confessions*. The story appeared in the press in 1925, (*World's Pictorial News*), and in Betty May's 1929 book, *Tiger Woman*. In 1965, it appeared in *The Magical Dilemma of Victor Neuburg* by Jean Overton Fuller, W.H. Allen, 1965. On pp 166-168: " One evening Donston had just come in from the theatre - in those days everyone dressed whether they liked it or not - and he found the women [Cremers and Collins] discussing this point. He gave a slight laugh, went into the passage, and returned in the opera cloak which he had been wearing to the theatre. He turned up the collar and pulled the cape across his shirtfront, made a slight gesture as if to say: 'You see how simple it is'..." and "'To return to this long explanatory digression, it was necessary in order to give the fair Cremers time to extricate the uniform case from its complex ropes, the knots being carefully memorised, and to pick the locks. During this process her mind had been far from at ease; first of all, there seemed to be no weight. Surely a trunk so carefully treasured could not be empty; but if there were a packet of letters more or less loose, there should have been some response to the process of shaking. Her curiosity rose to fever pitch; at last the lock yielded to her persuasive touch; she lifted the lid. The trunk was empty [sic], but its contents, although few, were striking. Five white dress ties soaked in blood." Crowley actually claimed in an interview with journalist Bernard O'Donnell that he knew Stephenson before he had died in 1912 and he claimed that Stephenson had given him the ties. *Unpublished Diary of September 13th 1933, p. 10 and November 1st 1933, p.272*. A version also appeared in the *East Anglian Daily Times* in 1929, the author, Pierre Girouard, ascribing it to Cremers.

209 Jean Overton Fuller, *The Magical Dilemma of Victor Neuburg*, W.H.

Allen, 1965. pp 166-168.

210 In 1896 he wrote an account of his experiences in India in WT Stead's *Borderland* entitled *A Modern Magician*. Although his stories were dismissed as fabrications, a few months later an interview with Mr Jacob of Simla, in the same publication verified the details but pointed out that Stephenson had been taken in by clever conjuring tricks.

211 Victoria Woodhull, began by giving fortune telling demonstrations. At 15 she married Dr. Canning Woodhull but continued to tour as a clairvoyant with her sister. In 1868, the sisters were backed in a brokerage venture by Cornelius Vanderbilt. In 1870, they became proprietors of *Woodhull and Claflin's Weekly*, a sensational journal in favour of suffrage, free love, and socialism. In 1872 the paper reported rumours of a love affair between Rev. Henry Ward Beecher and the wife of Theodore Tilton which provoked a national scandal. Also in 1872, the journal published the first English translation of *The Communist Manifesto*. In the same year Victoria became the first woman candidate for president. The two sisters moved to England in 1877. Victoria married John Biddulph Martin, a wealthy banker and became known as a philanthropist. See *Other Powers: The Age of Suffrage, Spiritualism and The Scandalous Victoria Woodhull*, Barbara Goldsmith, Alfred Knopf, New York, 1998.

212 Roslyn D'Onston, *The Patristic Gospels: An English Version of The Holy Gospels as They Existed in The Second Century*, Grant Richards, London, 1904.

213 Jean Overton Fuller, *The Magical Dilemma of Victor Neuburg*, Mandrake, 1990, p147.

214 Aleister Crowley, Ed. John Symonds and Kenneth Grant, *The Confessions of Aleister Crowley. An Autobiography*, Arkana, London, 1989, p690.

215 Ibid. p691.

216 Betty May, *Tiger Woman My Story*, Duckworth, London, 1929.

217 Aleister Crowley, *Jack The Ripper*, edited by J. Edward Cornelius, California, Thelema Lodge OTO, 1992.

218 http://www.violetbooks.com/index.html Hilton's book was

turned into a film by Frank Capra in 1933 and Shangri-la conceived by British author James Hilton in the 1933 novel *Lost Horizons*. It was immortalised by Frank Capra in the film of the same name, in 1933 leading to its land Shangri-La becoming synonymous in the English language with a mythical, utopian land.

219   *The Era*, London, 28th November 1891. p16.
220   http://members.tripod.com/~clairsedore/RazzleDazzle/my_cdnow_store.html
221   http://pages.prodigy.net/fljustice/hypatia.html
222   Mabel Collins, *Hypatia, a Drama of Today*, 1894.
223   do.
224   http://mysite.freeserve.com/arthurlloyd/Terrys.htm
225   *The Stage* London 20 June 1895 p10.
226   *The Sketch* London 26 June 1895 p464.
227   *The Era* London 22 June 1895 p11.
228   http://www.theosociety.org/pasadena/mahatma/ml-ccfor.htm
229   *Through The Gates of Gold*, Ward and Downey, London, 1887. p1.
230   The Edmonton Theosophical Society considered these points at one of their meetings and offered the following views.

- The writing must "feel right", it must stand on its own. Therefore one has a tendency to rely more on one's intuition.

- Ideally the writing should stand on its own but one has to admit that there will likely be some influence generated from the information known about the author.

- There is an expectation that consistency with the philosophy should be demonstrated in the author's life or one wonders where the information is really coming from.

- The writings should be judged on their own merits/value. [Example was given here of a Canadian singer, K.D. Lang, who has a beautiful voice and had much success but whose music was boycotted when she spoke out against 'factory farms' for raising beef and became a spokesperson for PETA (People for the Ethical Treatment of Animals); people could not separate the product (voice) from the individual's proclamations.]

- We all agreed (12 present) that reputation shouldn't matter.
- The Masters overlooked many things in certain persons and acknowledged the 'deeper' individual within (e.g., individuals whom the Mahatmas mention and support in "The Mahatma Letters"; also Moorad Ali Beg who was inspired to pen "The Elixir of Life".)
- One member present admitted to having chosen to discontinue reading a particular author after having read their autobiography while another member stated the biographical information actually caused her to read the writings more objectively.
- It was acknowledged that generally everyone present strives to weigh the writing for its own worth.
- The question arose "What are we judgmental of?" It was determined we each have a different level of prejudice. One tends to read a book by an ex-gang member to learn about gangs but why would one read spiritual philosophy written by one with a flawed lifestyle?
- In the "Collected Writings" HPB states that Mabel Collins was inspired in some areas of her writings and her imagination ran in others. Therefore, our intuition must remain our one true guide. One has to be aware whether our impressions are coming from the head or from the heart, and this ultimately depends on our individual spiritual development, that is, on one's ability to discern.
- It is helpful to know something about the author and then use discernment with regard to the writings.
- Having information about the author tends to make one more cautious but does not necessarily cause one to rule out or disregard their writings.
- It was agreed that it is helpful to know something about the author.
- It was ultimately agreed that the answer to your question is yes, one's perception of an author's work does change when one knows something about the author but it is not necessarily in a negative sense.

231   Mabel Cook, Simkin, Marshall, Hamilton, Kent and Company

Limited, London, 1901.

232 Margaret Oliphant, *Blackwood's*, 94 (August 1865): 168.

233 Margaret Oliphant, *Blackwood's*, 90 (May 1862): 565 - 74.

234 *The Theosophist* July 1927 p 390.

235 Whistler, James Abbott McNeill (1834-1903), the American-born painter and graphic artist was born in Lowell, Massachusetts. He first lived in London in 1848 with his sister and her husband. After time spent in Paris and the US, he returned in 1859. He soon made a name for himself, not just because of his talent, but also on account of his flamboyant personality. He was famous for his wit and dandyism, and loved controversy. His lifestyle was lavish and he was often in debt. Whistler was influenced by the Pre-Raphaelites, and he befriended Dante Gabriel Rossetti. Oscar Wilde was also among his famous friends. In 1877 he won a libel case against the art ctitic John Ruskin, but was ordered a farthing's damages with no costs. The expense of the trial led to Whistler's bankruptcy in 1879. During the late 1880s and 1890s Whistler achieved recognition as an artist of international stature. His paintings were acquired by public collections, he received awards at exhibitions, and he was elected to such prestigious professional associations as the Royal Academy of Fine Arts, Munich. He married Beatrix Godwin in 1888. On her death in 1896 he withdrew from an active social life.

236 Mary, or 'May' (1862-1938), was the second daughter of William and Jane Morris. D. G. Rossetti made a serious attempt to adopt May later in life. May, along with her father, was a member of the Hammersmith branch of the Democratic Federation. She worked consistently by his side in the Socialist cause. At the age of 23 she was her father's chief assistant in his decorative arts company. She eventually took over the management of the embroidery section of Morris and Company. Like her mother, May modelled at times for Dante Gabriel Rossetti. In 1885 May fell in love with Bernard Shaw. Together they formed a 'Mystic Betrothal'. In 1886 she became engaged to Henry Halliday Sparling, a Socialist comrade. She was married in June 1890 at Fulham Register Office. Shaw moved in, forming a ménage à

trois. May travelled to Zurich with Shaw to attend an International Socialist Workers' Congress without her husband. They eventually separated and divorced.

237 Thorp, Nigel, Centre for Whistler Studies, http://www.whistler.arts.gla.ac.uk/, *The Correspondence,* April 2004, http://www.whistler.arts.gla.ac.uk/letters/08089.asp?target=2

238 Louise Jopling, (1843-1933), was born in Manchester. In 1860 she married Frank Romer, a civil servant, who was appointed private secretary to Baron Rothschild in Paris in 1865. He died in 1872 and in 1874 Jopling was married for a second time, to Joseph Middlemore Jopling, a water colour painter and former civil servant. Together they had a son, Lindsay Millais. Her third husband was G.W. Rowe. Jopling was a writer, teacher and artist. She studied art in Paris under Charles Chaplin from 1867-8, and painted portraits, figure compositions, landscape and genre scenes. Later she set up her own art school. In 1880 she became a member of the Society of Women Artists and in 1891 of The Royal Society of Portrait Painters. She was the first woman to be elected to the Royal Society of British Artists in 1901. Jopling exhibited at the Royal Academy from 1870 to 1873, and at the Grosvenor Gallery from 1874 onwards. In 1877 Whistler painted a portrait of Louise Jopling, *Harmony in Flesh Colour and Black: Portrait of Mrs Louise Jopling.* She was also a supporter of the suffrage movement.

239 Lousie Jopling, *Twenty Years of My Life 1867-87,* John Lane, The Bodley Head, London, 1925.

240 *The World,* London, 10 July 1889, p35.

241 *The World,* "Tangerines", London, 18 August 1889.

242 Ibid p21

243 Op. Cit.

244 Op. Cit.

245 Op. Cit.

246 *The World,* London, 28th September 1889, p23

247 Member of a Caucasian people living in the Caucasus but not speaking an Indo-European language.

248 *Sword and Chatelaine: The Weekly Journal of The Services and Society*, London, 9 April 1892 to 17 December 1892.

249 *Sword and Chatelaine: The Weekly Journal of The Services and Society*, London, 9 April 1892.

250 *Sword and Chatelaine: The Weekly Journal of The Services and Society*, London, 16 April 1892.

251 *Sword and Chatelaine: The Weekly Journal of The Services and Society*, London, 23rd April 1892.

252 Ibid.

253 *Sword and Chatelaine: The Weekly Journal of The Services and Society*, London, 6th August 1892.

254 *Sword and Chatelaine: The Weekly Journal of The Services and Society*, London, 9th July 1892.

255 Mabel Collins, *Green Leaves*, Kegan Paul & Company, 1895.

256 *The Lamp*, Vol 1, 3rd October 1894, p44.

257 The owner of this house was a Mrs. Rhoda Robinson who shared it with her sons Charles, 19, an engineer turner and Augustus, 17 a florist's assistant. (Recorded in 1891 census records).

258 LN Fowler and Company, London, 1917, entry #200.

259 HP Blavatsky, "Have animals Souls?" *Theosophist,* January, February, and March, 1886. http://theosophy.org/tlodocs/hpb/HaveAnimalsSouls.htm

260 Frances Power Cobbe was raised in a privileged Anglo-Irish family. Her childhood was filled with family stories of adventures abroad, especially to India. Her family were deeply religious, and Frances began to question her religion in her teens. Her beliefs caused her father to banish her from his house although he let her return to be his housekeeper. Cobbe wrote her first book, *Essay On Intuitive Morals* in 1855. On her father's death in 1857, Cobbe received a small annuity. She met numerous independent and independent-minded women when travelling on the continent. Returning to England, Cobbe moved to Bristol and began to teach, working with girls released from prison, inmates of workhouses and prostitutes. Cobbe was

active in several social reform movements but is best known for her anti-vivisection work. An early British suffragist, she also supported higher education for women and the reform of poor laws. Her strongest efforts were directed to alleviating violence against women, especially violence by men against their wives. Frances Power Cobbe met the sculptor Mary Lloyd when she visited Rome between 1858-60, and by 1862 Mary and Frances had left to set up home together in London. Mary, a woman of inherited means, gave up her artistic pursuits and supported Frances in all her political activities. Mary died in 1898, but Frances lived on in their North Wales cottage until she died in 1904.

261 http://www.navs.org.uk/about/125/

262 Mabel Collins, (Mrs Keningale Cook), *The Anti-Vivisectionist Review*, No. 1.

263 *The Abolitionist* 15th May 1899.

264 *The Abolitionist*, Bristol, 15th May 1900, p156.

265 Ibid.

266 Charlotte Despard, (1844-1909), was a novelist and active in a number of reform movements. A member of the Social Democratic Federation, and later the Independent Labour Party, Despard was elected as a Poor Law Guardian in 1894. She became a member of the National Union of Women's Suffrage Societies and in 1906 joined the Women's Social and Political Union, being imprisoned for her activities in Holloway. Her objections to the way that the WSPU was run led her to becoming one of the founder members of the Women's Freedom League, which concentrated on using non-violent illegal methods. Despard urged members not to pay taxes and to boycott the 1911 Census. Like most members of the Women's Freedom League, Despard was a pacifist, and when war was declared in 1914 she refused to become involved in the British Army's recruitment campaign. After the passing of the Qualification of Women Act in 1918, Despard became the Labour Party candidate in Battersea in the post-war election. In the euphoria of victory, her anti-war views were very unpopular and like all the other pacifist candidates, who stood in the

election, she was defeated. Despard continued to be involved in politics after the war. In the 1920s she was involved in the Sinn Fein campaign for a united Ireland and in her eighties she joined the Communist Party.

267   *The Abolitionist*, Bristol, 15th May 1900, p250.

268   *The Abolitionist*, Bristol, 15th September 1900 p212.

269   Charlotte Despard, *The Abolitionist*, Bristol, 15th July 1901.

270   Some sources say 58,000.

271   Llewellyn Arthur Atherley-Jones. Liberal MP for North-Western Durham, a Barrister by profession.

272   Dr Walter Hadwen had been part of the anti-vivisection movement since 1875. He was a Gloucestershire doctor acclaimed for his campaign against compulsory inoculation, which he said could lead to the medical schools being taken over by drug companies. On Frances Power-Cobbe's death in 1904, Hadwen became president of the BUAV. He died in 1932.

273   http://www.online-literature.com/twain/316/

274   Pithing is the process of destroying nervous tissue in the region of the brain stem to ensure the death of the animal. It is usually done by inserting a rod through the hole made by the captive-bolt in the head or by severing the spinal cord between the atlas and axis, the first and second bones of the neck. It continues as a practice today.

275   Mabel Collins, *Confessions of A Woman*, Griffith Farrar & Company, London, 189 p2.

276   Ardat is the name of a female spirit and is used as a synonym for Lilith. It is associated with vampires.

277   John Lovell was an old friend of WQ Judge, and one of the original members of the early Theosophical Society. He was responsible for publishing a number of Mabel's books in the USA.

278   John Lovell to the Theosophical Publishing Company, Point Loma, California, 9th August 1913.

279   Letter to Royal Literary Fund from Mabel Collins dated 19th May 1912.

280 Letter to Royal Literary Fund from W Stebbing dated 27th May 1912.
281 Letter to Sylvester Baxter dated 5th August 1914.
282 The *Crucible,* Theosophical Publishing House, 1914, p20.
283 The *Crucible,* Theosophical Publishing House, 1914, p7.
284 Ibid. p123.
285 Letter to Royal Literary Fund from Mabel Collins dated 21 February 1916.
286 Letter to Royal Literary Fund from Mabel Collins dated 22 May 1917.
287 Catherine Metcalfe, *Occult Review,* Letter, London, September 1918, p173.
288 *Occult Review,* London, August 1918.
289 *Occult Review,* London, February 1919, p111.
290 *Occult Review,* London, March 1919, p168.
291 *Occult Review,* London, April 1919.
292 Grace Seton, was an active suffragette, and a prolific writer. She was renowned for her relief work in World War I and wrote a number of travel books. She married Ernest Thompson Seton in 1896. Grace Seton served as vice president and president of the Connecticut Woman's Suffrage Association, and with her husband, helped to organise the Girl Pioneers in 1910. During World War I, she organized and directed a women's motor unit to aid soldiers in France. She was president of the National League of Pen Women. In the 1920s and 1930s Seton visited Japan, China, Indochina, Hawaii, Egypt and Latin America, and wrote books about her travels, including *A Woman Tenderfoot* (1900) and *A Woman Tenderfoot in Egypt* (1923). The Setons divorced in 1935. In the 1940s she followed Paramhansa Yogananda, the Indian yogi, travelling to his ashrams. She died in Palm Beach, Florida, March 19, 1959. She was the mother of the writer Anya Seton.
293 *Lives of The Hunted: Containing a True Account of the Doings of Five Quadrupeds and Three Birds, And, in Elucidations of The Same, over 200 Drawings,* 1901, Scribners, New York, was actually the work

of Grace's husband, Ernest Thompson Seton (1860-1946). Illustrated by himself, Seton's books were all highly popular. He was co-founder of the Boy Scouts of America and founder of the Woodcraft League of America.

294   Letter dated 1 February 1925 from Mabel to Grace Seton from a collection held at Kent State University, Ohio, USA. Reproduced with kind permission.

295   Notes of Grace Seton from a collection held at Kent State University, Ohio, USA. Reproduced with kind permission.

296   Peter Ouspensky (1878-1947) was a major contributor to Twentieth century ideas. Born in Moscow and raised by an artistic and intellectual family, Ouspensky refused to follow conventional academic training. While employed as a journalist, his extensive travels, personal studies, and a quest for the miraculous resulted in the publication of *Tertium Organum* in 1912. He studied with Gurdjieff between 1915 and 1918. Ouspensky promoted Gurdjieff's system as the practical study of methods for developing consciousness. He lived in England after 1921, publishing *The New Model of The Universe* in 1931. In 1940, he moved to the United States with some of his London pupils and continued lecturing until his death in 1947, shortly after returning to England.

297   It appears likely that Mabel was referring to *Transcendental Physics* by Johann Zollner.

298   The theosophist and Freemason, Foster Bailey, worked at the Theosophical Society in New York. He was originally a lawyer but relinquished his practice at the start of World War I. He became National Secretary of the Theosophical Society in 1919 and never returned to law, preferring to work with Alice. A dispute within the Esoteric Section of the Theosophical Society in 1920 led to the Baileys leaving. At this time four of Alice Bailey's books were in print, with another twenty to appear in quick succession.

299   Alice Bailey (1880-1949) was born in England and became an active theosophist after moving to America with her first husband, Walter Evans. She became disillusioned with the Theosophical Society and in 1919 said that she was contacted by

a spirit who she called "The Tibetan". She wrote a series of books under his guidance. In 1920 Alice married Foster Bailey and in 1923 they started the Arcane School to teach disciples how to further the Great Universal Plan under the guidance of the inner hierarchy of spiritual masters led by Christ. After her death the school continued and is now under the auspices of the Lucis Trust. Bailey is a highly influential writer in the New Age movement and is particularly popular among esoteric astrologers.

300 *The Astral Tramp: A Biography of Sepharial,* Ascella, Nottingham, 1998.

KIM FARNELL

Index

A

Adelphi, The   45
Adyar   52
African Magic   109
alchemical symbolism   102
Alexandria   120
Alhambra Theatre   21
Anderson, Sir Robert   *12*
Animal magnetism   98
Arundale, Francesca   52, 56, 69
Arundale, George   52
Arundale, Mary   52
astrology   102
Athaeneum   30
Atherly-Jones, Llewellyn   147

B

Baal   110
Bailey, Alice   160, 228
Bailey, Foster   160
Banner of Light   54
Bath and Cheltenham Gazette   13
Bellett, John   *11*
Bentham, Jeremy   140
Bernhardt, Sarah   109
Besant, Annie   85, 87, 149, 150
Blackmore, R.D.
   Lorna Doone   23
Blavatsky, Helena Petrovna   9, 49, 50, 51, 52, 53, 55, 56, 57, 58, 59, 61, 64, 65, 66, 68, 69, 70, 71, 72, 73, 74, 75, 77, 80, 81, 82, 83, 84, 85, 86, 87, 88, 91, 92, 94, 95, 96, 97, 98, 101, 102, 108, 109, 111, 115, 117, 122, 123, 128, 135
   Isis Unveiled   53
   The Secret Doctrine   65, 66, 67, 70, 76, 81, 85, 86
Blavatsky Lodge   81
Bloody Sunday   61, 64
Bouchier, Dr Helen   47, 149
Braid, James   99
Branscombe, Elizabeth   11
British Library   135
British Museum   70, 122, 135
   Department of Manuscripts   135
Brodie-Innes, W.J.   84
Bromby, Dr   17, 18
Bulwer-Lytton, Edward   32, 50, 105, 106
Bundy, Colonel   94
Burrows, Herbert   86
Burton, Richard   83

C

Cameron, Robert   143
Caxton Hall   150
Channel Islands   16
Chatterji, Mohini   56
Chaucer, Geoffrey   22
Cheltenham Cemetery and Crematorium   161
Chicago Tribune   92
Cintra   161
Cleather, Alice Leighton   73
Cleopatra's Needle   45
Coleman, Emmette W.   95
Collings, Elizabeth   *11*, *12*, *13*, 14, 24, *195*
Collings, Francis   *10*
   Spiritual Poems   11
Collins, Mabel
   A Debt of Honour   119
   A Modern Hypatia: A Drama of Today   120, 121
   An Innocent Sinner   31, 32

At the shrine of Venus and the End of the Season   124
Blossom and the Fruit   94, 155
Cobwebs   32, 47
Flower o' the May   79
Green Leaves   135, 136
Ida: an adventure in Morocco   119
Idyll of the White Lotus   32, 45, 46
Illusions   33
In The Flower of Her Youth   12, 27, 32, 34, 39, 60, *192, 195*
In This World   32
Letters from England   157
Light on the Path   9, 45, 47, 55, 57, 58, 59, 82, 83, 93, 94, 95, 96, 125, 136, 155
Lord Vanecourt's Daughter   32, 60
Morial the Mahatma or, The Black Master of Tibet   119
One Life, One Law   151, 158
Our Bohemia   12
Our Glorious Future   157
Sensa   121
Star Sapphire   147, 155
Suggestion or The Modern Hypnotist   119
Tea Table Talk   79
The Blossom and the Fruit   79, 82, 84, 115, 122
The Confession of a Woman   119
The Crucible   155
The Idyll of the White Lotus   54, 58, 95, 122
The Mahatma   53
The Mahatma: A Tale of Modern Theosophy   55
The Prettiest Woman in Warsaw   32, 60, 61
The Scroll of the Disembodied Man   47
The Story of an Heiress   119
The Story of Helena Modjeska   32, 60
The Story of the Year   47
Through the Gates of Gold   97, 123
Too Red A Dawn   32
Viola Fanshawe   32, 60
Collins, Mortimer   9, 10, 11, 12, *13*, 14, *15, 16, 17, 18, 19, 20, 21, 23, 24, 25, 26, 27, 30*, 31, 32, 38, 83, 128, 153, *172, 173, 189, 193, 194, 195*
Collins, Wilkie   72
Cook, Keningale Robert   25, 27, 31, 32, 33, 34, 35, 38, 39, 42, 43, 48, 52, 53, 60, 84
Love in a Mist   34
Purpose and Passion   30, 32
The Fathers of Jesus   34
The Guitar Player   34
The King of Kent   34
Cook, Louisa   30, 74
Geometrical Psychology or the Science of Represent   60
Cooper Oakley, Isabel   71, 72, 75
copyright law   136
Corelli, Marie   147
Cotton, Frances   22, *23, 24*, 26, *31, 173, 193, 194, 195*
Coues, Elliott   91, 92, 93, 94, 96, 97, 119
Key to North American Birds   91
Coulomb, Edouard   74, 98
Coutts, Sir Lyndsay   128
Cremers, Vittoria   82, 84, 85, 107, 108, 109, 111, 112, 113, 114, 115, 116, 117, 124
Cronin, Edward   *11*
Crowley, Aleister   12, 84, 85, 107, 108, 115, 116, 117
Moonchild   107
Crump, Reverend JH   14
Crump, Susanna   14
Crystal Palace   67

D

Darby, John *11*
de Steiger, Isabelle 48, 53, 54, 56, 60, 101
Despard, Charlotte 145, 148, 150, 225
D'Onston, Roslyn
  The Patristic Gospels 115
Dublin Hermetic Society 70
Dublin University Magazine *23*, *31*, *35*, *193*, *196*

E

Edwards, W.H. 98, 100, 151
Egypt 37, 45, 46, 50, 54, 155
Ellis, Ashton 66
Embankment 45
Era, The 120

F

Fawcett, Douglas Edward 64
Finch, Gerard 54, 55, 74
First World War 39, 155
'Forbidden Banner, The' 150
Fraser's Magazine 14, 30

G

Garibaldi 106, 111
geomancy 102
Gibraltar 129, 130
Gilbert and Rivington printers 13
Gissing, George 147
Globe 20
Golden Dawn 60, 101, 102
Gothic novel 33
Guernsey *10*, *16*, *17*, *18*, *189*
Gurdjieff 122, 135

H

Hadwen, Dr 148
Hall, Marshall 141
Hamilton, W 74
Harbottle, Thomas 70, 74

Harris, Melvin 115
Harris, Reverend Richard 13
Hawker, Reverend Dr Robert 11
  The Poor Man's Commentary on the Bible 11
Heron, W Brown 119
Hilarion 53, 54, 55, 58, 59, 93, 161
Hilton, James
  Lost Horizons 119
Hodgson, Alice 161
Hodgson, Richard 52
Hoffman, Maud 122, 135
Hopkins, Ellen 88, 96
Horace 22
Horton, William 102
Hubbard, Susanna *10*, *14*, *15*, *16*, *17*, 19, 20, *21*, 22
Hutchinson, Francis *11*

I

India 50, 51, 52, 57, 58, 95

J

Jack the Ripper *9*, 12, 102, 103, 104, 106, 112, 113, 114, 115, 116, 117
James, William 40
Johnson, Charles 70, 71
Jopling, Louise 128
Judge, William Quan 50, 51, 66, 87, 92, 97

K

Kama Sutra, The 83
Kardec, Allan 52
Keightley, Archibald 57, 64, 65, 66, 68, 97
Keightley, Bertram 55, 56, 57, 64, 65, 66, 68, 71, 72, 73, 74, 86, 97
Keightleys 64, 66, 68, 70, 77, 80, 82, 84, 85
King of Bohemia 21, 23

Kingscombe   10
Kingsford, Dr Anna   51, 52, 55, 56
Knowl Hill   15, 20, 21, 23, *24,
      25, 192*
Koot Hoomi   96, 119

L

Ladies Mirror and Review, The   133
Lancaster Gazette   15
Lane, Michael Angelo   83
Leamington   *19, 20*
Lechdale   *14*
Leo, Alan   12, 140, *189*
   1001 Notable Nativities   140
Lesser Banishing Ritual of the
      Pentagram   102
Light   34, 35, 87, 93, 96, 97
Lillie, John   32, 61
Lloyd, Mary   85
London Dialectical Society   40, 42
London Gazette, The   136
Lovell, John   153
Lucifer   75, 76, 77, 79, 80, 81,
      109, 122.

M

Madras   52
Magendie, Francois   141
magic   102, 109, 110, 113, 115
magnetic healing   98
Mahatmas   55
   Letters   135
Maitland, Mr.   56
Marryat, Florence   42, 43, 44
Martin's Act   140
Maskelyne, John   88
Massey, Charles Carlton   51, 52
Masters   55, 59, 60
Matthews, Henry   64
May, Betty   116, 117
   Tiger Woman   117
'Maycot'   66, 67, 69, 72, 75, 77,
      80, 85, 97
Mead, George R.S.   81
Mediumship   41

Mesmer, Franz   98
Metcalfe, Catherine   156, 161
Metropolitan Federation of Radical
      Clubs   64
Morecambe   *15*
Morning Leader   147
Morris, Mary   127, 128
Morroco   129
Morya   50, 119

N

National Secular Society   40
New York   51, 54
New York Sun   97
Newcastle Daily Leader   143
Nottingham   *20*

O

Obeeyah   104, 110
Occult Review, The   151, 158
Occult World, The   51
O'Connell, Bernard   116
Odyssey   22
Olcott, Colonel Henry Steel   50, 51,
      54, 55, 56, 75, 91, 92
Old, Walter   73
O'Leary, John   83
Our Bohemia   32, *192, 195*
Ouspensky   135
Owen, Robert   41

P

Pall Mall Gazette   81, 85, 104, 110
Palmer, Ralph Thomas   60, 101
Paylton, J.M.   143
Payne, Bertrand   21
Pease, A.E.   143
Pease, Joseph   143
Pekinese   156
Pickering, William Hodgson   161
Pierrepoint, Helen   146, 147
Pioneer, The   51
Plymouth Brethren   11, *12*, 39, *41*
Plymouth Mail   *19*

Pompadour Cosmetique
    Company 109, 112, 114
Power-Cobbe, Frances 85, 141, 142,
    149
Price, Harry 84, 108
Pugs 156
Punch 14
Pythagoras 110

Q

Qabalah 102
Queen Elizabeth College 17

R

Ramsgate 49, 50
Religio-Philosophical Journal 91, 94
Richardson, Sir Thomas 143
Rider Haggard, H 104
Ross-Church, Mrs 42. *See also*
    Marryat, Florence
Rossetti, Christina 31
Rossetti, Dante Gabriel 21, *193*
Royal Literary Fund 153
Russell, Alfred Wallace 147
Russell, George W (AE) 81
Russia 50

S

Salcombe *10*
Sandys, Col. 147
Sappho 32
Scotland Yard 103, 107
Sepharial 73
Seton, Grace 160
    The Lives of the Hunted 160
Shakespeare 22
Shewar, Lady Helen 143
Short Cuts 32
Shrewsbury *19*
Sinnett, A.P. 42, 52, 53, 54, 55,
    56, 57, 59, 65, 74, 75, 80,
    88, 102, 122, 135
    Esoteric Buddhism 51, 65, 70,
    88

Mrs 70
Social Democratic Federation 64
Society for Psychical Research 40,
    52, 98, 99
South London Press 144, 146
Spiritualism 40, 41, 88
    British National Association of
    Spiritualists 51
    Cook, Florence 42
    Fox family 40
    Home, Daniel Dunglas 40
St Peters Church 25
St Peters Port 17
Stage, The 120
Stead, W.T. 81, 85, 114
Stebbing, W 153
Steele, Dr *24*
Stephenson, Robert Donston 9, 106,
    107, 109, 110, 111, 112,
    113, 114, 115, 117, 124
Sunday World, The 88
Swedenborg, Emmanuel 64
Sword and Chatelaine, The 133

T

Tangier 129, 130, 133
Tantra 83
Tarot 102
Tau-Triadelta 109, 110
Temple Bar 32, 61
Theosophical Society 9, 47, 50, 51,
    52, 54, 55, 56, 57, 59, 60,
    61, 65, 71, 81, 86, 91, 93,
    94, 95, 97, 98, 101, 119,
    122, 128, 149, 150, 161
    Blavatsky Lodge 75
    Esoteric Section 60, 81, 83, 101
    The Theosophical Publishing
    Company 76
    The Theosophist 75, 161
Theosophical Publishing House 86
Theosophy 50, 51, 53, 60, 65,
    86, 88, 101, 122
Transactions of the Blavatsky
    Lodge 74

Thornton, G   74
Tibet   50, 55, 119
Times, The   38
Totteridge Park School   *12*
Twain, Mark   148
Tynan, Katherine   83

V

Vaccination   144, 145
Varley, John   128
Vivisection   140, 141, 143, 148
   animal experimentation   141
   Animal Protection Congress   150
   anti vivisection   144, 149
   British Union for the Abolition of Vivisection   142
   BUAV   143, 145, 146, 147, 148, 149.   *See* British Union for the Abolition of Vivisection
   The Abolitionist   142
   Cruelty to Animals Act   141
   'Have Pity' poster   144
   International Anti-Vivisection Council   149
   International Congress of the World League for th   148
   Journal of Pathology and Bacteriology   146
   Journal of Physiology   146
   National Anti-Vivisection Society   142, 148
   Royal Society for the Prevention of Cruelty to An   141
   Second Royal Commission on Vivisection   149
   Society for the Prevention of Cruelty to Animals   141
   The Abolitionist   147, 149
   The Dog's Tale   148
   Victoria St. Society for the Protection of Animals   141

W

Wachtmeister, Countess Constance   64, 77, 80, 86
Wargrave Church   15
Warren, Sir Charles   64, 103, 104, 107
Whistler, James Abbott McNeil   127, 128
Whitman, Walt   34
Wilde, Oscar   31, 81
Woman   30, 38
Woodhull, Victoria   115
Woodridge, May   146
World, The   79, 122, 127, 129, 133
World's Pictorial News   116
Wright, Claude   70
Wyld, George   51

Y

Yates, Edmund   23, 127, 128
Yates, Francis   *23*
Yeats, William Butler   70, 71, 81, 82, 83, 84, 102

Z

Zhelihovsky, Vera   71

Mandrake

Other Related Titles of Interest

Sybarite Among the Shadows
by Richard McNeff
ISBN 1869928-, $8.99/$18

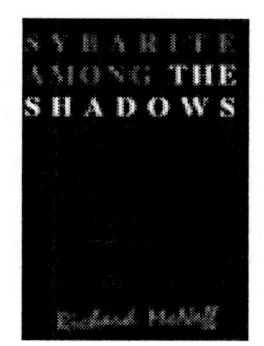

What if the Beast returned and you were not sure if he were the best or worst thing that had ever happened to you?

Sybarite among the Shadows finds Victor Neuburg on June 11 1936 with the poet he discovered, Dylan Thomas. They embark on a quest whose object is Neuburg's old master, the Great Beast 666; settings, the Surrealist Exhibition, and pubs and clubs of bohemian London; characters, Augustus John, Nina Hamnett and Tom Driberg. Neuburg confronts his demons; Crowley does too. They also meet something far more menacing: MI5's plot to avert the Abdication.

"To use Aleister Crowley in a work of 'faction' is brave indeed. Just his name casts a spell over the page. Richard McNeff has faced up to the task with aplomb and realistically recreates him, in all his bizarre, mesmerizing complexity." - Martin Booth

Sickert and the Ripper Crimes
Jean Overton Fuller
284pp, 1869928687 £12.99/$20

A new chapter for Jean Overton Fuller's ground breaking study of murder. The *original* investigation into the 1888 Ripper Murders and the artist Walter Richard Sickert.

Her story begins in the 1920s, when the artist Walter Richard Sickert (one of Britain's finest) confessed something truly spine chilling to his artist/colleague Florence Pash, also the confident of Jean Overton Fuller's mother. Sickert told Florence that he was painting into his pictures clues to the murders, as he wished people to know the truth after his death. But it was not to be until 1990, that Jean was able to again pick up the thread. In the meantime, she had built a formidable reputation as an expert on war time espionage. Using these skills and her artist's eye, she read the riddle. Now twelve years after original publication, she returns to tell the fascinating story of what happened next, including reviews of material by Joseph Sickert and Patrica Cornwell.

'timely and welcome . . . remains a curious and important book.'
Paul Begg in *The Ripperologist*, April 2002

The Magical Dilemma of Victor Neuburg
By Jean Overton Fuller
ISBN 1869928792, 334pp 152x229mm, 10 illustrations
13.99 in paperback original

Really two books in one. Firstly a record of one man's extraordinary journey to magical enlightenment. Secondly the story of Aleister Crowley, the magus who summoned Neuburg to join him in the quest. The book opens with the author's entry into the group of young poets including Dylan Thomas and Pamela Hansford Johnson. They gather around Victor Neuburg in 1935 when he is poetry editor of the *Sunday Referee*. Gradually the author becomes aware of his strange and sinister past, in which Neuburg was associated in magick with Aleister Crowley. Neuburg had been Crowley's partner in magical rituals in the desert and in rites even more dangerous and controversial.

JSM - Journal for the Academic Study of Magick
(eds) Dave Evans & Alison Butler

A multidisciplinary, peer-reviewed
print publication, covering all areas of magick, witchcraft, paganism etc; all geographical regions and all historical periods.

Issue 1
ISBN 1869928 679, £13.99, Airmail $25, 200pp
Beyond Attribution: The Importance of Barrett's Magus/Alison Butler * Shadow over Philistia: A review of the Cult of Dagon/John C. Day   * A History of Otherness:Tarot and Playing Cards from Early Modern Europe/Joyce Goggin * Opposites Attract: magical identity and social uncertainty/Dave Green * 'Memories of a sorcerer': notes on Gilles Deleuze-Felix Guattari, Austin Osman Spare and Anomalous Sorceries./Matt Lee * Le Streghe Son Tornate: The Reappearance of Streghe in Italian American Queer Writings/Ilaria Serra * Controlling Chance, Creating Chance: Magical Thinking in Religious Pilgrimage/Deana Weibel

Issue 2
ISBN 1869928 725,, £19.99, 420pp
Alien Selves: Modernity and the Social Diagnostics of the Demonic in 'Lovecraftian Magick': Woodman/Wishful Thinking Notes towards a psychoanalytic sociology of Pagan magick: Green/A Shell with my Name on it: The Reliance on the Supernatural During the First World War. Chambers/The Metaphysical Relationship between Magick and Miracles: Morgan Luck/Demonic Possession, and Spiritual Healing in Nineteenth-Century Devon: Semmens/ Human Body in Southern Slavic Folk Sorcery: Filipovic & Rader/Four Glasses Of Water: Snell/The Land Near the Dark Cornish

For these & other titles contact:
Mogg Morgan, (01865) 243671
mandrake@mandrake.uk.net
web: mandrake.uk.net
PO Box 250, Oxford, OX1 1AP (UK)

Printed in the United Kingdom
by Lightning Source UK Ltd.
109762UKS00001B/112-150